In Defense of Marxism

In Defense of Marxism

Against the Petty-Bourgeois Opposition
in the Socialist Workers Party

Leon Trotsky

PATHFINDER

NEW YORK   LONDON   MONTREAL   SYDNEY

ISBN 978-0-87348-789-4
Library of Congress Catalog Card Number 94-65039
Manufactured in the United States of America

First edition, 1942
Second edition, 1973
Third edition, 1990
Fourth edition, 1995
Seventh printing, 2011
Eighth printing, 2012

Cover painting: Howard Hodgkin, *Patrick Caulfield in Italy*,
1972–92, oil on wood, 43½ x 57½ inches. Private collection,
Mexico, courtesy of Knoedler and Co., New York and Anthony
d'Offay Gallery, London.

Cover and book design: Eric Simpson

Pathfinder
www.pathfinderpress.com
E-mail: pathfinder@pathfinderpress.com

Contents

Preface to the fourth edition, *by Doug Jenness*   9

Introduction to the second edition, *by George Novack
    and Joseph Hansen*   21

1. Letter to James P. Cannon, *September 12, 1939*   45
2. The USSR in war, *September 25, 1939*   47
3. Letter to Sherman Stanley, *October 8, 1939*   74
4. Again and once more again on the nature of the USSR,
   October 18, 1939   77
5. The referendum and democratic centralism,
   October 21, 1939   90
6. Letter to Sherman Stanley, *October 22, 1939*   92
7. Letter to James P. Cannon, *October 28, 1939*   96
8. Letter to Max Shachtman, *November 6, 1939*   99
9. Letter to James P. Cannon, *December 15, 1939*   106
10. A petty-bourgeois opposition in the Socialist
    Workers Party, *December 15, 1939*   108
11. Letter to John G. Wright, *December 19, 1939*   136

12. Letter to Max Shachtman, *December 20, 1939* 138

13. Four letters to the National Committee majority,
    *December 26, 1939; December 27, 1939;
    January 3, 1940; January 4, 1940* 139

14. Letter to Joseph Hansen, *January 5, 1940* 146

15. An open letter to Comrade Burnham,
    January 7, 1940 148

16. Letter to James P. Cannon, *January 9, 1940* 180

17. Letter to Farrell Dobbs, *January 10, 1940* 181

18. Letter to John G. Wright, *January 13, 1940* 183

19. Letter to James P. Cannon, *January 16, 1940* 184

20. Letter to George Novack, *January 16, 1940* 185

21. Letter to Joseph Hansen, *January 18, 1940* 186

22. From a scratch—to the danger of gangrene,
    January 24, 1940 188

23. Letter to Martin Abern, *January 29, 1940* 253

24. Two letters to Albert Goldman, *February 10, 1940;
    February 19, 1940* 255

25. Back to the party!, *February 21, 1940* 258

26. 'Science and style', *February 23, 1940* 263

27. Letter to James P. Cannon, *February 27, 1940* 265

28. Letter to Joseph Hansen, *February 29, 1940* 267

29. Three letters to Farrell Dobbs, *March 4, 1940;
    April 4, 1940; April 16, 1940* 270

30. Petty-bourgeois moralists and the proletarian party,
    April 23, 1940 277

31. Balance sheet of the Finnish events, *April 25, 1940* 283

32. Letter to James P. Cannon, *May 28, 1940* 296

33. Letter to Albert Goldman, *June 5, 1940* 297

34. On the 'Workers' Party, *August 7, 1940*   298

35. Letter to Albert Goldman, *August 9, 1940*   303

36. Letter to Chris Andrews, *August 17, 1940*   305

APPENDIX

Science and style: A reply to Comrade Trotsky,
    February 1, 1940   307

Letter of resignation of James Burnham from
    the Workers Party, *May 21, 1940*   341

Glossary of names and terms   351

Index   365

Preface to the fourth edition

Following the disintegration of the Stalinist parties in the former Soviet Union and Eastern Europe in 1989–90, the new petty-bourgeois regimes in these countries have staked their fortunes on integrating their economies into the declining world system dominated by the imperialist powers and reestablishing capitalism. Dumping any pretense of building socialism, these crisis-ridden governments have sought to defend their grip on political power and its accompanying privileges by expanding capitalist trade and enterprise within their borders and stepping up the use of market methods and incentives.

The various petty-bourgeois layers heading these regimes have pressed ahead—without much success—to privatize their economies. In their view, the only road forward is to seek incorporation into the world capitalist system, including imperialist institutions of debt slavery such as the International Monetary Fund and the World Bank, and even the European Community.

Far from providing the promised abundance of affordable food, fiber, and goods, however, this course has only deepened the economic and social inequalities built up by more than six decades of anti-working-class methods of planning and management. And far from providing a boost to the imperialist economies, it has placed new economic strains on the world capitalist system.

Throughout Eastern Europe and the former USSR structural unemployment is widespread and large inflationary swings are endemic. Food shortages and malnourishment are increasing. Production has plummeted since the early 1990s—by some 40 percent in Russia, 50 percent in Ukraine, and almost 25 percent in Hungary.

Living and working conditions of the producing majority are deteriorating and cuts in the social wage are mounting. Infant mortality has risen sharply and life expectancy has dropped. For example, in Russia infant mortality jumped from 17.4 per 1,000 newborn babies in 1990 to 19.1 in 1993. And life expectancy of males born today is lower than it was in the mid-1960s. A UNICEF report in October 1994 noted that in Russia and Eastern Europe there has been a resurgence of infectious, parasitic, and nutritionally related diseases such as tuberculosis and diphtheria.

Moreover, there is no prospect that conditions will improve or that any significant economic aid from the richest capitalist powers will be forthcoming. To the contrary, the situation for working people continues to worsen as this part of the world is increasingly swept into the maelstrom of capitalism's deepest economic and social crisis since the 1930s. Politically the trend in these countries, as it will become increasingly so in the capitalist countries too, is toward strong-arm Bonapartist regimes, rather than toward bourgeois democracy.

In the face of fierce price competition, rival imperialist governments are being drawn into sharper and sharper conflicts. The governments of Eastern Europe and those of the countries that once made up the USSR will inevitably be drawn into these disputes. In the now-dissolved Yugoslavia, for example, we can see how the interests of the ruling rich in the United States, Germany, France, and Britain come into conflict as they jockey for position among warring gangs who are attempting by means of "ethnic cleansing" to build capitalism in the territory they control.

The process that toppled or deeply shook the Stalinist regimes in Eastern Europe culminated in mass protests that began in 1989–90. Unleashing decades of pent-up anger and frustration, millions across these countries took to the streets demanding justice and political rights. The USSR, a prisonhouse of nations under Stalinist rule, was broken up.

The disintegration of the Stalinist parties and the formation of weaker and more unstable regimes opened the way for workers and farmers to take the first steps toward becoming involved in public life, organizing to defend their class interests, and viewing as their own the struggles of working people and fighters for national liberation in other countries.

The euphoria of 1989 and 1990 has since been swept away by the intensifying assault on workers' and farmers' social rights, and protest actions today by workers are less frequent. The struggles of the future, however, were foreshadowed in Germany, where workers in the east and west joined forces in 1993 to rally against cuts in social benefits and to strike against wage inequality in the east.

Despite the goal of reestablishing capitalism—including schemes to privatize basic industry, transportation, and banking, which were nationalized decades ago following the expropriation of the capitalist class in the former USSR and Eastern Europe—none of these regimes can simply reimpose the market system. Only when capitalist ownership in the steel, auto, mining, and other basic industries is reintroduced can competition between large capitals be reestablished, making it possible in turn for prices of production to regulate the social allocation of labor, raw materials, and production goods among various sectors of the economy, as is the case in all capitalist countries.

Extended moves to overturn the social relations connected with nationalized property, which is what the restoration of capitalist ownership would mean, will meet with stiffening resistance from working people. The violence and repression that would be needed to carry this out, and the level to which living standards and job conditions would have to be driven down, would pose bigger and bigger risks of political upheavals. The consequences of such assaults would be unacceptable to the international working class and even to sectors of bourgeois opinion.

These momentous changes taking place in the former USSR and Eastern Europe are stimulating interest and discussion among working people, students, and others around the world. There is a thirst for a clear explanation of the economic, social, and political contradictions in the structures of these countries.

Questions include: What is the social character of these countries? What is the class character of these states? Is capitalism being restored? What, if anything, is there for workers to defend in these societies? What is the logic of workers' struggles? What should be the stance of working people in the United States and other countries to these developments? How will workers in Eastern Europe and the former Soviet Union be affected by struggles against capitalist exploitation and imperialist domination around the world?

This book by Leon Trotsky is a helpful guide for working through answers to these and other questions. Trotsky was a member of the central leadership team of the Soviet workers and peasants republic and of the Communist International assembled by V.I. Lenin in the early years after the October 1917 revolution. Trotsky provides a materialist analysis reinforced by direct experience. Although the articles and letters in this volume were written more than fifty years ago, their evaluation of Soviet society and its contradictory place in world politics is not only accurate but *essential* to understanding the permanent crisis of the Stalinist parties and the growing instability of the regimes in Eastern Europe and in the former USSR.

In the late 1920s Trotsky had been expelled from the Soviet Communist Party and forced into exile by Joseph Stalin. Trotsky's "crime" was to have continued to fight for the communist course that V.I. Lenin and the Bolsheviks had followed before the bureaucratic degeneration of the revolution under Stalin. "Stalinism" refers to the counterrevolutionary policies and murderous factional practices of the privileged social caste that emerged and consolidated its power at that time and continues its domination in the countries of the former Soviet Union to this day. These Stalinist policies and organizational methods were endorsed and emulated by the leaderships of parties that called themselves "Communist" around the world. They subordinated workers' struggles to serving the diplomatic needs of the caste in the Soviet Union and, after World War II, of the castes that exercised power in other countries where capitalism had been overturned in the decade following the war.

In 1939–40, when the materials in this book were written, Trotsky was living in exile in Mexico. In August 1940 he was assassinated by an agent of Stalin.

Trotsky wrote these articles and letters as part of a debate inside the Socialist Workers Party during the opening stages of the second interimperialist world war. The key issue in dispute was what kind of party needed to be built in the United States and around the world: a revolutionary party that was truly part of the working class and its struggles, or a petty-bourgeois radical party calling itself working-class in words while buckling in deeds to bourgeois public opinion? What kind of party could stand up to the pressures of the capitalists' intensifying prowar propaganda and anticommunist hysteria?

Trotsky's standpoint was that of the historic line of march of the working class, both inside the Soviet Union and internationally. He explained that clarity on the class character and contradictions of the Soviet Union was interlinked with the political tasks and orientation of revolutionary workers the world over. It was necessary to distinguish between the nationalized property relations that resulted from the expropriation of the capitalist class, which were conquests of the workers and peasants during the opening years of the Russian revolution, and the counterrevolutionary policies of the privileged social caste. Only by doing so could working people around the world know what they should do to defend the Soviet Union against impending military attack (which came with imperialist Germany's invasion in June 1941, less than a year after the final items in this collection were written).

The underlying cause of World War II was the rivalry among the competing capitalist ruling families for world domination, Trotsky explained. A manifesto on the war drafted by Trotsky and adopted by the SWP and other communist organizations in May 1940 outlined the tasks of working people as they were dragged into the slaughter by the capitalist rulers. (See *Writings of Leon Trotsky [1939–40]*, Pathfinder, 1973, pp. 183–222.)

Trotsky's analysis of the economic and social structures of the Soviet Union and the counterrevolutionary character of the Stalinist bureaucracy, which the SWP shared, has been tested by history and confirmed. Trotsky insisted that this question came down to one of politics, of the class struggle. The international working-class movement could not stop fighting to maintain ground that had been conquered by workers in struggle without unimpeachable evidence that the propertied class had taken it back. This was true no matter how much the workers' conquests had been besmirched by petty-bourgeois social parasites who sought only—and ineffectively—to defend the trough from which they derived their own material privileges and comforts.

Moreover, the prognosis that the war would lead to a new wave of working-class revolutions and anticolonial uprisings was richly borne out, if in ways that Trotsky and the SWP did not and could not have foreseen.

Despite the Stalin regime's continuing counterrevolutionary course during the war, the workers and peasants of the Soviet Union in a heroic effort successfully beat back the German imperialist invasion. The military turning point came in early 1943, when Soviet resistance broke the siege of Stalingrad.

The victories of Soviet workers and farmers, won at great human and material cost, prevented the restoration of capitalism and imperialist domination in the Soviet Union. They also gave a powerful impulse to anticolonial and other national liberation struggles throughout Africa, Asia, the Pacific, and the Caribbean. Capitalist property relations were overturned in the late 1940s and early 1950s in Eastern and Central Europe, North Korea, China, and then North Vietnam. And the victory of Cuban workers and peasants in 1959 over the U.S.-backed Batista regime opened the socialist revolution in the Americas and for the first time since the Stalinist counterrevolution resulted in the establishment of a workers state guided by a proletarian internationalist leadership that used state power to advance the interests of the working class at home and abroad. Aside from Cuba, however, the postwar extension of the socialist revolution occurred not under the guidance of revolutionary proletar-

ian leadership but under the domination of the Stalinists.
Moreover, the strength of Stalinism in the workers movement
in Western Europe, especially France and Italy, blocked any
chance for socialist victories in a major imperialist power.
Thus, the revolutionary advances impelled by the triumph
of Soviet working people over imperialist aggression did not
"inevitably lead to the overthrow of the bureaucracy in the
USSR and regeneration of Soviet democracy," as Trotsky
had anticipated. Nor did these advances result in a political
revolution that restored power to the Soviet working class
under the leadership of a renewed communist party.

In Trotsky's 1936 book *The Revolution Betrayed: What
Is the Soviet Union and Where Is It Going?* (Pathfinder,
1972), which is an essential complement to *In Defense of
Marxism*, he based his prognosis of a political revolution
in the Soviet Union on the communist consciousness that
still existed among tens of thousands of workers who had
gone through the October revolution or had been deeply
influenced by its revolutionary leadership.

In the decades since, however, this political consciousness has eroded so much under the stultifying conditions
imposed by the Stalinist regimes that today there is no organized communist working-class vanguard in the former
Soviet Union or anywhere in Central or Eastern Europe.
Instead, there has been a break in continuity with the rich
communist traditions of the early Soviet government under
Lenin's leadership and the first five years of the Communist
International.

Workers throughout Eastern Europe and the former Soviet Union, however, are regaining political room to organize and become involved in politics. They are beginning to
resist attacks on their economic and social conquests. It is
through struggles like these that working people from Berlin to the Pacific coast of Russia will link up with fights by

other workers and farmers the world over, test alternative strategies and ideas, and begin anew the building of proletarian communist leaderships.

The political crisis in the Socialist Workers Party discussed by Trotsky in these pages was precipitated by the signing of the "nonaggression" pact between the governments of the Soviet Union and Germany (the Stalin-Hitler pact) on August 22, 1939, and the outbreak of war a week later with the invasion of Poland by German imperialism. Far from being surprised, a majority of the SWP were well-equipped for the Stalin-Hitler pact—an event Trotsky anticipated as early as 1933. Despite this, a substantial minority in the SWP leadership and membership concluded that there was no longer anything progressive in the Soviet Union to defend. This panicky turning away from historic conquests of the international workers movement reflected a more fundamental retreat from any perspective of building a revolutionary proletarian party in the United States and worldwide.

For several years, Trotsky had been urging the SWP to adopt an "orientation of the whole party toward factory work" and to deepen its active involvement in the industrial trade unions. He called for systematic political activity among workers who are Black. "They are convoked by the historic development to become a vanguard of the working class," Trotsky said. His views on these questions can be found in *Background to 'The Struggle for a Proletarian Party'* and *Leon Trotsky on Black Nationalism and Self-Determination*, both published by Pathfinder.

Many questions of communist leadership and party building that arose in the 1939–40 debate were also addressed in *The Struggle for a Proletarian Party* (Pathfinder, 1972) by

James P. Cannon, SWP national secretary at the time. This book remains an invaluable companion volume to *In Defense of Marxism* and should be studied along with it.

For a broader picture of the effort to forge a party of the working-class vanguard in the United States, Pathfinder's four-volume series on the struggle to organize the Teamsters union in the Midwest is especially useful: *Teamster Rebellion, Teamster Power, Teamster Politics,* and *Teamster Bureaucracy.* The series was written by Farrell Dobbs, the central leader of the Teamster organizing drives in the second half of the 1930s who later served for two decades as the SWP's national secretary. Dobbs describes the hard-fought labor battles through which an entire layer of working-class fighters learned how to carry out serious revolutionary work in the trade unions and were won to socialism. The impact of this Teamsters experience on the evolution and development of the forces that founded the SWP was deeply felt in the 1939–40 struggle, in which the proletarian character of the party was challenged and successfully defended.

During the period of capitalist expansion following World War II, the labor movement was pushed out of the center of politics in the United States. This began to change as the 1974–75 international recession, the deepest since 1937, registered the scope of the economic crisis that was going to face the capitalist rulers. To bolster declining profit rates, employers began squeezing more out of working people in every way possible and launched an assault on the unions.

Labor's resistance to this assault, which has gone through ups and downs, has moved the unions back into a central place in U.S. and world politics. Moreover, the unions have been deeply affected by the conquests of social and political battles of recent decades (the struggle for Black rights, the anti–Vietnam War movement, fights for women's rights, etc.) and by the changing composition of the working class in the United States (growing numbers of immigrant workers, the increasing percentage of women).

In response, the Socialist Workers Party entered a new stage of its evolution by once again turning its face and activity to work in the industrial trade unions. The 1978 report by Jack Barnes for the SWP National Committee that adopted this perspective explained that this turn was necessary to "carry forward the basic proletarian orientation the party has had for decades." That report and other documents outlining a course to build a proletarian party in the closing decades of the twentieth century are contained in *The Changing Face of U.S. Politics: Working-Class Politics and the Trade Unions*, published by Pathfinder in a new edition in 1994.

In Defense of Marxism was first published in 1942 with an introduction by George Novack and Joseph Hansen, two leaders of the SWP. Hansen had been a member of Trotsky's secretariat in Mexico during much of the time the 1939–40 discussion in the SWP was taking place. Novack and Hansen updated their introduction for the second edition of the book in 1973.

Doug Jenness
MAY 1995

Introduction to the second edition

by George Novack and Joseph Hansen*

I

For more than forty years Leon Trotsky defended and developed the ideas and methods of Marxism. In early manhood he undertook their defense against the tsarist regime and the whole bourgeois world. During the First World War he defended revolutionary internationalism against the social patriots and revisionists of the Second International. In the Russian revolution, side by side with Lenin, he defended the program of bolshevism against the Mensheviks and Social Revolutionaries. After the victorious October 1917 revolution, as the leading Soviet propagandist he defended Marxist principles in the field of political polemics as vigorously and brilliantly as he led the defense of the workers state on the military fronts. With Lenin he founded the Third International to spread the ideas of Marxism throughout the world.

Trotsky's greatest battles in defense of Marxism came after

---

* George Novack and Joseph Hansen were longtime leaders of the Socialist Workers Party in the United States. Hansen served as secretary to Leon Trotsky from 1937 until the latter's assassination in 1940.

21

Lenin's death. When the first signs of bureaucratic reaction appeared within the Russian Communist Party, Trotsky organized the Left Opposition, which sought to maintain the Bolshevik program against the backslidings toward petty-bourgeois politics of the Stalin-Zinoviev-Kamenev bloc. Despite his deportation to Alma-Ata, he continued the struggle of the Russian Communist Left Opposition against the growing revisionist tendencies of the degenerating Stalinist clique. In exile in Turkey he organized the Communist Left Opposition on an international scale. When the Third International capitulated to fascism without a struggle in Germany in 1933, Trotsky called for the formation of the Fourth International, which was founded in 1938.

During the last decade of his life, Trotsky defended Marxism against fascism, against bourgeois-democratic public opinion, against all varieties of petty-bourgeois politics from the virulent Stalinism of the Third International and the senile social reformism of the Second International to impotent centrism, ultraleftism, and anarcho-syndicalism. There was no significant anti-Marxist tendency that did not have to reckon with Trotsky and that he did not analyze and answer in his writings. In the universal reaction culminating in the Second World War, Trotsky stood forth as the foremost champion of revolutionary socialism.

At the beginning of the Second World War, Trotsky was again called upon to give battle in defense of Marxism. This time the struggle took place in the ranks of the American section of his own Fourth International. Unbalanced by the impact of the war in Europe and the pressure of alien class influences and ideas, a group of leaders within the Socialist Workers Party made what Trotsky characterized as "an attempt to reject, disqualify, and overthrow the theoretical foundations, the political principles and organizational methods of our movement." (See page 177 of this volume.)

They and their followers failed. They failed because Trotsky, basing himself upon the experiences of the Bolshevik Party and its predecessors, had forewarned the Trotskyist movement that the outbreak of another imperialist war would inevitably precipitate a crisis in its ranks; that under the onslaught of bourgeois public opinion the petty-bourgeois elements in the party would become disoriented; that the proletarian wing must prepare itself against the dangers of this demoralization. They failed because, when that crisis did break out Trotsky detected its first symptoms, diagnosed the nature of the disease, and prognosticated its further development. They failed because Trotsky was able to lead the proletarian majority in the ensuing factional conflict.

This volume is the most valuable product of that struggle which tested and tempered the ranks of our party. Here are many of Trotsky's most mature contributions to Marxist thought. To this last battle in defense of Marxism, Trotsky devoted the best energies of the last year of his life. He wrote the final item in this collection on August 17, 1940—three days before the Stalinist assassin struck him down.

II

As Trotsky demonstrated in his article, "From a Scratch—To the Danger of Gangrene," the elements of a petty-bourgeois deviation had long been germinating within the American Trotskyist movement. This tendency did not dare assert itself in an organized and open political shape until it was impelled to do so by the events leading up to and directly following the outbreak of the Second World War.

The immediate occasion for the formation of the petty-bourgeois opposition and its assault upon Marxism revolved around the question of the USSR. This was no accident. Since November 7, 1917, the question of the Russian revolution—and the Soviet state, which is its creation—has drawn a sharp dividing line through the labor movement of all countries. The attitude taken toward the Soviet Union throughout all these years has been the decisive criterion separating the genuine revolutionary tendency from all shades and degrees of waverers, backsliders, and capitulators to the pressure of the bourgeois world—the Mensheviks, Social Democrats, anarchists and syndicalists, centrists, Stalinists.

The development of the discussion quickly revealed that all the fundamental issues were involved.

On August 22, 1939, came the announcement of the Soviet-German pact. Thereupon a great wave of anti-Soviet propaganda swept through the "democracies." The petty-bourgeois wing of the Socialist Workers Party was shaken to the core. The same day at the meeting of the SWP Political Committee, Shachtman made the following motion: "That the next meeting of the Political Committee begin with a discussion of our estimate of the Stalin-Hitler pact *as related to our evaluation of the Soviet state* and the perspectives for the future." Shachtman still affirmed defense of the USSR. But his motion indicated that he was now approaching James Burnham's views on the nature of the USSR, which he had previously opposed. In several documents written two years before, Burnham—like Shachtman a member of the Political Committee—had already questioned the fundamental principle of the Fourth International that the Soviet Union is a workers state which, though degenerated under the Stalinist regime, must be unconditionally defended against imperialist attack by the world working class. Thus the pact which ushered in the war likewise ushered in our inner-party crisis.

A week later the Second World War began. The hitherto pent-up petty-bourgeois tendency now broke out of bonds. At the September 3 Political Committee meeting Burnham made a motion to convene a full session of the National

Committee the following week and to place on its agenda a reconsideration of the Russian question. The majority agreed and demanded that the opposition first put its new ideas in written form. The majority also asked for sufficient time to invite Trotsky to acquaint us with his views. Characteristic of the opposition's hostility to Trotsky from the outset was the fact that it voted against this proposal.

On September 5 Burnham submitted his document "On the Character of the War" for the plenum meeting of the National Committee. Its essence is in the following sentences: "It is impossible to regard the Soviet Union as a workers state in any sense whatever. . . . Soviet intervention [in the war] will be wholly subordinated to the general imperialist character of the conflict as a whole; and will be in no sense a defense of the remains of the Socialist economy." A week later, in the letter with which this volume begins, Trotsky began laying bare the real implications of Burnham's doctrine: "that all the revolutionary potentialities of the world proletariat are exhausted, that the socialist movement is bankrupt, and that the old capitalism is transforming itself into 'bureaucratic collectivism' with a new exploiting class."

Trotsky expanded upon Burnham's position in his first important document of the faction struggle, "The USSR in War," which arrived in time for discussion at the plenum. Since the petty-bourgeois opposition had not yet openly constituted itself as a faction, Trotsky utilized arguments similar to theirs that had been advanced by the Italian ex-communist Bruno R. and others, and he developed their logical conclusions. This document constituted a stern warning to Burnham and his followers that in challenging the program of the Fourth International on the Russian question, they thereby actually challenged the basic postulates of scientific socialism.

Three different groupings came together in the petty-bourgeois opposition. Burnham was its ideological leader, expressing most completely its anti-Marxist character. Abern's clique ostensibly agreed with Trotsky's views and disclaimed Burnham's. Shachtman, occupying an intermediate position, was beset with doubts and reservations, which he applied indiscriminately to both Trotsky's and Burnham's positions.

These last two tendencies in the bloc—those of Abern and Shachtman—were not yet ready to take their stand on Burnham's ground. They still pretended allegiance to the program of the Fourth International. How did they get around these contradictions in their position in order to form a common faction with Burnham? They conspired with Burnham to suppress his real views. Then they found a common formula for their unprincipled combination by refusing to consider basic principles and demanding that the discussion be limited to immediate "concrete" issues.

At the plenum which convened on September 30, when the time came for Burnham to speak for his document, he blandly announced that he had withdrawn it! Instead, his attorney Shachtman produced a resolution as to the joint platform of the opposition which attempted to evade and postpone discussion of the fundamental dispute on the class nature of the Soviet state by limiting the struggle to "immediate answers to the concrete questions raised by the Hitler-Stalin pact." The resolution nevertheless failed to adhere to its own aims and conditions. The Red Army invasion of Poland was termed an act of *"imperialist policy"* which necessitated a "revision of our previous concept of the 'unconditional defense of the Soviet Union.'"

The Abern clique exposed its unprincipled character by voting for both Shachtman's resolution and the motion of the party majority to "reaffirm our basic analysis of the nature of the Soviet state and the role of Stalinism" and to "endorse the political conclusions" of Trotsky's "The USSR in War."

From all appearances, at this stage of their flight from Marxism, the opposition simply differed with Trotsky's interpretation of current events and the "organizational methods" of the leadership of the Socialist Workers Party, which they attributed to Cannon. But Trotsky and his co-thinkers discerned the anti-Marxist tendency concealed within this entire unprincipled combination. The ideological parentage of Shachtman's resolution was clear. Its question mark over the class nature of the Soviet Union was a bridge leading to Burnham's answer. That answer was foreshadowed in his characterization of the Red Army's actions as "acts of imperialist policy." As Trotsky explained in his first letter to Sherman Stanley and in his article, "Again and Once More Again on the Nature of the USSR," *imperialism* is a term Marxists reserve for the expansionist politics of monopoly capitalism. The plenum accordingly condemned the resolution of the opposition "as an attempt in part to revise the fundamental position of the party, and in part to shield the position of those who aim at a revision of our policy on the question of the Soviet Union in a fundamental sense," and accepted the position put forward in Trotsky's article "The USSR in War."

The opposition organized on a national scale and sought support in other national sections of the Fourth International. At a series of membership meetings in New York, the majority continued its efforts to bring the fundamental issues to the surface.

In his next article "Again and Once More Again on the Nature of the USSR," Trotsky dealt more specifically and sharply with the arguments being circulated by Burnham's followers, warning those who cared to heed: "If we are to speak of a revision of Marx, it is in reality the revision of those comrades who project a new type of state, 'nonbourgeois' and 'nonworker.'" Stenograms of a speech by James P. Cannon in support of the Fourth International position and of a speech by Shachtman which tried to cover up Burnham and maintain the highly unstable position of his plenum resolution were sent to Trotsky. Upon receipt of the two stenograms, Trotsky immediately dictated a letter to Shachtman, printed on page 99 of this volume, answering in detail the revisionist ideas which Shachtman had up to this time tried to palm off as being in agreement with Trotsky's "The USSR in War."

The majority printed articles in the internal bulletin of the Socialist Workers Party during the next weeks further clarifying the deep-going character of the differences, but the opposition stubbornly refused to accept battle on this principled basis. Trotsky decided that the time had come to cut through the rationalizations of the minority and to open up the abscess from which the infection was flowing— Burnham's ideological leadership. In the famous first paragraph of his next article, "A Petty-Bourgeois Opposition in the Socialist Workers Party" (page 108), he declared:

"It is necessary to call things by their right names. Now that the positions of both factions in the struggle have become determined with complete clearness, it must be said that the minority of the National Committee is leading a typical petty-bourgeois tendency. Like any petty-bourgeois group inside the socialist movement, the present opposition is characterized by the following features: a disdainful attitude toward theory and an inclination toward eclecticism; disrespect for the tradition of their own organization; anxiety for personal 'independence' at the expense of anxiety for objective truth; nervousness instead of consistency; readiness to jump from one position to another; lack of understanding of revolutionary centralism and hostility toward it; and finally, inclination to substitute clique ties and personal relationships for party discipline. . . ."

These words cut like a scalpel through the pretensions of the minority. The full implications of the faction struggle had now been posed point-blank by the leader of the Fourth International. The article, mainly directed against Burnham, brought forward before the entire Fourth International the question of Burnham's method in arriving at his theoretical and political conclusions. Trotsky showed that Burnham and Shachtman's rejection of dialectics and their substitution of the pragmatic method had inexorably led to incorrect political conclusions. For the benefit of workers unacquainted with dialectical materialism, Trotsky outlined the elementary ideas of the method in lucid terms.

Trotsky followed up his analysis of the petty-bourgeois opposition with "An Open Letter to Comrade Burnham." This was designed as a deliberate challenge to force Burnham into the open and compel him to defend his real views. Burnham did not dare remain silent any longer under Trotsky's concentrated fire for fear of losing influence over his personal following. Moreover, Trotsky's thrusts had hit him in the vitals. As Burnham subsequently confessed in his letter of resignation, Trotsky dealt with the very beliefs that were determining Burnham's course and of which he was conscious long before his public break with the Fourth International.

Why did not a large part of the opposition leave Burnham and return to Marxism at this point? The answer can be found in the social pressure bearing down upon them as the war encircled the globe. This was the period when Baron Mannerheim's "poor little Finland" was the object of commiseration and the Soviet Union the object of virulent hatred in England and the United States.

Shachtman came out in defense of Burnham in an open letter attacking Trotsky. In line with Burnham's contention that the method of dialectical materialism—the method employed by Trotsky—was of no use in answering the political problems of the day, he utilized the Polish and Finnish events to cast aspersions upon Trotsky's interpretations of current events.

Trotsky answered Shachtman in "From a Scratch—To the Danger of Gangrene." In this article Trotsky's attack on Burnham—always his main attack throughout the fight— is supplemented by a powerful and devastating analysis of Shachtman's past and his role as Burnham's attorney. Burnham now came out in his own defense. He replied to Trotsky's open letter with his notorious document "Science and Style," which has been appended to this volume.*

"Science and Style" was the crassest expression of the anti-Marxist character and tendency of the opposition. Trotsky's success in smoking Burnham out and forcing him to divulge his real views was the turning point in the struggle. With Burnham's answer the struggle became clearly defined for

---

* Burnham's "Science and Style" was issued by the opposition in mimeographed form during the factional struggle in the Socialist Workers Party, but they never ventured to make it public after the split although challenged by Trotsky to do so.

Trotsky wrote: "Let the readers demand of these editors that they publish the sole programmatic work of the minority, namely Burnham's article, 'Science and Style.' If the editors were not preparing to emulate a peddler who markets rotten merchandise under fancy labels, they would themselves have felt obliged to publish this article. Everybody could then see for himself just what kind of 'revolutionary Marxism' is involved here. But they *will not dare* do so. They are ashamed to show their true faces. Burnham is skilled at hiding his all-too-revealing articles and resolutions in his briefcase, while Shachtman has made a profession of serving as an attorney for other people's views through lack of any views of his own." (page 279)

the whole Fourth International. Here was empirical proof that the fight centered between revisionism and Marxism! Burnham's document, which appeared on the crest of the wave of Anglo-American war hysteria against the Soviet Union, rendered *explicit* what Trotsky and others with a dialectical understanding of the deeper structure of the party had seen as *implicit* for a long time.

Trotsky had achieved his main aim: to prove to the Fourth International that the heavy proportion of petty-bourgeois elements in its membership had thrown the SWP into a crisis with the outbreak of the Second World War and that this crisis concerned the most fundamental propositions of scientific socialism. When "Science and Style" appeared, Trotsky explicitly stated this in his letter of February 23: "The abscess is open. Abern and Shachtman can no longer repeat that they wish only to discuss Finland and Cannon a bit. They can no longer play blindman's buff with Marxism and with the Fourth International. Should the Socialist Workers Party remain in the tradition of Marx, Engels, Franz Mehring, Lenin, and Rosa Luxemburg—a tradition which Burnham proclaims 'reactionary'—or should it accept Burnham's conceptions which are only a belated reproduction of pre-Marxian petty-bourgeois socialism?" He invited Abern and Shachtman to speak up: "What do you think of Burnham's 'science' and of Burnham's 'style'? . . . Comrades Abern and Shachtman, you have the floor!" They remained silent.

When Abern and Shachtman refused to disavow Burnham and his doctrines, including his "science" and his "style," it became obvious that they were preparing to split from the Fourth International. The majority endeavored to maintain unity, acting under the conviction that the unity of the revolutionary party and the inculcation of party patriotism are among its most precious assets. The majority likewise had two objectives: (1) to keep wavering elements in the minority under the maximum influence of our program; (2) to prove conclusively to the other sections of the Fourth International that if matters came to a split the responsibility for the split rested wholly with the minority. "We must do everything in order to convince also the other sections that the majority exhausted all the possibilities in favor of unity," Trotsky explained in his letter on page 265. "The happenings in the Socialist Workers Party have now a great international importance. . . . You must act not only on the basis of your subjective appreciations, as correct as they may be, but on the basis of objective facts available to everyone."

All the objective facts demonstrate that the minority's break with Marxism was the primary reason for the split. The discussion—which continued for more than six months—was the fullest ever undertaken in our movement. There was complete freedom for every viewpoint to express itself. The opposition was given every opportunity to win a majority and leadership in the party. "Even as an eventual minority," Trotsky wrote to the majority on December 19, "you should in my opinion remain disciplined and loyal towards the party as a whole. It is extremely important for the education in genuine party patriotism, about the necessity for which Cannon wrote me one time very correctly" (page 136). At the convention where Trotsky's followers succeeded in winning a majority of the party to their position, they did not expel the minority from the party, deprive them of a share in leadership, of responsible posts, or demand that they renounce their beliefs. On the contrary, representation corresponding to their actual strength was offered on all the bodies of the party; only observance of the principle of democratic centralism was demanded, that the minority abide loyally by the decision of the majority and confine its activity to further attempts to win the party to its position. The convention majority even agreed to a continuation of the discussion in the internal bulletin.

The conduct of the majority in this respect, guided at every step by Trotsky, serves as a model of correct bolshevik tactics in building the proletarian party. Trotsky draws the balance sheet of this aspect of the struggle in his article, "Petty-Bourgeois Moralists and the Proletarian Party" (page 277).

At the SWP convention which convened on April 5, 1940, the majority of the party reaffirmed its support of the Fourth International program. On April 16 the Political Committee met and moved: "That the committee accepts the convention decisions and obligates itself to carry them out in a disciplined manner." The minority bloc leaders refused to vote for this motion. Instead of expelling them, as would have been wholly justified, the majority still waited. The record was made clear to the other sections of the Fourth International to the very end. Burnham and his followers were simply suspended until they would indicate "their intention to comply with convention decisions."

The minority, however, had already rented a separate headquarters. They set up a separate organization, which they named the "Workers Party," began printing a public newspaper, and stole the party's theoretical organ, the *New International*. These actions of the minority are dealt with in Trotsky's article, "Petty-Bourgeois Moralists and the Proletarian Party" (page 277) which, together with the "Balance Sheet of the Finnish Events" (page 283), tersely sums up the political lessons of the struggle.

Such was the sequence of events in the factional struggle from August 1939, when the minority leaders started to attack and revise the Fourth International program, to April 1940 when they broke away from the Socialist Workers Party.

III

Burnham was far from an isolated figure. He not only had followers inside the Socialist Workers Party; he had a host of kindred spirits outside amongst the ex-radical petty-bourgeois intellectuals. Most prominent among them were Sidney Hook, Max Eastman, Lewis Corey, Louis Hacker. These forerunners of Burnham had already revised Marxism all along the line, beginning with its theoretical foundations and ending with its politics. They constituted the American section of an international brotherhood of renegades from Marxism headed by Souvarine, Victor Serge, Bruno R., etc.

As Trotsky pointed out in "A Petty-Bourgeois Opposition in the Socialist Workers Party," Burnham and Shachtman had endeavored to analyze this tendency in an article in the January 1939 issue of the *New International*: "Intellectuals in Retreat." Their analysis proved inadequate for the same reasons that later induced them to join this procession of fugitives from the revolutionary movement. Hook, Eastman, Corey blazed the trail for Burnham and Shachtman. Indeed, the petty-bourgeois opposition drew their arguments and ideas and received moral encouragement and inspiration from this "League of Abandoned Hopes," which they had previously criticized.

Most of these renegades had begun their careers as revisionists with a *philosophical* struggle against materialist dialectics. To conceal the extent and profundity of their opposition to Marxism from themselves as well as from others, one and all protested that their differences were "purely philosophical" and that such abstract differences in theory need not affect their specific political ideas and actions. Logic and philosophy in general, they held, had no organic connection with politics. Consequently, they argued, the Marxist philosophy of dialectical materialism had no bearing on concrete political parties, programs, and struggles. Burnham and Shachtman first enunciated this attitude in their article "Intellectuals in Retreat." They jointly maintained it during the faction struggle. Burnham disclosed his irreconcilable hostility to Marxist theory in "Science and Style" when he accused Trotsky of dragging dialectics into the political controversy as a "red herring." "There is no sense *at all*," declared Burnham, "in which dialectics . . . is fundamental in *politics*, none at all." Burnham and Shachtman had simply taken over this position from Eastman and Hook. Eastman had long contended that Marxism should purge itself of dialectical materialism which, he alleged, was nothing but a remnant of religion and Hegelian metaphysics, and adopt his "common sense" approach. Hook, echoing these arguments, scoffed at "the fancied political implications of the doctrine of dialectical materialism."

This divorce of logic from politics, this rejection of dialectical materialism as the theoretical foundation of Marxism, is alien to Marxist thought and tradition. Marxism is a unified, consistent, and comprehensive world conception. Its method of thought, the materialist dialectic, as distinguished from Hegel's idealist dialectics, is essentially the logic of *revolutionary* change. The principal laws of this logic rationally explain not only the course of gradual changes in natural, social, and mental processes but also the sharp breaks and qualitative leaps whereby things are transformed into their own opposites.

Why are bourgeois thinkers repelled from the materialist dialectic? Mainly because, as a logic of *history*, it recognizes the seeds and roots of *social revolutions* within gradual changes in social life. At a certain stage in the accumulation of these changes, a qualitative leap occurs, a great break with the past, a revolution. Thus, according to the dialectic, social and political revolutions are not accidental aberrations or avoidable detours in history but materially caused and lawfully determined stages in the cycle of development of class societies. Finally—and to bourgeois ideologists and their petty-bourgeois shadows, this is its most horrifying feature—the materialist dialectic explains the *logical* evolution of the class struggles of our own epoch. It demonstrates why progressive capitalism became transmuted into reactionary monopoly capitalism with its imperialist politics and wars; it demonstrates the inevitability of the overthrow of monopoly capitalism by the social revolution of the international working class, and the transformation of dying capitalism into living socialism.

The materialist dialectic cannot be severed from social life or political thought because it formulates those general laws of social movement which give rise to the class struggle, govern its course, and determine its outcome. When Lenin remarked, and Trotsky in these writings reiterated, "There can be no revolutionary practice without revolutionary theory," they meant specifically: there can be no consistent revolutionary proletarian politics without the materialist dialectic which is the essence of scientific socialism.

This is the key to the significance of materialist dialectics to the revolutionary socialist movement and to the opposition it arouses among such enemies of that movement as the renegade petty-bourgeois doctrinaires. To accept the logic of Marxism—to study, master, and use it—is to embrace and advance the revolution. Indifference or opposition to the logical foundations of Marxism, if consistently developed, must and will lead to a repudiation of Marxism—as it did in the cases of Burnham, Shachtman, Hook, Eastman, and other high priests of "common sense"—not simply in philosophical theory but in political practice. Their desertion of socialism and their prostration before bourgeois thought was implicit from the beginning, as Trotsky foresaw, in their hostility toward materialist dialectics. The antagonism to Marxism they first manifested in the apparently unrelated field of philosophical controversy reached fruition in their political program. Obviously logic and philosophy are not so far removed from practical reality as they claimed.

History itself speaks most strongly against any such attempts to split Marxist method from practical politics. Under Lenin and Trotsky the Bolshevik Party realized in social and political action what Marx and Engels with the aid of their dialectical method had explained and forecast in *The Communist Manifesto* and *Capital*. What the Bolsheviks proved in the most positive manner in the Russian revolution of 1917—the harmonious integration of Marxist theory and revolutionary action—the subsequent careers of Hook, Eastman, Burnham, and Shachtman amply demonstrated in negative ways. Eastman and Burnham unreservedly repudiated Marxism and socialism while Hook and Shachtman espoused proimperialist policies as spokesmen for the right-wing Social Democracy in the United States. These renegades conducted a spiteful struggle against the revolutionary Marxist movement with which they once identified themselves.

Burnham's flight into the camp of the class enemy was the most precipitate and thoroughgoing of them all. One month after departing from the Trotskyist movement he disdainfully resigned from his new "party." Burnham's resignation and his letter of apology to his dupes involuntarily confirmed all that Trotsky had said about Burnham in the course of the controversy. This letter is republished in the appendix for the information and enlightenment of students of the dialectic.*

A few months later Burnham expounded his new ideas on world politics in the book *The Managerial Revolution*, which enjoyed wide popularity in big-business, bureaucratic, and petty-bourgeois intellectual circles. While Trotsky was warning of the impending assault by the Nazi armies and girding the class-conscious workers for the defense of the first workers state, Burnham set forth the thesis that Hitler and Stalin, the chief representatives of the coming managerial society, had joined forces in the August 1939 pact to "drive death wounds into capitalism." This "concrete" political proposition was shattered by Hitler's attack in June 1941 to "drive death wounds" into the Soviet Union.

In the following decades Burnham stepped forward as one of the most fanatical anti-Soviet ideologists. His calls for an armed crusade against the worldwide "Communist conspiracy" were proclaimed in a series of books extending from *The Struggle for World Power* (1947) to *The Suicide of the West* (1964). He gave anticommunist lectures at the U.S. War College and testified that Shachtman's group was "subversive" at a U.S. Department of Justice hearing in the late 1950s. (Despite his efforts, the Independent Socialist League and its predecessor, the Workers Party, were removed from the Attorney General's list.) Burnham is now editor

---

* During the faction fight in the SWP the opposition demanded the right to publish an organ of their own so that the public might be informed of their views. After they had established their own press, however, following the split, they never saw fit to publish this letter and thus to inform the public of the reasons their most prominent leader had given for deserting the ranks of socialism. Burnham's letter of resignation was published for the first time in the *Fourth International*, August 1940.

of the *National Review*, an ultraright organ, where he has condemned the Nixon administration for its appeasement of Moscow and Peking and called for a benevolent reevaluation of fascism.

Whereas Burnham wholeheartedly embraced imperialism, Shachtman characteristically drifted step by step toward reconciliation with the powers that be. He went as far to the right as it is possible to go in the United States and retain the label of "socialist."

In the article he and Burnham wrote in the January 1939 *New International* analyzing the retrogression of the anti-Stalinist intellectuals into anti-Leninism and anti-Trotskyism, they stated that "the main intellectual disease from which these intellectuals suffer may be called Stalinophobia, or vulgar anti-Stalinism. The malady was superinduced by the universal revulsion against Stalin's macabre system of frame-ups and purges. And the result has been that most of the writing done on the subject since then has been less a product of cold social analysis than of mental shock, and where there is analysis it is moral rather than scientific and political."

After warning others of its dire consequences, Shachtman himself became infected with this disease. Malignant Stalinophobia ravaged the remnants of his previous Marxist positions piece by piece until nothing was left of his former political self. He abandoned the defense of the Soviet Union in its hour of mortal peril during the Second World War. In justification he borrowed the theory of the nature of the Soviet Union as a country completely owned as well as politically controlled by a unique new class that was designated as "bureaucratic collectivist."

He characterized the degenerated workers state as a retrogressive "new form of class society" that was neither capitalist nor socialist but something far below the level of a democratic capitalism. According to his view, all the successful worker-peasant revolutions from the Russia of 1917 to the Cuba of 1959 have been not only anticapitalist but antisocialist.

This theory misrepresented the highly contradictory reality of Soviet society under Stalinism, which combined the fundamental socialist achievements of the October revolution—the elimination of capitalist ownership and the establishment of a planned economy and foreign trade monopoly—with an antisocialist totalitarian political structure in which the ruling bureaucracy excluded the working class from all decision-making powers.

By making the possession of political authority the prime determinant of the class nature of a social formation, Shachtman broke with the Marxist method of historical materialism, which, as Trotsky emphasized, singles out the property forms based on the predominant relations of production as the decisive criterion. Italy, for example, has remained capitalist under the Savoy monarchy, Mussolini's fascism, and the present parliamentary republic; the Soviet Union has retained its essentially proletarian economic base under Stalin and his successors as well as under the regime of Lenin and Trotsky.

His arbitrary conception of the postcapitalist states facilitated the transition of Shachtman and his disciples from a "third camp" position, which presumably elevated them above the opposing class forces struggling on the world arena, over to direct support of imperialist policy. Since he maintained that "democracy" in the abstract took precedence over socioeconomic relations, and liberal capitalism was more democratic than the Stalinized regimes, Shachtman was led after the war to support the bourgeois nationalist Mickolajczyk against the Moscow-supported Osubka-Morawski government in Poland.

As the cold war deepened, Shachtman shifted further

and further to the right. After converting his Workers Party
into the Independent Socialist League, he took part of his
disintegrating forces into the Socialist Party in 1958. There
he functioned as a spokesman for the right wing, which
backed Washington's Bay of Pigs invasion, the intervention
in Vietnam, and the bombing of North Vietnam—all in the
name of defending the "free world" against totalitarianism.
He nestled up to such ultraconservative union officials as
AFL-CIO president George Meany and was an adviser to
United Federation of Teachers president Albert Shanker,
the foe of Black and Puerto Rican control of the schools in
their communities.

In 1972, the year of his death at the age of sixty-eight,
Shachtman supported the Hubert Humphrey elements in the
Democratic Party. (Hook voted for Nixon that year.)

The evolution of Shachtman and Burnham from 1940 on
confirmed Trotsky's prediction that the abandonment of
Marxism and rejection of solidarity with the workers state
would logically lead to accommodation with the imperialists. In the end the difference in the positions of the two men
came down to a matter of degree: Shachtman stood for a
liberal capitalism under a pseudosocialist guise, Burnham
for extreme capitalist reaction. The sole opposition leader
who remained by and large faithful to his past, Martin Abern, faded from political activity and died in 1949.

The precedent of Trotsky's dialectical materialist approach
to the 1939–40 events in Poland and Finland proved helpful
as a guide to the Fourth International in interpreting the
postwar developments in Eastern Europe. Trotsky carefully
distinguished between the reactionary aims and actions of
the Soviet bureaucracy and the revolutionary significance
of the transformation of property relations in the territories
occupied by its armed forces.

With this compass in hand, the Trotskyists were able to

discern the essential difference between the policies of the Kremlin bureaucrats and the progressive changes introduced in the economic foundations of the East European countries. These were defined as deformed workers states since, unlike the degenerated Soviet Union, their political structures were marred by grave bureaucratic distortions from birth.

The peoples in the Soviet bloc have ever since been struggling to throw off the despotic rule of the Kremlin and its satellite regimes and move forward to a "socialism with a human face" in which the masses of workers and peasants will actually exercise political and economic supremacy.

By repelling the assault of the petty-bourgeois opposition of 1939–40 upon dialectical materialism and the political program for the world socialist revolution, the Socialist Workers Party took a big step forward in assimilating the fundamental method of Marxism. In the third of a century since, our party has systematically educated its members in these ideas and defended them against philosophical revisionists on one side and sectarian phrasemongers on the other.

Trotsky's writings during his last great ideological battle, gathered here in one volume, have been indispensable in accomplishing this work. They provide an exemplary case study, showing how an expert exponent of the Marxist dialectic applies its teachings to unravel the intricacies of some of the most puzzling phenomena and complex political problems of our era.

JANUARY 1973

In Defense of Marxism

1

Letter to James P. Cannon[‡]

SEPTEMBER 12, 1939

Dear Jim:

I am writing now a study on the social character of the USSR in connection with the war question. The writing, with its translation, will take at least one week more. The fundamental ideas are as follows:

1. Our definition of the USSR can be right or wrong, but I do not see any reason to make this definition dependent on the German-Soviet pact.

2. The social character of the USSR is not determined by her friendship with democracy or fascism. Who adopts such a point of view becomes a prisoner of the Stalinist conception of the People's Front epoch.

3. Who says that the USSR is no more a degenerate workers state, but a new social formation, should clearly say what he adds to our *political conclusions*.

4. The USSR question cannot be isolated as unique from the whole historic process of our times. Either the Stalin state is a transitory formation, it is a deformation of a worker

---

[‡] Documents in this volume marked with this symbol were written by Leon Trotsky in English; the others are English translations of the original Russian text.

state in a backward and isolated country, or "bureaucratic collectivism" (Bruno R., *La Bureaucratisation du monde*; Paris, 1939) is a new social formation which is replacing capitalism throughout the world (Stalinism, fascism, New Deal, etc.). The terminological experiments (workers state, not workers state; class, not class; etc.) receive a sense only under this historic aspect. Who chooses the second alternative admits, openly or silently, that all the revolutionary potentialities of the world proletariat are exhausted, that the socialist movement is bankrupt, and that the old capitalism is transforming itself into "bureaucratic collectivism" with a new exploiting class.

The tremendous importance of such a conclusion is self-explanatory. It concerns the whole fate of the world proletariat and mankind. Have we the slightest right to induce ourselves by purely terminological experiments in a new historic conception which occurs to be in an absolute contradiction with our program, strategy, and tactics? Such an adventuristic jump would be doubly criminal now in view of the world war when the perspective of the socialist revolution becomes an imminent reality and when the case of the USSR will appear to everybody as a transitorial episode in the process of world socialist revolution.

I write these lines in haste, which explains their insufficiency, but in a week I hope to send you my more complete thesis.

Comradely greetings,

*V.T.O. [Leon Trotsky]**

---

* Because of the conditions of his residence in the various countries in which he lived after his exile, Trotsky often used pseudonyms in his letters. His letters were frequently signed with the name of his English secretary.

2

The USSR in war

SEPTEMBER 25, 1939

The German-Soviet pact and the character of the USSR

Is it possible after the conclusion of the German-Soviet pact to consider the USSR a workers state? The future of the Soviet state has again and again aroused discussion in our midst. Small wonder; we have before us the first experiment in the workers state in history. Never before and nowhere else has this phenomenon been available for analysis. In the question of the social character of the USSR, mistakes commonly flow, as we have previously stated, from replacing the historical fact with the programmatic norm. Concrete fact departs from the norm. This does not signify, however, that it has overthrown the norm; on the contrary, it has reaffirmed it, from the negative side. The degeneration of the first workers state, ascertained and explained by us, has only the more graphically shown what the workers state should be, what it could and would be under certain historical conditions. The contradiction between the concrete fact and the norm constrains us not to reject the norm but, on the contrary, to fight for it by means of the revolutionary road. The program of the approaching revolution in the USSR is determined on the one hand by our appraisal of the USSR as an objective historical *fact,* and on the other hand, by a *norm* of the workers state. We do not say: "Everything is lost, we must begin all over again." We clearly indicate those elements of the workers state which at the given stage can be salvaged, preserved, and further developed.

Those who seek nowadays to prove that the Soviet-German pact changes our appraisal of the Soviet state take their stand, in essence, on the position of the Comintern—to put it more correctly, on yesterday's position of the Comintern. According to this logic, the historical mission of the workers state is the struggle for imperialist democracy. The "betrayal" of the democracies in favor of fascism divests the USSR of its being considered a workers state. In point of fact, the signing of the treaty with Hitler supplies only an extra gauge with which to measure the degree of degeneration of the Soviet bureaucracy, and its contempt for the international working class, including the Comintern, but it does not provide any basis whatsoever for a reevaluation of the sociological appraisal of the USSR.

Are the differences political or terminological?

Let us begin by posing the question of the nature of the Soviet state not on the abstract-sociological plane but on the plane of concrete-political tasks. Let us concede for the moment that the bureaucracy is a new "class" and that the present regime in the USSR is a special system of class exploitation. What new political conclusions follow for us from these definitions? The Fourth International long ago recognized the necessity of overthrowing the bureaucracy by means of a revolutionary uprising of the toilers. Nothing else is proposed or can be proposed by those who proclaim the bureaucracy to be an exploiting "class." The goal to be attained by the overthrow of the bureaucracy is the reestablishment of the rule of the soviets, expelling from them

the present bureaucracy. Nothing different can be proposed
or is proposed by the leftist critics.* It is the task of the re-
generated soviets to collaborate with the world revolution
and the building of a socialist society. The overthrow of
the bureaucracy therefore presupposes the preservation of
state property and of planned economy. Herein is the nub
of the whole problem.

Needless to say, the distribution of productive forces
among the various branches of economy and generally the
entire content of the plan will be drastically changed when
this plan is determined by the interests not of the bureaucracy but of the producers themselves. But inasmuch as the
question of overthrowing the parasitic oligarchy still remains linked with that of preserving the nationalized (state)
property, we called the future revolution *political*. Certain
of our critics (Ciliga, Bruno, and others) want, come what
may, to call the future revolution *social*. Let us grant this
definition. What does it alter in essence? To those tasks of
the revolution which we have enumerated it adds nothing
whatsoever.

Our critics as a rule take the facts as we long ago established them. They add absolutely nothing essential to the
appraisal either of the position of the bureaucracy and the
toilers, or of the role of the Kremlin on the international
arena. In all these spheres, not only do they fail to challenge
our analysis, but on the contrary they base themselves completely upon it and even restrict themselves entirely to it. The
sole accusation they bring against us is that we do not draw
the necessary "conclusions." Upon analysis it turns out, however, that these conclusions are of a purely terminological

---

* We recollect that some of those comrades who are inclined to
consider the bureaucracy a new class, at the same time objected strenu-
ously to the exclusion of the bureaucracy from the soviets.—L.T.

character. Our critics refuse to call the degenerated workers state—a workers state. They demand that the totalitarian bureaucracy be called a ruling class. The revolution against this bureaucracy they propose to consider not political but social. Were we to make them these terminological concessions, we would place our critics in a very difficult position, inasmuch as they themselves would not know what to do with their purely verbal victory.

Let us check ourselves once again

It would therefore be a piece of monstrous nonsense to split with comrades who on the question of the sociological nature of the USSR have an opinion different from ours, insofar as they solidarize with us in regard to the political tasks. But on the other hand, it would be blindness on our part to ignore purely theoretical and even terminological differences, because in the course of further development they may acquire flesh and blood and lead to diametrically opposite political conclusions. Just as a tidy housewife never permits an accumulation of cobwebs and garbage, just so a revolutionary party cannot tolerate lack of clarity, confusion, and equivocation. Our house must be kept clean!

Let me recall for the sake of illustration, the question of Thermidor. For a long time we asserted that Thermidor in the USSR was only being prepared but had not yet been consummated. Later, investing the analogy to Thermidor with a more precise and well-deliberated character, we came to the conclusion that Thermidor had already taken place long ago. This open rectification of our own mistake did not introduce the slightest consternation in our ranks. Why? Because the *essence* of the processes in the Soviet Union was appraised identically by all of us, as we jointly studied day by day the growth of reaction. For us it was only a question of rendering more precise a historical analogy, nothing more.

I hope that still today despite the attempt of some comrades to uncover differences on the question of the "defense of the USSR"—with which we shall deal presently—we shall succeed by means of simply rendering our own ideas more precise to preserve unanimity on the basis of the program of the Fourth International.

Is it a cancerous growth or a new organ?

Our critics have more than once argued that the present Soviet bureaucracy bears very little resemblance to either the bourgeois or labor bureaucracy in capitalist society; that to a far greater degree than fascist bureaucracy it represents a new and much more powerful social formation. This is quite correct and we have never closed our eyes to it. But if we consider the Soviet bureaucracy a "class," then we are compelled to state immediately that this class does not at all resemble any of those propertied classes known to us in the past; our gain consequently is not great. We frequently call the Soviet bureaucracy a caste, underscoring thereby its shut-in character, its arbitrary rule, and the haughtiness of the ruling stratum which considers that its progenitors issued from the divine lips of Brahma whereas the popular masses originated from the grosser portions of his anatomy. But even this definition does not of course possess a strictly scientific character. Its relative superiority lies in this, that the makeshift character of the term is clear to everybody, since it would enter nobody's mind to identify the Moscow oligarchy with the Hindu caste of Brahmins. The old sociological terminology did not and could not prepare a name for a new social event which is in process of evolution (degeneration) and which has not assumed stable forms. All of us, however, continue to call the Soviet bureaucracy a bureaucracy, not being unmindful of its historical peculiarities. In our opinion this should suffice for the time being.

Scientifically and politically—and not purely terminological-ly—the question poses itself as follows: Does the bureaucracy represent a temporary growth on a social organism or has this growth already become transformed into a historically indispensable organ? Social excrescences can be the product of an "accidental" (i.e., temporary and extraordinary) en-meshing of historical circumstances. A social organ (and such is every class, including an exploiting class) can take shape only as a result of the deeply rooted inner needs of produc-tion itself. If we do not answer this question, then the entire controversy will degenerate into sterile toying with words.

The early degeneration of the bureaucracy

The historical justification for every ruling class consisted in this—that the system of exploitation it headed raised the development of the productive forces to a new level. Beyond the shadow of a doubt, the Soviet regime gave a mighty im-pulse to economy. But the source of this impulse was the nationalization of the means of production and the planned beginnings, and by no means the fact that the bureaucracy usurped command over the economy. On the contrary, bu-reaucratism, as a system, became the worst brake on the technical and cultural development of the country. This was veiled for a certain time by the fact that Soviet economy was occupied for two decades with transplanting and assimilating the technology and organization of production in advanced capitalist countries. The period of borrowing and imitation still could, for better or for worse, be accommodated to bu-reaucratic automatism, i.e., the suffocation of all initiative and all creative urge. But the higher the economy rose, the more complex its requirements became, all the more un-bearable became the obstacle of the bureaucratic regime. The constantly sharpening contradiction between them leads to uninterrupted political convulsions, to systematic annihilation of the most outstanding creative elements in all spheres of activity. Thus, before the bureaucracy could succeed in exuding from itself a "ruling class," it came into irreconcilable contradiction with the demands of development. The explanation for this is to be found precisely in the fact that the bureaucracy is not the bearer of a new system of economy peculiar to itself and impossible without itself, but is a parasitic growth on a workers state.

The conditions for the omnipotence and fall of the bureaucracy

The Soviet oligarchy possesses all the vices of the old ruling classes but lacks their historical mission. In the bureaucratic degeneration of the Soviet state it is not the general laws of modern society from capitalism to socialism which find expression but a special, exceptional, and temporary refraction of these laws under the conditions of a backward revolutionary country in a capitalist environment. The scarcity in consumer goods and the universal struggle to obtain them generate a policeman who arrogates to himself the function of distribution. Hostile pressure from without imposes on the policeman the role of "defender" of the country, endows him with national authority, and permits him doubly to plunder the country.

Both conditions for the omnipotence of the bureaucracy—the backwardness of the country and the imperialist environment—bear, however, a temporary and transitional character and must disappear with the victory of the world revolution. Even bourgeois economists have calculated that with a planned economy it would be possible to raise the national income of the United States rapidly to $200 billion a year and thus assure the entire population not only the satisfaction of its primary needs but real comforts. On the other hand, the world revolution would do away with the

danger from without as a supplementary cause of bureau-
cratization. The elimination of the need to expend an enormous share of the national income on armaments would raise
even higher the living and cultural level of the masses. In
these conditions the need for a policeman-distributor would
fall away by itself. Administration as a gigantic cooperative
would very quickly supplant state power. There would be no
room for a new ruling class or for a new exploiting regime,
located between capitalism and socialism.

And what if the socialist revolution is not accomplished?

The disintegration of capitalism has reached extreme limits,
likewise the disintegration of the old ruling class. The further
existence of this system is impossible. The productive forces
must be organized in accordance with a plan. But who will
accomplish this task—the proletariat or a new ruling class
of "commissars"—politicians, administrators, and techni-
cians? Historical experience bears witness, in the opinion
of certain rationalizers, that one cannot entertain hope in
the proletariat. The proletariat proved "incapable" of avert-
ing the last imperialist war although the material prerequi-
sites for a socialist revolution already existed at that time.
The successes of fascism after the war were once again the
consequence of the "incapacity" of the proletariat to lead
capitalist society out of the blind alley. The bureaucratiza-
tion of the Soviet state was in its turn the consequence of
the "incapacity" of the proletariat itself to regulate society
through the democratic mechanism. The Spanish revolution was strangled by the fascist and Stalinist bureaucracies before the very eyes of the world proletariat.* Finally,

---

* Trotsky's writings on the revolutionary upsurge in Spain and the
1936–39 civil war are collected in *The Spanish Revolution 1931–39*
(New York: Pathfinder, 1973).

the last link in this chain is the new imperialist war, the preparation of which took place quite openly, with complete impotence on the part of the world proletariat. If this conception is adopted, that is, if it is acknowledged that the proletariat does not have the forces to accomplish the socialist revolution, then the urgent task of the statification of the productive forces will obviously be accomplished by somebody else. By whom? By a new bureaucracy, which will replace the decayed bourgeoisie as a new ruling class on a world scale. That is how the question is beginning to be posed by those "leftists" who do not rest content with debating over words.

The present war and the fate of modern society

By the very march of events this question is now posed very concretely. The Second World War has begun. It attests incontrovertibly to the fact that society can no longer live on the basis of capitalism. Thereby it subjects the proletariat to a new and perhaps decisive test.

If this war provokes, as we firmly believe, a proletarian revolution, it must inevitably lead to the overthrow of the bureaucracy in the USSR and regeneration of Soviet democracy on a far higher economic and cultural basis than in 1918. In that case the question as to whether the Stalinist bureaucracy was a "class" or a growth on the workers state will be automatically solved. To every single person it will become clear that in the process of the development of the world revolution the Soviet bureaucracy was only an *episodic* relapse.

If, however, it is conceded that the present war will provoke not revolution but a decline of the proletariat, then there remains another alternative: the further decay of monopoly capitalism, its further fusion with the state and the replacement of democracy wherever it still remained by a totalitarian regime. The inability of the proletariat to take into its hands the leadership of society could actually lead under these conditions to the growth of a new exploiting class from the Bonapartist fascist bureaucracy. This would be, according to all indications, a regime of decline, signalizing the eclipse of civilization.

An analogous result might occur in the event that the proletariat of advanced capitalist countries, having conquered power, should prove incapable of holding it and surrender it, as in the USSR, to a privileged bureaucracy. Then we would be compelled to acknowledge that the reason for the bureaucratic relapse is rooted not in the backwardness of the country and not in the imperialist environment but in the congenital incapacity of the proletariat to become a ruling class. Then it would be necessary in retrospect to establish that in its fundamental traits the present USSR was the precursor of a new exploiting regime on an international scale.

We have diverged very far from the terminological controversy over the nomenclature of the Soviet state. But let our critics not protest; only by taking the necessary historical perspective can one provide himself with a correct judgment upon such a question as the replacement of one social regime by another. The historic alternative, carried to the end, is as follows: either the Stalin regime is an abhorrent relapse in the process of transforming bourgeois society into a socialist society, or the Stalin regime is the first stage of a new exploiting society. If the second prognosis proves to be correct, then, of course, the bureaucracy will become a new exploiting class. However onerous the second perspective may be, if the world proletariat should actually prove incapable of fulfilling the mission placed upon it by the course of development, nothing else would remain except only to recognize that the socialist program, based on the internal contradictions of capitalist society, ended as a utopia. It is self-evident that a new "minimum" program would be required—for the defense of the interests of the slaves of the totalitarian bureaucratic society.

But are there such incontrovertible or even impressive objective data as would compel us today to renounce the prospect of the socialist revolution? That is the whole question.

The theory of 'bureaucratic collectivism'

Shortly after the assumption of power by Hitler, a German "left-communist," Hugo Urbahns, came to the conclusion that in place of capitalism a new historical era of "state capitalism" was impending. The first examples of this regime he named as Italy, the USSR, Germany. Urbahns, however, did not draw the political conclusions of his theory. Recently, an Italian "left-communist," Bruno R., who formerly adhered to the Fourth International, came to the conclusion that "bureaucratic collectivism" was about to replace capitalism. (Bruno R., *La Bureaucratisation du monde*; Paris, 1939, 350 pp.) The new bureaucracy is a class, its relation to the toilers is collective exploitation, the proletarians are transformed into the slaves of totalitarian exploiters.

Bruno R. brackets together planned economy in the USSR, fascism, National Socialism and Roosevelt's "New Deal." All these regimes undoubtedly possess common traits, which in the last analysis are determined by the collectivist tendencies of modern economy. Lenin even prior to the October revolution formulated the main peculiarities of imperialist capitalism as follows: gigantic concentration of productive forces, the heightening fusion of monopoly capitalism with the state, an organic tendency toward naked dictatorship as a result of this fusion. The traits of centralization and collectivization determine both the politics of revolution and the politics of counterrevolution; but this by no means signifies that it is possible to equate revolution, Thermidor, fascism, and American "reformism." Bruno has caught on to the fact that the tendencies of collectivization assume, as a result of the political prostration of the working class, the form of "bureaucratic collectivism." The phenomenon in itself is incontestable. But where are its limits, and what is its historical weight? What we accept as the deformity of a transitional period, the result of the unequal development of multiple factors in the social process, is taken by Bruno R. for an independent social formation in which the bureaucracy is the ruling class. Bruno R. in any case has the merit of seeking to transfer the question from the charmed circle of terminological copybook exercises to the plane of major historical generalizations. This makes it all the easier to disclose his mistake.

Like many ultralefts, Bruno R. identifies in essence Stalinism with fascism. On the one side the Soviet bureaucracy has adopted the political methods of fascism; on the other side the fascist bureaucracy, which still confines itself to "partial" measures of state intervention, is heading toward and will soon reach complete statification of economy. The first assertion is absolutely correct. But Bruno's assertion that fascist "anticapitalism" is capable of arriving at the expropriation of the bourgeoisie is completely erroneous. "Partial" measures of state intervention and of nationalization in reality differ from planned state economy just as reforms differ from revolution. Mussolini and Hitler are only "coordinating" the interests of the property owners and "regulating" capitalist economy, and, moreover, primarily for war purposes. The Kremlin oligarchy is something else again: it has the opportunity of directing economy as a body only owing to the fact that the working class of Russia accomplished the greatest overturn of property relations in history. This difference must not be lost sight of.

But even if we grant that Stalinism and fascism from opposite poles will some day arrive at one and the same type of exploitive society ("bureaucratic collectivism" according to Bruno R.'s terminology) this still will not lead humanity out of the blind alley. The crisis of the capitalist system is produced not only by the reactionary role of private property but also by the no less reactionary role of the national state. Even if the various fascist governments did succeed in establishing a system of planned economy at home then, aside from the, in the long run, inevitable revolutionary movements of the proletariat unforeseen by any plan, the struggle between the totalitarian states for world domination would be continued and even intensified. Wars would devour the fruits of planned economy and destroy the bases of civilization. Bertrand Russell thinks, it is true, that some victorious state may, as a result of the war, unify the entire world in a totalitarian vise. But even if such a hypothesis should be realized, which is highly doubtful, military "unification" would have no greater stability than the Versailles treaty. National uprisings and pacifications would culminate in a new world war, which would be the grave of civilization. Not our subjective wishes but the objective reality speaks for it, that the only way out for humanity is the world socialist revolution. The alternative to it is the relapse into barbarism.

The proletariat and its leadership

We shall very soon devote a separate article to the question of the relation between the class and its leadership. We shall confine ourselves here to the most indispensable. Only vulgar "Marxists" who take it that politics is a mere and direct "reflection" of economics, are capable of thinking that leadership reflects the class directly and simply. In reality leadership, having risen above the oppressed class, inevitably succumbs to the pressure of the ruling class. The leadership of the American trade unions, for instance, "reflects" not so much the proletariat, as the bourgeoisie. The selection and education of a truly revolutionary leadership, capable of withstanding the pressure of the bourgeoisie, is an extraordinarily difficult task. The dialectics of the historic process expressed itself most brilliantly in the fact that the proletariat of the most backward country, Russia, under certain historic conditions, has put forward the most farsighted and courageous leadership. On the contrary, the proletariat in the country of the oldest capitalist culture, Great Britain, has even today the most dull-witted and servile leadership.

The crisis of capitalist society which assumed an open character in July 1914, from the very first day of the war produced a sharp crisis in the proletarian leadership. During the twenty-five years that have elapsed since that time, the proletariat of the advanced capitalist countries has not yet created a leadership that could rise to the level of the tasks of our epoch. The experience of Russia testifies, however, that such a leadership can be created. (This does not mean, of course, that it will be immune to degeneration.) The question consequently stands as follows: Will objective historical necessity in the long run cut a path for itself in the consciousness of the vanguard of the working class; that is, in the process of this war and those profound shocks which it must engender, will a genuine revolutionary leadership be formed capable of leading the proletariat to the conquest of power?

The Fourth International has replied in the affirmative to this question, not only through the text of its program, but also through the very fact of its existence. All the various types of disillusioned and frightened representatives of pseudo-Marxism proceed *on the contrary* from the assumption that the bankruptcy of the leadership only "reflects" the incapacity of the proletariat to fulfill its revolutionary mission. Not all our opponents express this thought clearly, but all of them—ultralefts, centrists, anarchists, not to mention Stalinists and Social Democrats—shift the responsibility for the defeats from themselves to the shoulders of the proletariat. None of them indicate under precisely what conditions the proletariat will be capable of accomplishing the socialist overturn.

If we grant as true that the cause of the defeats is rooted in the social qualities of the proletariat itself then the position of modern society will have to be acknowledged as hopeless. Under conditions of decaying capitalism the proletariat grows neither numerically nor culturally. There are no grounds, therefore, for expecting that it will sometime rise to the level of the revolutionary tasks. Altogether differently does the case present itself to him who has clarified in his mind the profound antagonism between the organic, deep-going, insurmountable urge of the toiling masses to tear themselves free from the bloody capitalist chaos, and the conservative, patriotic, utterly bourgeois character of the outlived labor leadership. We must choose one of these two irreconcilable conceptions.

Totalitarian dictatorship—a condition of acute crisis and not a stable regime

The October revolution was not an accident. It was forecast long in advance. Events confirmed this forecast. The degeneration does not refute the forecast, because Marxists never believed that an isolated workers state in Russia could maintain itself indefinitely. True enough, we expected the wrecking of the Soviet state, rather than its degeneration; to put it more correctly, we did not sharply differentiate between those two possibilities. But they do not at all contradict each other. Degeneration must inescapably end at a certain stage in downfall.

A totalitarian regime, whether of Stalinist or fascist type, by its very essence can be only a temporary transitional regime. Naked dictatorship in history has generally been the product and the symptom of an especially severe social crisis, and not at all of a stable regime. Severe crisis cannot be a permanent condition of society. A totalitarian state is capable of suppressing social contradictions during a certain period, but it is incapable of perpetuating itself. The monstrous purges in the USSR are most convincing testimony of the fact that Soviet society organically tends toward ejection of the bureaucracy.

It is an astonishing thing that Bruno R. sees precisely in the Stalinist purges proof of the fact that the bureaucracy has become a ruling class, for in his opinion only a ruling class is capable of measures on so large a scale.* He forgets however that tsarism, which was not a "class," also permitted itself rather large-scale measures in purges and moreover precisely in the period when it was nearing its doom. Symptomatic of his oncoming death agony, by the sweep and monstrous fraudulence of his purge, Stalin tes-

---

* True enough, in the last section of his book, which consists of fantastic contradictions, Bruno R. quite consciously and articulately refutes his own theory of "bureaucratic collectivism" unfolded in the first section of the book and declares that Stalinism, fascism, and nazism are transitory and parasitic formations, historic penalties for the impotence of the proletariat. In other words, after having subjected the views of the Fourth International to the sharpest kind of criticism, Bruno R. unexpectedly returns to those views, but only in order to launch a new series of blind fumblings. We see no grounds for following in the footsteps of a writer who has obviously lost his balance. We are interested in those of his arguments by means of which he seeks to substantiate his views that the bureaucracy is a class.—L.T.

tifies to nothing else but the incapacity of the bureaucracy to transform itself into a stable ruling class. Might we not place ourselves in a ludicrous position if we affixed to the Bonapartist oligarchy the nomenclature of a new ruling class just a few years or even a few months prior to its inglorious downfall? Posing this question clearly should alone in our opinion restrain the comrades from terminological experimentation and overhasty generalizations.

The orientation toward world revolution and the regeneration of the USSR

A quarter of a century proved too brief a span for the revolutionary rearming of the world proletarian vanguard, and too long a period for preserving the soviet system intact in an isolated backward country. Mankind is now paying for this with a new imperialist war; but the basic task of our epoch has not changed, for the simple reason that it has not been solved. A colossal asset in the last quarter of a century and a priceless pledge for the future is constituted by the fact that one of the detachments of the world proletariat was able to demonstrate in action *how* the task must be solved.

The second imperialist war poses the unsolved task on a higher historical stage. It tests anew not only the stability of the existing regimes but also the ability of the proletariat to replace them. The results of this test will undoubtedly have a decisive significance for our appraisal of the modern epoch as the epoch of proletarian revolution. If contrary to all probabilities the October revolution fails during the course of the present war, or immediately thereafter, to find its continuation in any of the advanced countries; and if, on the contrary, the proletariat is thrown back everywhere and on all fronts—then we should doubtlessly have to pose the question of revising our conception of the present epoch and its driving forces. In that case it would be a question not of slapping a copybook label on the USSR or the Stalinist gang but of reevaluating the world historical perspective for the next decades if not centuries: Have we entered the epoch of social revolution and socialist society, or on the contrary the epoch of the declining society of totalitarian bureaucracy?

The twofold error of schematists like Hugo Urbahns and Bruno R. consists, first, in that they proclaim this latter regime as having been already finally installed; secondly, in that they declare it a prolonged transitional state of society between capitalism and socialism. Yet it is absolutely self-evident that if the international proletariat, as a result of the experience of our entire epoch and the current new war, proves incapable of becoming the master of society, this would signify the foundering of all hope for a socialist revolution, for it is impossible to expect any other more favorable conditions for it; in any case no one foresees them now, or is able to characterize them. Marxists do not have the slightest right (if disillusionment and fatigue are not considered "rights") to draw the conclusion that the proletariat has forfeited its revolutionary possibilities and must renounce all aspirations to hegemony in an era immediately ahead. Twenty-five years in the scales of history, when it is a question of profoundest changes in economic and cultural systems, weigh less than an hour in the life of man. What good is the individual who, because of empirical failures in the course of an hour or a day, renounces a goal that he set for himself on the basis of the experience and analysis of his entire previous lifetime? In the years of darkest Russian reaction (1907 to 1917) we took as our starting point those revolutionary possibilities which were revealed by the Russian proletariat in 1905. In the years of world reaction we must proceed from those possibilities which the Russian proletariat revealed in 1917.

The Fourth International did not by accident call itself the world party of the socialist revolution. Our road is not to be changed. We steer our course toward the world revolution and by virtue of this very fact toward the regeneration of the USSR as a workers state.

Foreign policy is the continuation of domestic policy

What do we defend in the USSR? Not that in which it resembles the capitalist countries but precisely that in which it differs from them. In Germany also we advocate an uprising against the ruling bureaucracy, but only in order immediately to overthrow capitalist property. In the USSR the overthrow of the bureaucracy is indispensable for the preservation of state property. Only in this sense do we stand for the defense of the USSR.

There is not one among us who doubts that the Soviet workers should defend the state property, not only against the parasitism of the bureaucracy, but also against the tendencies toward private ownership, for example, on the part of the kolkhoz aristocracy. But after all, foreign policy is the continuation of policy at home. If in domestic policy we correlate defense of the conquests of the October revolution with irreconcilable struggle against the bureaucracy, then we must do the same thing in foreign policy as well. To be sure, Bruno R., proceeding from the fact that "bureaucratic collectivism" has already been victorious all along the line, assures us that no one threatens state property, because Hitler (and Chamberlain?) is as much interested, you see, in preserving it as Stalin. Sad to say, Bruno R.'s assurances are frivolous. In event of victory Hitler will in all probability begin by demanding the return to German capitalists of all the property expropriated from them; then he will secure a similar restoration of property for the English, the French, and the Belgians so as to reach an agreement with them at the expense of the USSR; finally, he will make Germany the contractor of the most important state enterprises in the USSR in the interests of the German military machine. Right now Hitler is the ally and friend of Stalin; but should Hitler, with the aid of Stalin, come out victorious on the western front, he would on the morrow turn his guns against the USSR. Finally Chamberlain, too, in similar circumstances would act no differently from Hitler.

The defense of the USSR and the class struggle

Mistakes on the question of defense of the USSR most frequently flow from an incorrect understanding of the methods of "defense." Defense of the USSR does not at all mean rapprochement with the Kremlin bureaucracy, the acceptance of its politics, or a conciliation with the politics of her allies. In this question, as in all others, we remain completely on the ground of the international class struggle.

In the tiny French periodical, *Que Faire*, it was recently stated that inasmuch as the "Trotskyites" are defeatists in relation to France and England they are therefore defeatists also in relation to the USSR. In other words: If you want to defend the USSR you must stop being defeatists in relation to her imperialist allies. *Que Faire* calculated that the "democracies" would be the allies of the USSR. What these sages will say now we don't know. But that is hardly important, for their very method is rotten. To renounce defeatism in relation to that imperialist camp to which the USSR adheres today or might adhere tomorrow is to push the workers of the enemy camp to the side of their government; it means to renounce defeatism in general. The renunciation of defeatism under the conditions of imperialist war, which is tantamount to the rejection of the socialist revolution—rejection of revolution in the name of "defense of the USSR"—would sentence the USSR to final decomposition and doom.

"Defense of the USSR," as interpreted by the Comintern, like yesterday's "struggle against fascism," is based on renunciation of independent class politics. The proletariat is transformed—for various reasons in varying circumstances, but always and invariably—into an auxiliary force of one bourgeois camp against another. In contradistinction to this, some of our comrades say: Since we do not want to become tools of Stalin and his allies we therefore renounce the defense of the USSR. But by this they only demonstrate that their understanding of "defense" coincides essentially with the understanding of the opportunists; they do not think in terms of the independent politics of the proletariat. As a matter of fact, we defend the USSR as we defend the colonies, as we solve all our problems, not by supporting some imperialist governments against others, but by the method of international class struggle in the colonies as well as in the metropolitan centers.

We are not a government party; we are the party of irreconcilable opposition, not only in capitalist countries but also in the USSR. Our tasks, among them the "defense of the USSR," we realize not through the medium of bourgeois governments and not even through the government of the USSR, but exclusively through the education of the masses through agitation, through explaining to the workers what they should defend and what they should overthrow. Such a "defense" cannot give immediate miraculous results. But we do not even pretend to be miracle workers. As things stand, we are a revolutionary minority. Our work must be directed so that the workers on whom we have influence should correctly appraise events, not permit themselves to be caught unawares, and prepare the general sentiment of their own class for the revolutionary solution of the tasks confronting us.

The defense of the USSR coincides for us with the preparation of world revolution. Only those methods are permissible which do not conflict with the interests of the revolution. The defense of the USSR is related to the world socialist revolution as a tactical task is related to a strategic one. A tactic is subordinated to a strategic goal and in no case can be in contradiction to the latter.

The question of occupied territories

As I am writing these lines the question of the territories occupied by the Red Army still remains obscure.* The cable dispatches contradict each other, since both sides lie a great deal; but the actual relationships on the scene are no doubt still extremely unsettled. Most of the occupied territories will doubtlessly become part of the USSR. In what form?

Let us for a moment conceive that in accordance with the treaty with Hitler, the Moscow government leaves un-touched the rights of private property in the occupied areas and limits itself to "control" after the fascist pattern. Such a concession would have a deep-going principled character and might become a starting point for a new chapter in the history of the Soviet regime; and consequently a starting point for a new appraisal on our part of the nature of the Soviet state.

It is more likely, however, that in the territories scheduled to become a part of the USSR, the Moscow government will carry through the expropriation of the large landowners and statification of the means of production. This variant

---

* On September 17, 1939, two and a half weeks after German troops invaded Poland, Soviet forces invaded and occupied the east-ern part of the country; Moscow formally annexed the occupied territory later in the year. During September and October the Baltic countries of Estonia, Latvia, and Lithuania were forced to accept the presence of Soviet bases, leading to their total occupation in mid-1940. Shortly thereafter, they were also annexed.

is most probable not because the bureaucracy remains true to the socialist program but because it is neither desirous nor capable of sharing the power, and the privileges the latter entails, with the old ruling classes in the occupied territories. Here an analogy literally offers itself. The first Bonaparte halted the revolution by means of a military dictatorship. However, when the French troops invaded Poland, Napoleon signed a decree: "Serfdom is abolished." This measure was dictated not by Napoleon's sympathies for the peasants, nor by democratic principles, but rather by the fact that the Bonapartist dictatorship based itself not on feudal, but on bourgeois property relations. Inasmuch as Stalin's Bonapartist dictatorship bases itself not on private but on state property, the invasion of Poland by the Red Army should, in the nature of the case, result in the abolition of private capitalist property, so as thus to bring the regime of the occupied territories into accord with the regime of the USSR.

This measure, revolutionary in character—"the expropriation of the expropriators"—is in this case achieved in a military-bureaucratic fashion. The appeal to independent activity on the part of the masses in the new territories— and without such an appeal, even if worded with extreme caution it is impossible to constitute a new regime—will on the morrow undoubtedly be suppressed by ruthless police measures in order to assure the preponderance of the bureaucracy over the awakened revolutionary masses. This is one side of the matter. But there is another. In order to gain the possibility of occupying Poland through a military alliance with Hitler, the Kremlin for a long time deceived and continues to deceive the masses in the USSR and in the whole world, and has thereby brought about the complete disorganization of the ranks of its own Communist International. The primary political criterion for us is not the transformation of property relations in this or another area, however important these may be in themselves, but rather the change in the consciousness and organization of the world proletariat, the raising of their capacity for defending former conquests and accomplishing new ones. From this one, and the only decisive standpoint, the politics of Moscow, taken as a whole, completely retains its reactionary character and remains the chief obstacle on the road to the world revolution.

Our *general* appraisal of the Kremlin and the Comintern does not, however, alter the *particular* fact that the statification of property in the occupied territories is in itself a progressive measure. We must recognize this openly. Were Hitler on the morrow to throw his armies against the east to restore "law and order" in eastern Poland, the advanced workers would defend against Hitler these new property forms established by the Bonapartist Soviet bureaucracy.

We do not change our course!

The statification of the means of production is, as we said, a progressive measure. But its progressiveness is relative; its specific weight depends on the sum-total of all the other factors. Thus, we must first and foremost establish that the extension of the territory dominated by bureaucratic autocracy and parasitism, cloaked by "socialist" measures, can augment the prestige of the Kremlin, engender illusions concerning the possibility of replacing the proletarian revolution by bureaucratic maneuvers, and so on. This evil by far outweighs the progressive content of Stalinist reforms in Poland. In order that nationalized property in the occupied areas, as well as in the USSR, become a basis for genuinely progressive, that is to say socialist development, it is necessary to overthrow the Moscow bureaucracy. Our program retains, consequently, all its validity. The events did not catch us unawares. It is necessary only to interpret them correctly. It is necessary to understand clearly that sharp contradictions are contained in the character of the USSR and in her international position. It is impossible to free oneself from those contradictions with the help of terminological sleight-of-hand ("workers state"—"not workers state"). We must take the facts as they are. We must build our policy by taking as our starting point the real relations and contradictions.

We do not entrust the Kremlin with any historic mission. We were and remain against seizures of new territories by the Kremlin. We are for the independence of Soviet Ukraine, and if the Byelorussians themselves wish—of Soviet Byelorussia. At the same time, in the sections of Poland occupied by the Red Army, partisans of the Fourth International must play the most decisive part in expropriating the landlords and capitalists, in dividing the land among the peasants, in creating soviets and workers committees, etc. While so doing, they must preserve their political independence, they must fight during elections to the soviets and factory committees for the complete independence of the latter from the bureaucracy, and they must conduct revolutionary propaganda in the spirit of distrust toward the Kremlin and its local agencies.

But let us suppose that Hitler turns his weapons against the east and invades territories occupied by the Red Army. Under these conditions, partisans of the Fourth International, without changing in any way their attitude toward the Kremlin oligarchy, will advance to the forefront, as the most urgent task of the hour, the military resistance against Hitler. The workers will say: "We cannot cede to Hitler the overthrowing of Stalin; that is *our own task*." During the military struggle against Hitler, the revolutionary workers will strive to enter into the closest possible comradely relations with the rank-and-file fighters of the Red Army. While arms in hand they deal blows to Hitler, the Bolshevik-Leninists will at the same time conduct revolutionary propaganda against Stalin preparing his overthrow at the next and perhaps very near stage.

This kind of "defense of the USSR" will naturally differ, as heaven does from earth, from the official defense which is now being conducted under the slogan: "For the fatherland! For Stalin!" *Our* defense of the USSR is carried on under the slogan: "For socialism! For the world revolution! Against Stalin!" In order that these two varieties of "defense of the USSR" do not become confused in the consciousness of the masses it is necessary to know clearly and precisely how to formulate slogans which correspond to the concrete situation. But above all it is necessary to establish clearly just *what* we are defending, just *how* we are defending it, against *whom* we are defending it. Our slogans will create confusion among the masses only if we ourselves do not have a clear conception of our tasks.

Conclusions

We have no reasons whatsoever at the present time for changing our principled position in relation to the USSR.

War accelerates the various political processes. It may accelerate the process of the revolutionary regeneration of the USSR. But it may also accelerate the process of its final degeneration. For this reason it is indispensable that we follow painstakingly and without prejudice these modifications which war introduces into the internal life of the USSR so that we may give ourselves a timely accounting of them.

Our tasks in the occupied territories remain basically the same as in the USSR itself; but inasmuch as they are posed by events in an extremely sharp form, they enable us all the better to clarify our general tasks in relation to the USSR.

We must formulate our slogans in such a way that the workers see clearly just what we are defending in the USSR (state property and planned economy), and against whom we are conducting a ruthless struggle (the parasitic bureaucracy and its Comintern). We must not lose sight for a single moment of the fact that the question of overthrowing the Soviet bureaucracy is for us subordinate to the question of preserving state property in the means of production in the USSR; that the question of preserving state property in the means of production in the USSR is subordinate for us to the question of the world proletarian revolution.

3

Letter to Sherman Stanley‡

OCTOBER 8, 1939

Dear Comrade Stanley,

I received your letter to O'Brien in view of his departure. The letter produced upon me a strange impression, because in opposition to your very good articles, it is full of contradictions.

I didn't receive as yet any material about the plenum and don't know either the text of the majority resolution or that of M.S. [Max Shachtman] but you affirm that there is not an irreconcilable opposition between the two texts. At the same time you affirm that a "disaster" approaches the party. Why? Even if there have been two *irreconcilable* positions, it would signify not a "disaster" but a necessity to fight out the political struggle to the end. But if both motions represent only nuances of the same point of view expressed in the program of the Fourth International, how can arise from this unprincipled (in your opinion) divergence, a catastrophe? That the majority preferred their own nuance (if it is only a nuance) is natural. But what is absolutely unnatural is that the minority proclaims: "because you, the majority, accept your own nuance and not ours we foretell catastrophe." From the side of whom??? . . . And you affirm that you "look objectively upon the different groupings." It is not my impression at all.

You write for example that from my article "one page *for some reason or other* was missing." You express in this way a very venomous suspicion towards responsible comrades. The page was missing by a regrettable nonchalance in our office here, and we sent already a new, complete text for translation.*

Your argument about the degenerated "workers *empire*" seems to me not a very happy invention. "Tsarist expansion program" was objected to [charged against] the Bolsheviks almost from the first day of the October revolution. Even a sound workers state would tend toward expansion, and the geographical lines would inevitably coincide with the general lines of the tsarist expansion because revolutions don't ordinarily change geographical conditions. What we object to about the Kremlin gang is not the expansion and not the geographical direction of the expansion but the bureaucratic, counterrevolutionary methods of the expansion. But at the same time because we as Marxists "look objectively" upon historic happenings we recognize that neither the tsar, nor Hitler, nor Chamberlain had or have the custom of abolishing, in the occupied countries, capitalist property, and this fact, a very progressive one, depends upon another fact; namely, that the October revolution is not definitely assassinated by the bureaucracy, and that the last is forced by its position to take measures which we must defend in a given situation against imperialist enemies. These progressive measures are, of course, incomparably less important

---

* The document, "The USSR in War," arrived while the plenum of the National Committee of the Socialist Workers Party was in session. One page was missing. The political line of this document was endorsed by the majority of the plenum. The minority raised a hue and cry about the missing page, charging, among other things, that it was being deliberately suppressed.

than the general counterrevolutionary activity of the bureaucracy: it is why we find it necessary to overthrow the bureaucracy. . . .

The comrades are very indignant about the Stalin-Hitler pact. It is comprehensible. They wish to get revenge on Stalin. Very good. But today we are weak, and we cannot immediately overthrow the Kremlin. Some comrades try then to find a purely verbalistic satisfaction: they strike out from the USSR the title, workers state, as Stalin deprives a disgraced functionary of the Order of Lenin. I find it, my dear friend, a bit childish. Marxist sociology and hysteria are absolutely irreconcilable.

With best comradely greetings,

Crux [Leon Trotsky]

4

Again and once more again on the nature of the USSR

OCTOBER 18, 1939

Psychoanalysis and Marxism

Certain comrades, or former comrades, such as Bruno R., having forgotten the past discussions and decisions of the Fourth International, attempt to explain my personal estimate of the Soviet state psychoanalytically. "Since Trotsky participated in the Russian revolution, it is difficult for him to lay aside the idea of the workers state inasmuch as he would have to renounce his whole life's cause," etc. I think that the old Freud, who was very perspicacious, would have cuffed the ears of psychoanalysts of this ilk a little. Naturally I would never risk taking such action myself. Nevertheless I dare assure my critics that subjectivity and sentimentality are not on my side but on theirs.

Moscow's conduct, which has passed all bounds of abjectness and cynicism, calls forth an easy revolt within every proletarian revolutionary. Revolt engenders need for rejection. When the forces for immediate action are absent, impatient revolutionaries are inclined to resort to artificial methods. Thus arises, for example, the tactic of individual terror. More frequently resort is taken to strong expressions, to insults, and to imprecation. In the case which concerns us certain comrades are manifestly inclined to seek com-

pensation through "terminological" terror. However, even
from this point of view the mere fact of qualifying the bureaucracy as a class is worthless. If the Bonapartist riffraff
is a class this means that it is not an abortion but a viable
child of history. If its marauding parasitism is "exploitation" in the scientific sense of the term, this means that the
bureaucracy possesses a historical future as the ruling class
indispensable to the given system of economy. Here we have
the end to which impatient revolt leads when it cuts itself
loose from Marxist discipline!

When an emotional mechanic considers an automobile in
which, let us say, gangsters have escaped from police pursuit
over a bad road, and finds the frame bent, the wheels out
of line, and the motor partially damaged, he might quite
justifiably say: "It is not an automobile—devil knows what
it is!" Such an estimate would lack any technical and scientific value, but it would express the legitimate reaction
of the mechanic at the work of the gangsters. Let us suppose, however, that this same mechanic must recondition
the object which he named "devil-knows-what-it-is." In this
case he will start with the recognition that it is a damaged
automobile before him. He will determine which parts are
still good and which are beyond repair in order to decide
how to begin work. The class-conscious worker will have
a similar attitude toward the USSR. He has full right to say
that the gangsters of the bureaucracy have transformed the
workers state into "devil-knows-what-it-is." But when he
passes from this explosive reaction to the solution of the political problem, he is forced to recognize that it is a damaged
workers state before him, in which the motor of economy
is damaged, but which still continues to run and which can
be completely reconditioned with the replacement of some
parts. Of course this is only an analogy. Nevertheless it is
worth reflecting over.

'A counterrevolutionary workers state'

Some voices cry out: "If we continue to recognize the USSR as a workers state, we will have to establish a new category: the counterrevolutionary workers state." This argument attempts to shock our imagination by opposing a good programmatic norm to a miserable, mean, even repugnant reality. But haven't we observed from day to day since 1923 how the Soviet state has played a more and more counterrevolutionary role on the international arena? Have we forgotten the experience of the Chinese revolution, of the 1926 general strike in England, and finally the very fresh experience of the Spanish revolution?* There are two completely counterrevolutionary workers Internationals. These critics have apparently forgotten this "category." The trade unions of France, Great Britain, the United States, and other countries support completely the counterrevolutionary politics of their bourgeoisie. This does not prevent us from labeling them trade unions, from supporting their progressive steps, and from defending them against the bourgeoisie. Why is it impossible to employ the same method with the counterrevolutionary workers state? In the last analysis a workers state is a trade union which has conquered power. The difference in attitude in these two cases is explainable by the simple fact that the trade unions have a long history and we have become accustomed to consider them as realities and not simply as "categories" in our program. But, as regards the workers state there is being evinced an inability to learn to approach it as a real historical fact which has not subordinated itself to our program.

---

* Trotsky's writings on the Chinese revolution of 1925–27 and on the British general strike of 1926 are collected in *Leon Trotsky on China* (New York: Pathfinder, 1976) and *Leon Trotsky on Britain* (New York: Pathfinder, 1973).

'Imperialism'?

Can the present expansion of the Kremlin be termed imperialism? First of all we must establish what social content is included in this term. History has known the "imperialism" of the Roman state based on slave labor, the imperialism of feudal land ownership, the imperialism of commercial and industrial capital, the imperialism of the tsarist monarchy, etc. The driving force behind the Moscow bureaucracy is indubitably the tendency to expand its power, its prestige, its revenues. This is the element of "imperialism" in the widest sense of the word which was a property in the past of all monarchies, oligarchies, ruling castes, medieval estates, and classes. However, in contemporary literature, at least Marxist literature, imperialism is understood to mean the *expansionist policy of finance capital*, which has a very sharply defined economic content. To employ the term "imperialism" for the foreign policy of the Kremlin—without elucidating exactly what this signifies—means simply to identify the policy of the Bonapartist bureaucracy with the policy of monopolistic capitalism on the basis that both one and the other utilize military force for expansion. Such an identification, capable of sowing only confusion, is much more proper to petty-bourgeois democrats than to Marxists.

Continuation of the policy of tsarist imperialism

The Kremlin participates in a new division of Poland, the Kremlin lays hands upon the Baltic states, the Kremlin orients toward the Balkans, Persia, and Afghanistan; in other words, the Kremlin continues the policy of tsarist imperialism. Do we not have the right in this case to label the policy of the Kremlin itself imperialist? This historical-geographical argument is no more convincing than any of the others. The proletarian revolution, which occurred on the territory of the tsarist empire, attempted from the very beginning to conquer and for a time conquered the Baltic countries; attempted to penetrate Romania and Persia and at one time led its armies up to Warsaw (1920). The lines of revolutionary expansion were the same as those of tsarism, since revolution does not change geographical conditions. That is precisely why the Mensheviks at that time already spoke of Bolshevik imperialism as borrowed from the traditions of tsarist diplomacy. The petty-bourgeois democracy willingly resorts to this argument even now. We have no reason, I repeat, for imitating them in this.

Agency of imperialism?

However, aside from the manner in which to appraise the expansionist policy of the USSR itself, there remains the question of the help which Moscow provides the imperialist policy of Berlin. Here first of all, it is necessary to establish that under certain conditions—up to a certain degree and in a certain form—the support of this or that imperialism would be inevitable even for a completely healthy workers state—in virtue of the impossibility of breaking away from the chains of world imperialist relations. The Brest-Litovsk peace without the least doubt temporarily reinforced German imperialism against France and England.* An isolated workers state cannot fail to maneuver between the hostile imperialist camps. Maneuvering means temporarily supporting one of them against the other. To know exactly which one of the two camps it is more advantageous or less dan-

---

* The Brest-Litovsk peace treaty ended Berlin's war against the new Soviet government in March 1918. The highly unfavorable terms imposed by the German capitalists had to be accepted, Lenin explained, because to continue the war would have torn apart the worker-peasant alliance on which rested the Soviet state and its capacity for self-defense.

gerous to support at a certain moment is not a question of principle but of practical calculation and foresight. The inevitable disadvantage which is engendered as a consequence of this constrained support of one bourgeois state against another is more than covered by the fact that the isolated workers state is thus given the possibility of continuing its existence.

But there is maneuvering and maneuvering. At Brest-Litovsk the Soviet government sacrificed the national independence of the Ukraine in order to salvage the workers state. Nobody could speak of treason toward the Ukraine, since all the class-conscious workers understood the forced character of this sacrifice. It is completely different with Poland. The Kremlin has never and at no place represented the question as if it had been *constrained* to sacrifice Poland. On the contrary, it boasts cynically of its combination, which affronts, rightfully, the most elementary democratic feelings of the oppressed classes and peoples throughout the world and thus weakens extremely the international situation of the Soviet Union. The economic transformations in the occupied provinces do not compensate for this by even a tenth part!

The entire foreign policy of the Kremlin in general is based upon a scoundrelly embellishment of the "friendly" imperialism and thus leads to the sacrifice of the fundamental interests of the world workers movement for secondary and unstable advantages. After five years of duping the workers with slogans for the "defense of the democracies" Moscow is now occupied with covering up Hitler's policy of pillage. This in itself still does not change the USSR into an imperialist state. But Stalin and his Comintern are now indubitably the most valuable agency of imperialism.

If we want to define the foreign policy of the Kremlin exactly, we must say that it is the policy of the *Bonapartist bureaucracy of a degenerated workers state in imperialist encirclement.* This definition is not as short or as sonorous as "imperialist policy," but in return it is more precise.

'The lesser evil'

The occupation of eastern Poland by the Red Army is to be sure a "lesser evil" in comparison with the occupation of the same territory by Nazi troops. But this lesser evil was obtained because Hitler was assured of achieving a greater evil. If somebody sets or helps to set a house on fire and afterward saves five out of ten of the occupants of the house in order to convert them into his own semi-slaves, that is to be sure a lesser evil than to have burned the entire ten. But it is dubious that this firebug merits a medal for the rescue. If nevertheless a medal were given to him he should be shot immediately after as in the case of the hero in one of Victor Hugo's novels.

'Armed missionaries'

Robespierre once said that people do not like missionaries with bayonets. By this he wished to say that it is impossible to impose revolutionary ideas and institutions on other people through military violence. This correct thought does not signify of course the inadmissibility of military intervention in other countries in order to cooperate in a revolution. But such an intervention, as part of a revolutionary international policy, must be understood by the international proletariat, must correspond to the desires of the toiling masses of the country on whose territory the revolutionary troops enter. The theory of socialism in one country is not capable, naturally, of creating this active international solidarity which alone can prepare and justify armed intervention. The Kremlin poses and resolves the question of military intervention, like all other questions of its policy, absolutely independently of the ideas and feelings of the international working class. Because of this, the latest diplomatic "successes" of the Kremlin monstrously compromise the USSR and introduce extreme confusion into the ranks of the world proletariat.

Insurrection on two fronts

But if the question thus shapes itself—some comrades say—is it proper to speak of the defense of the USSR and the occupied provinces? Is it not more correct to call upon the workers and peasants in both parts of former Poland to arise against Hitler as well as against Stalin? Naturally, this is very attractive. If revolution surges up simultaneously in Germany and in the USSR, including the newly occupied provinces, this would resolve many questions at one blow. But our policy cannot be based upon only the most favorable, the most happy combination of circumstances. The question is posed thus: What to do if Hitler, before he is crushed by revolution, attacks the Ukraine before revolution has smashed Stalin? Will the partisans of the Fourth International in this case fight against the troops of Hitler as they fought in Spain in the ranks of the Republican troops against Franco? We are completely and wholeheartedly for an independent (of Hitler as well as of Stalin) Soviet Ukraine. But what to do if, before having obtained this independence, Hitler attempts to seize the Ukraine which is under the domination of the Stalinist bureaucracy? The Fourth International answers: Against Hitler we will defend this Ukraine enslaved by Stalin.

'Unconditional defense of the USSR'

What does "unconditional" defense of the USSR mean? It means that we do not lay any conditions upon the bureaucracy. It means that independently of the motive and causes of the war we defend the social basis of the USSR, if it is menaced by danger on the part of imperialism.

Some comrades say: "And if the Red Army tomorrow invades India and begins to put down a revolutionary movement there, shall we in this case support it?" Such a way of posing a question is not at all consistent. It is not clear above all why India is implicated. Is it not simpler to ask: If the Red Army menaces workers' strikes or peasant protests against the bureaucracy in the USSR, shall we support it or not? Foreign policy is the continuation of the internal. We have never promised to support *all* the actions of the Red Army, which is an instrument in the hands of the Bonapartist bureaucracy. We have promised to defend only the USSR as a workers state and solely those things within it which belong to a workers state.

An adroit casuist can say: If the Red Army, independently of the character of the "work" fulfilled by it, is beaten by the insurgent masses in India, this will weaken the USSR. To this we will answer: The crushing of a revolutionary movement in India, with the cooperation of the Red Army, would signify an incomparably greater danger to the social basis of the USSR than an episodical defeat of counterrevolutionary detachments of the Red Army in India. In every case the Fourth International will know how to distinguish where and when the Red Army is acting solely as an instrument of the Bonapartist reaction and where it defends the social basis of the USSR.

A trade union led by reactionary fakers organizes a strike against the admission of Negro workers into a certain branch of industry. Shall we support such a shameful strike? Of course not. But let us imagine that the bosses, utilizing the given strike, make an attempt to crush the trade union and to make impossible in general the organized self-defense of the workers. In this case we will defend the trade union as a matter of course in spite of its reactionary leadership. Why is not this same policy applicable to the USSR?

The fundamental rule

The Fourth International has established firmly that in all imperialist countries, independent of the fact as to whether they are in alliance with the USSR or in a camp hostile to it, the proletarian parties during the war must develop the class struggle with the purpose of seizing power. At the same time the proletariat of the imperialist countries must not lose sight of the interests of the USSR's defense (or of that of colonial revolutions) and in case of real necessity must resort to the most decisive action, for instance, strikes, acts of sabotage, etc. The groupings of the powers since the time the Fourth International formulated this rule have changed radically. But the rule itself retains all its validity. If England and France tomorrow menace Leningrad or Moscow, the British and French workers should take the most decisive measures in order to hinder the sending of soldiers and military supplies. If Hitler finds himself constrained by the logic of the situation to send Stalin military supplies, the German workers, on the contrary, would have no reason for resorting in this concrete case to strikes or sabotage. Nobody, I hope, will propose any other solution.

'Revision of Marxism'?

Some comrades evidently were surprised that I spoke in my article ("The USSR in War") of the system of "bureaucratic collectivism" as a theoretical possibility. They discovered in this even a complete revision of Marxism. This is an apparent misunderstanding. The Marxist comprehension of historical necessity has nothing in common with fatalism. Socialism is not realizable "by itself," but as a result of the struggle of living forces, classes, and their parties.

The proletariat's decisive advantage in this struggle resides in the fact that it represents historical progress, while the bourgeoisie incarnates reaction and decline. Precisely in this is the source of our conviction in victory. But we have full right to ask ourselves: What character will society take if the forces of reaction conquer?

Marxists have formulated an incalculable number of times the alternative: either socialism or return to barbarism. After the Italian "experience" we repeated thousands of times: either communism or fascism. The real passage to socialism cannot fail to appear incomparably more complicated, more heterogeneous, more contradictory than was foreseen in the general historical scheme. Marx spoke about the dictatorship of the proletariat and its future withering away but said nothing about bureaucratic degeneration of the dictatorship. We have observed and analyzed for the first time in experience such a degeneration. Is this revision of Marxism?

The march of events has succeeded in demonstrating that the delay of the socialist revolution engenders the indubitable phenomena of barbarism—chronic unemployment, pauperization of the petty bourgeoisie, fascism, finally wars of extermination which do not open up any new road. What social and political forms can the new "barbarism" take, if we admit theoretically that mankind should not be able to elevate itself to socialism? We have the possibility of expressing ourselves on this subject more concretely than Marx. Fascism on one hand, degeneration of the Soviet state on the other, outline the social and political forms of a neobarbarism. An alternative of this kind—socialism or totalitarian servitude—has not only theoretical interest, but also enormous importance in agitation, because in its light the necessity for socialist revolution appears most graphically.

If we are to speak of a revision of Marx, it is in reality

the revision of those comrades who project a new type of state, "nonbourgeois" and "nonworker." Because the alternative developed by me leads them to draw their own thoughts up to their logical conclusion, some of these critics, frightened by the conclusions of their own theory, accuse me . . . of revising Marxism. I prefer to think that it is simply a friendly jest.

The right of revolutionary optimism

I endeavored to demonstrate in my article "The USSR in War" that the perspective of a nonworker and nonbourgeois society of exploitation, or "bureaucratic collectivism," is the perspective of complete defeat and the decline of the international proletariat, the perspective of the most profound historical pessimism.

Are there any genuine reasons for such a perspective? It is not superfluous to inquire about this among our class enemies.

In the weekly of the well-known newspaper *Paris-Soir* of August 31, 1939, an extremely instructive conversation is reported between the French ambassador Coulondre and Hitler on August 25, at the time of their last interview. (The source of the information is undoubtedly Coulondre himself.) Hitler sputters, boasts of the pact which he concluded with Stalin ("a realistic pact"), and "regrets" that German and French blood will be spilled.

"But," Coulondre objects, "Stalin displayed great doubledealing. The real victor (in case of war) will be Trotsky. Have you thought this over?"

"I know," Der Führer responds, "but why did France and Britain give Poland complete freedom of action?" etc.

These gentlemen like to give a personal name to the specter of revolution. But this of course is not the essence of this dramatic conversation at the very moment when diplomatic relations were ruptured. "War will inevitably provoke revolution," the representative of imperialist democracy, himself chilled to the marrow, frightens his adversary.

"I know," Hitler responds, as if it were a question decided long ago. "I know." Astonishing dialogue!

Both of them, Coulondre and Hitler, represent the barbarism which advances over Europe. At the same time neither of them doubts that their barbarism will be conquered by socialist revolution. Such is now the awareness of the ruling classes of all the capitalist countries of the world. Their complete demoralization is one of the most important elements in the relation of class forces. The proletariat has a young and still weak revolutionary leadership. But the leadership of the bourgeoisie rots on its feet. At the very outset of the war which they could not avert, these gentlemen are convinced in advance of the collapse of their regime. This fact alone must be for us the source of invincible revolutionary optimism!

5

The referendum and democratic centralism*

OCTOBER 21, 1939

We demand a referendum on the war question because we want to paralyze or weaken the centralism of the imperialist state. But can we recognize the referendum as a normal method for deciding issues in our own party? It is not possible to answer this question except in the negative.

Whoever is in favor of a referendum recognizes by this that a party decision is simply an arithmetical total of local decisions, every one of the locals being inevitably restricted by its own forces and by its limited experience. Whoever is in favor of a referendum must be in favor of imperative mandates; that is, in favor of such a procedure that every local has the right to *compel* its representative at a party convention to vote in a definite manner. Whoever recognizes imperative mandates automatically denies the significance of conventions as the highest organ of the party. Instead of a convention it is sufficient to introduce a counting of local votes. The party as a centralized whole disappears. By

---

* In the course of its factional struggle, the minority put forward the demand for a referendum on the issue in dispute concerning the USSR. The majority opposed this. Trotsky came out in support of the majority's rejection of a referendum.

accepting a referendum the influence of the most advanced locals and most experienced and farsighted comrades of the capital or industrial centers is substituted for the influence of the least experienced, backward sections, etc.

Naturally we are in favor of an all-sided examination and of voting upon every question by each party local, by each party cell. But at the same time every delegate chosen by a local must have the right to weigh all the arguments relating to the question in the convention and to vote as his political judgment demands of him. If he votes in the convention against the majority which delegated him, and if he is not able to convince his organization of his correctness after the convention, then the organization can subsequently deprive him of its political confidence. Such cases are inevitable. But they are incomparably a lesser evil than the system of referendums or imperative mandates which completely kill the party as a whole.

COYOACÁN, D.F.

6

Letter to Sherman Stanley‡

OCTOBER 22, 1939

Dear Comrade Stanley:

It is with some delay that I answer your letter of October 11.

1. You say that "there can be no serious differences or disagreements" on the Russian question. If this is so, why the terrible alarm in the party against the National Committee, i.e., its majority? You should not substitute your own conceptions for that of the minority members of the National Committee who considered the question serious and burning enough to provoke a discussion just at the threshold of the war.

2. I cannot agree with you that my statement does not contradict that of Comrade M.S. The contradiction concerns two fundamental points:

(a) The class nature of the USSR.

(b) The defense of the USSR.

On the first question, Comrade M.S. places a question mark, which signifies that he denies the old decision and postpones making a new decision. A revolutionary party cannot live between two decisions, one annihilated, the other not presented. In the question of the defense of the USSR or the new occupied territories against Hitler's (or Great Britain's) attack, Comrade M.S. proposes a revolution against Stalin and Hitler. This abstract formula signifies negating the defense in a concrete situation. I attempted to analyze this question in a new article sent yesterday by airmail to the National Committee.

3. I agree with you completely that only a serious discussion can clarify the matter, but I don't believe that voting simultaneously for the statement of the majority and that of Comrade M.S. could contribute to the necessary clarification.

4. You state in your letter that the main issue is not the Russian question but the "internal regime." I have heard this accusation often since almost the very beginning of the existence of our movement in the United States. The formulations varied a bit, the groupings too, but a number of comrades always remained in opposition to the "regime." They were, for example, against the entrance into the Socialist Party (not to go further into the past).* However it immediately occurred that not the entrance was the "main issue" but the regime. Now the same formula is repeated in connection with the Russian question.

5. I for my part believe that the passage through the Socialist Party was a salutary action for the whole development of our party and that the "regime" (or the leadership) which assured this passage was correct against the opposition which at that time represented the tendency of stagnation.

6. Now at the beginning of the war a new sharp opposition

---

* In mid-1936 members of the Workers Party of the U.S., predecessor of the SWP, joined the Socialist Party to fuse with revolutionary-minded workers and youth then joining it in large numbers. After winning over many of these forces, former Workers Party members and other militants were expelled by the SP leadership in mid-1937. The expelled members formed the Socialist Workers Party on January 1, 1938.

arises on the Russian question. It concerns the correctness of our program elaborated through innumerable disputes, polemics, and discussions during at least ten years. Our decisions are of course not eternal. If somebody in a leading position has doubts and only doubts, it is his duty toward the party to clarify himself by fresh studies or by discussions inside the leading party bodies before throwing the question into the party—not in the form of elaborated new decisions, but in the form of doubts. Of course from the point of view of the statutes of the party, everybody, even a member of the Political Committee, has the right to do so, but I don't believe that this right was used in a sound manner which could contribute to the amelioration of the party regime.

7. Often in the past I have heard accusations from comrades against the National Committee as a whole—its lack of initiative, and so on. I am not the attorney of the National Committee and I am sure that many things have been omitted which should have been done. But whenever I insisted upon concretization of the accusations, I learned often that the dissatisfaction with their own local activity, with their own lack of initiative, was transformed into an accusation against the National Committee which was supposed to be Omniscient, Omnipresent, Omnibenevolent.

8. In the present case the National Committee is accused of "conservatism." I believe that to defend the old programmatic decision until it is replaced by a new one is the elementary duty of the National Committee. I believe that such "conservatism" is dictated by the self-preservation of the party itself.

9. Thus in two most important issues of the last period comrades dissatisfied with the "regime" have had in my opinion a false political attitude. The regime must be an instrument for correct policy and not for false. When the

incorrectness of their policy becomes clear, then its protagonists are often tempted to say that not this special issue is decisive but the general regime. During the development of the Left Opposition and the Fourth International we opposed such substitutions hundreds of times. When Vereecken or Sneevliet or even Molinier were beaten on all their points of difference, they declared that the genuine trouble with the Fourth International is not this or that decision but the bad regime.

10. I don't wish to make the slightest analogy between the leaders of the present opposition in our American party and the Vereeckens, Sneevliets, and so on; I know very well that the leaders of the opposition are highly qualified comrades and I hope sincerely that we will continue to work together in the most friendly manner. But I cannot help being disquieted by the fact that some of them repeat the same error at every new stage of the development of the party with the support of a group of personal adherents. I believe that in the present discussion this kind of procedure must be analyzed and severely condemned by the general opinion of the party which now has tremendous tasks to fulfill.

With best comradely greetings,

Crux [Leon Trotsky]

P.S.—In view of the fact that I speak in this letter about the majority and the minority of the National Committee, especially of the comrades of the M.S. resolution, I am sending a copy of this letter to Comrades Cannon and Shachtman.

C.

7

Letter to James P. Cannon[‡]

OCTOBER 28, 1939

Dear Jim:

Two things are clear to me from your letter of October 24: (1) that a very serious ideological fight has become inevitable and politically necessary; (2) that it would be extremely prejudicial if not fatal to connect this ideological fight with the perspective of a split, of a purge, or expulsions, and so on and so forth.

I heard for example that Comrade Gould proclaimed in a membership meeting: "You wish to expel us." But I don't know what reaction came from the other side to this. I for my part would immediately protest with the greatest vehemence such suspicions. I would propose the creation of a special control commission in order to check such affirmations and rumors. If it happens that someone of the majority launches such threats I for my part would vote for a censure or severe warning.

You have many new members and uneducated youth. They need a serious educational discussion in the light of the great events. If their thoughts at the beginning are obsessed by the perspective of personal *degradation*, i.e., demotions, loss of prestige, disqualifications, eliminations from Central Committee, etc., and so, the whole discussion would become envenomed and the authority of the leadership would be compromised.

If the leadership on the contrary opens a ruthless fight against petty-bourgeois idealistic conceptions and organizational prejudices but at the same time assures all the necessary guarantees for the discussion itself and for the minority, the result would be not only an ideological victory but an important growth in the authority of the leadership.

"A conciliation and compromise at the top" on the questions which form the matter of divergences would of course be a crime. But I for my part would propose to the minority at the top an agreement, if you wish, a compromise on the methods of the discussion and parallelly on the political collaboration. For example, (a) both sides eliminate from the discussion any threats, personal denigration, and so on; (b) both sides take the obligation of loyal collaboration during the discussion; (c) every false move (threats, or rumors of threats, or a rumor of alleged threats, resignations, and so on) should be investigated by the National Committee or a special commission as a particular fact and not thrown into the discussion and so on.

If the minority accepts such an agreement you will have the possibility of disciplining the discussion and also the advantage of having taken a good initiative. If they reject it you can at every party membership meeting present your written proposition to the minority as the best refutation of their complaints and as a good example of "our regime."

It seems to me that the last convention failed at a very bad moment (the time was not ripe) and became a kind of abortion.* The genuine discussion comes some time after

---

* The SWP's Second National Convention in early July 1939 was the scene of a preliminary struggle between the two future factions, over the organization report and the makeup of the new National Committee.

the convention. This signifies that you can't avoid a new convention at Christmas or so. The idea of a referendum is absurd. It could only facilitate a split on local lines. But I believe that the majority in the above-mentioned agreement can propose to the minority a new convention on the basis of two platforms with all the organizational guarantees for the minority.

The convention is expensive but I don't see any other means of concluding the present discussion and the party crisis it produces.

J. Hansen [Leon Trotsky]

P.S. Every serious and sharp discussion can of course lead to some desertions, departures, or even expulsions, but the whole party should be convinced from the logic of the facts that they are inevitable results occurred in spite of the best will of the leadership, and not an objective or aim of the leadership, and not the point of departure of the whole discussion. This is in my mind the decisive point of the whole matter.

J.H. [Leon Trotsky]

8

Letter to Max Shachtman‡

Dear Comrade Shachtman:

I received the transcript of your speech of October 15* which you sent me, and I read it, of course, with all the attention it deserves. I found a lot of excellent ideas and formulations which seemed to me in full accordance with our common position as it is expressed in the fundamental documents of the Fourth International. But what I could not find was an explanation for your attack upon our previous position as "insufficient, inadequate, and outdated."

You say that "It is the concreteness of the events which differ from our theoretical hypothesis and predictions that changes the situation." (Page 17.) But unfortunately you speak about the "concreteness" of the events very abstractly so that I cannot see in what respect they change the situation and what are the consequences of these changes for our politics. You mention some examples from the past. Hence, according to you, we "saw and foresaw" the degeneration of the Third International (page 18); but only after the Hit-

* This speech was delivered to a membership meeting of the New York organization of the Socialist Workers Party. It is reproduced in *Internal Bulletin*, vol. 2, no. 3, dated November 14, 1939.

ler victory did we find it necessary to proclaim the Fourth
International. This example is not formulated exactly. We
foresaw not only the degeneration of the Third International
but also the possibility of its regeneration. Only the German
experience of 1929–1933 convinced us that the Comintern
was doomed and nothing could regenerate it. But then we
changed our policy fundamentally: to the Third International we opposed the Fourth International.

But we did not draw the same conclusions concerning the
Soviet state. Why? The Third International was a party, a
selection of people on the basis of ideas and methods. This
selection became so fundamentally opposed to Marxism
that we were obliged to abandon all hope of regenerating it.
But the Soviet state is not only an ideological selection, it is
a complex of social institutions which continues to persist
in spite of the fact that the ideas of the bureaucracy are now
almost the opposite of the ideas of the October revolution.
That is why we did not renounce the possibility of regenerating the Soviet state by political revolution. Do you believe
now that we must change this attitude? If not, and I am sure
that you don't propose it, where is the fundamental change
produced by the "concreteness" of events?

In this connection you quote the slogan of the *independent Soviet Ukraine* which, as I see with satisfaction, you
accept. But you add: "As I understand our basic position
it always was to oppose separatist tendencies in the Feder-
ated Soviet Republic." (Page 19.) In respect to this you see
a fundamental "change in policy." But: (1) The slogan of an
independent Soviet Ukraine was proposed before the Hitler-
Stalin pact.* (2) This slogan is only an application on the

---

* Trotsky had raised the demand for an independent Ukraine in
1939. See *Writings of Leon Trotsky [1938–39]*, pp. 301–7; and *Writings of Leon Trotsky [1939–40]*, pp. 44–54, 74–75, and 90–92.

field of the national question of our general slogan for the revolutionary overthrow of the bureaucracy. You could with the same right say: "As I understand our basic position it was always to oppose any rebellious acts against the Soviet government." Of course, but we changed this basic position several years ago. I don't really see what new change you propose in this connection now.

You quote the march of the Red Army in 1920 into Poland and into Georgia and you continue: "Now, if there is nothing new in the situation, why does not the majority propose to hail the advance of the Red Army into Poland, into the Baltic countries, into Finland. . . ." (Page 20.) In this decisive part of your speech you establish that something is "new in the situation" between 1920 and 1939. Of course! This newness in the situation is the bankruptcy of the Third International, the degeneracy of the Soviet state, the development of the Left Opposition, and the creation of the Fourth International. This "concreteness of events" occurred precisely between 1920 and 1939. And these events explain sufficiently why we have radically changed our position toward the politics of the Kremlin, including its military politics.

It seems that you forget somewhat that in 1920 we supported not only the deeds of the Red Army but also the deeds of the GPU. From the point of view of our appreciation of the state there is no principled difference between the Red Army and the GPU. In their activities they are not only closely connected but intermeshed. We can say that in 1918 and the following years we hailed the Cheka in their fight against Russian counterrevolutionaries and imperialist spies but in 1927 when the GPU began to arrest, to exile, and to shoot the genuine Bolsheviks we changed our appreciation of this institution. This concrete change occurred at least eleven years before the Soviet-German pact. That is why I am astonished when you speak sarcastically about "the refusal even (!) of the majority to take the same position today that we all took in 1920. . . ." (Page 20.) We began to change this position in 1923. We proceeded by stages more or less in accordance with the objective developments. The decisive point of this evolution was for us 1933–34. If we fail to see just what the new fundamental changes are which you propose in our policy, it doesn't signify that we go back to 1920!

You insist especially on the necessity of abandoning the slogan for the unconditional defense of the USSR, whereupon you interpret this slogan in the past as our unconditional support of every diplomatic and military action of the Kremlin; i.e., of Stalin's policy. No, my dear Shachtman, this presentation doesn't correspond to the "concreteness of events." Already in 1927 we proclaimed in the Central Committee: "For the socialist fatherland? Yes! For the Stalinist course? No!"* Then you seem to forget the so-called "thesis on Clemenceau" which signified that in the interests of the genuine defense of the USSR, the proletarian vanguard can be obliged to eliminate the Stalin government and replace it with its own. This was proclaimed in 1927!† Five years later we explained to the workers that this change of government can be effectuated only by political revolution. Thus we separated fundamentally our defense of the USSR

---

* Contained in Trotsky, *The Stalin School of Falsification*, (New York: Pathfinder, 1971), p. 177.

† The Clemenceau thesis was an analogy used by Trotsky in 1927 to explain why the Bolshevik-Leninist Opposition should not renounce the struggle to change the line of the Communist Party in time of war or war danger. Georges Clemenceau had sharply criticized the ineffectual policies of the French capitalist government during World War I, becoming its leader in 1917 when it became apparent that he was its best defender.

as a workers state from the bureaucracy's defense of the USSR. Whereupon you interpret our past policy as unconditional support of the diplomatic and military activities of Stalin! Permit me to say that this is a horrible deformation of our whole position not only since the creation of the Fourth International but since the very beginning of the Left Opposition.

Unconditional defense of the USSR signifies, namely, that our policy is not determined by the deeds, maneuvers, or crimes of the Kremlin bureaucracy but only by our conception of the interests of the Soviet state and world revolution.

At the end of your speech you quote Trotsky's formula concerning the necessity of subordinating the defense of the nationalized property in the USSR to the interests of the world revolution, and you continue: "Now my understanding of our position in the past was that we vehemently deny any possible conflict between the two. . . . I never understood our position in the past to mean that we *subordinate* the one to the other. If I understand English, the term implies either that there is a conflict between the two or the possibility of such a conflict." (Page 37.) And from this you draw the impossibility of maintaining the slogan of unconditional defense of the Soviet Union.

This argument is based upon at least two misunderstandings. How and why could the interests of maintaining the nationalized property be in "conflict" with the interests of the world revolution? Tacitly you infer that the *Kremlin's* (not our) policy of defense can come into conflict with the interests of the world revolution. Of course! At every step! In every respect! However, our policy of defense is not conditioned by the Kremlin's policy. This is the first misunderstanding. But, you ask, if there is not a conflict why the necessity of subordination? Here is the second misunderstanding. We must subordinate the defense of the USSR to the world revolution insofar as we subordinate a *part* to a *whole*. In 1918 in the polemics with Bukharin, who insisted upon a revolutionary war against Germany, Lenin answered approximately: "If there should be a revolution in Germany now, then it would be our duty to go to war even at the risk of losing. Germany's revolution is more important than ours and we should if necessary sacrifice the Soviet power in Russia (for a while) in order to help establish it in Germany." A strike in Chicago at this time could be unreasonable in and of itself, but if it is a matter of helping a general strike on the national scale, the Chicago workers should subordinate their interests to the interests of their class and call a strike. If the USSR is involved in the war on the side of Germany, the German revolution could certainly menace the immediate interests of the defense of the USSR. Would we advise the German workers not to act? The Comintern would surely give them such advice, but not we. We will say: "We must subordinate the interests of the defense of the Soviet Union to the interests of the world revolution."

Some of your arguments are, it seems to me, answered in Trotsky's last article, "Again and Once More Again on the Nature of the USSR," which was written before I received the transcript of your speech.

You have hundreds and hundreds of new members who have not passed through our common experience. I am fearful that your presentation can lead them into the error of believing that we were unconditionally for the support of the Kremlin, at least on the international field, that we didn't foresee such a possibility as the Stalin-Hitler collaboration, that we were taken unawares by the events, and that we must fundamentally change our position. That is not true! And independently from all the other questions which are discussed or only touched upon in your speech (leadership, conservatism, party regime, and so on) we must, in my opinion, again check our position on the Russian question with all the necessary carefulness in the interest of the American section as well as of the Fourth International as a whole.

The real danger now is not the "unconditional" defense of that which is worthy of defense, but direct or indirect help to the political current which tries to identify the USSR with the fascist states for the benefit of the democracies, or to the related current which tries to put all tendencies in the same pot in order to compromise bolshevism or Marxism with Stalinism. We are the only party which really foresaw the events, not in their empirical concreteness, of course, but in their general tendency. Our strength consists in the fact that we do not need to change our orientation as the war begins. And I find it very false that some of our comrades, moved by the factional fight for a "good regime" (which they, so far as I know, have never defined), persist in shouting: "We were taken unawares! Our orientation turned out to be false! We must improvise a new line! And so on." This seems to me completely incorrect and dangerous.

With warmest comradely greetings,

Lund [Leon Trotsky]

CC: J.P. CANNON

P.S. The formulations in this letter are far from perfect since it is not an elaborated article, but only a letter dictated by me in English and corrected by my collaborator during the dictation.

L.

9

Letter to James P. Cannon‡

DECEMBER 15, 1939

Dear Comrade Cannon,

The leaders of the opposition have not accepted the struggle upon a principled plane up to now and will undoubtedly attempt to avoid it even in the future. It is not difficult consequently to guess what the leaders of the opposition will say in regard to the enclosed article. "There are many correct elementary truths in the article," they will say; "we don't deny them at all, but the article fails to answer the burning 'concrete' questions. Trotsky is too far from the party to be able to judge correctly. Not all petty-bourgeois elements are with the opposition, not all workers with the majority." Some of them will surely add that the article "ascribes" ideas to them which they have never entertained, etc.

For answers to "concrete" questions, the oppositionists want recipes from a cookbook for the epoch of imperialist wars. I don't intend to write such a cookbook. But from our principled approach to the fundamental questions we shall always be able to arrive at a correct solution for any concrete problem, complicated though it might be. Precisely in the Finnish problem the opposition demonstrated its incapacity to answer concrete questions.

There are never factions which are chemically pure in their

composition. Petty-bourgeois elements find themselves necessarily in every workers party and faction. The question is
only who sets the tone. With the opposition the tone is set
by the petty-bourgeois elements.

The inevitable accusation that the article ascribes to the
opposition ideas which they never entertained is explained by
the formlessness and contradictory character of the opposition's ideas which cannot bear the touch of critical analysis.
The article "ascribes" nothing to the leaders of the opposition, it only develops their ideas to the end. Naturally I can
see the development of the struggle only from the sidelines.
But the general traits of the struggle can often be better observed from the sidelines.

I clasp your hand warmly,

L. Trotsky
COYOACÁN, D.F.

10

A petty-bourgeois opposition in the Socialist Workers Party

DECEMBER 15, 1939

It is necessary to call things by their right names. Now that the positions of both factions in the struggle have become determined with complete clearness, it must be said that the minority of the National Committee is leading a typical petty-bourgeois tendency. Like any petty-bourgeois group inside the socialist movement, the present opposition is characterized by the following features: a disdainful attitude toward theory and an inclination toward eclecticism; disrespect for the tradition of their own organization; anxiety for personal "independence" at the expense of anxiety for objective truth; nervousness instead of consistency; readiness to jump from one position to another; lack of understanding of revolutionary centralism and hostility toward it; and finally, inclination to substitute clique ties and personal relationships for party discipline. Not all the members of the opposition of course manifest these features with identical strength. Nevertheless, as always in a variegated bloc the tinge is given by those who are most distant from Marxism and proletarian policy. A prolonged and serious struggle is obviously before us. I make no attempt to exhaust the problem in this article, but I will endeavor to outline its general features.

Theoretical skepticism and eclecticism

In the January 1939 issue of the *New International* a long article was published by Comrades Burnham and Shachtman, "Intellectuals in Retreat." The article, while containing many correct ideas and apt political characterizations, was marred by a fundamental defect if not flaw. While polemicising against opponents who consider themselves—without sufficient reason—above all as proponents of "theory," the article deliberately did not elevate the problem to a theoretical height. It was absolutely necessary to explain why the American "radical" intellectuals accept Marxism without the dialectic (a clock without a spring). The secret is simple. In no other country has there been such rejection of the class struggle as in the land of "unlimited opportunity." The denial of social contradictions as the moving force of development led to the denial of the dialectic as the logic of contradictions in the domain of theoretical thought. Just as in the sphere of politics it was thought possible everybody could be convinced of the correctness of a "just" program by means of clever syllogisms and society could be reconstructed through "rational" measures, so in the sphere of theory it was accepted as proved that Aristotelian logic, lowered to the level of "common sense," was sufficient for the solution of all questions.

Pragmatism, a mixture of rationalism and empiricism, became the national philosophy of the United States. The theoretical methodology of Max Eastman is not fundamentally different from the methodology of Henry Ford—both regard living society from the point of view of an "engineer" (Eastman—platonically). Historically the present disdainful attitude toward the dialectic is explained simply by the fact that the grandfathers and great-grandmothers of Max Eastman and others did not need the dialectic in order to conquer territory and enrich themselves. But times have changed and the philosophy of pragmatism has entered a period of bankruptcy just as has American capitalism.

The authors of the article did not show, could not and did not care to show, this internal connection between philosophy and the material development of society, and they frankly explained why.

"The two authors of the present article," they wrote of themselves, "differ thoroughly on their estimate of the general theory of dialectical materialism, one of them accepting it and the other rejecting it. . . . There is nothing anomalous in such a situation. Though theory is doubtless always in one way or another related to practice, the relation is not invariably direct or immediate; and as we have before had occasion to remark, human beings often act inconsistently. From the point of view of each of the authors there is in the other a certain such inconsistency between 'philosophical theory' and political practice, which might on some occasion lead to decisive concrete political disagreement. But it does not now, nor has anyone yet demonstrated that agreement or disagreement on the more abstract doctrines of dialectical materialism necessarily affects today's and tomorrow's concrete political issues—and political parties, programs, and struggles are based on such concrete issues. We all may hope that as we go along or when there is more leisure, agreement may also be reached on the more abstract questions. Meanwhile there is fascism and war and unemployment."

What is the meaning of this thoroughly astonishing reasoning? Inasmuch as *some* people through a bad method *sometimes* reach correct conclusions, and inasmuch as some people through a correct method *not infrequently* reach incorrect conclusions, therefore . . . the method is not of great importance. We shall meditate upon methods sometime

when we have more leisure, but now we have other things
to do. Imagine how a worker would react upon complain-
ing to his foreman that his tools were bad and receiving the
reply: With bad tools it is possible to turn out a good job,
and with good tools many people only waste material. I am
afraid that such a worker, particularly if he is on piecework,
would respond to the foreman with an unacademic phrase.
A worker is faced with refractory materials which show resistance and which because of that compel him to appreciate
fine tools, whereas a petty-bourgeois intellectual—alas!—
utilizes as his "tools" fugitive observations and superficial
generalizations—until major events club him on the head.

To demand that every party member occupy himself
with the philosophy of dialectics naturally would be lifeless
pedantry. But a worker who has gone through the school
of the class struggle gains from his own experience an inclination toward dialectical thinking. Even if unaware of
this term, he readily accepts the method itself and its conclusions. With a petty bourgeois it is worse. There are of
course petty-bourgeois elements organically linked with
the workers, who go over to the proletarian point of view
without an internal revolution. But these constitute an insignificant minority. The matter is quite different with the
academically trained petty bourgeoisie. Their theoretical
prejudices have already been given finished form at the
school bench. Inasmuch as they succeeded in gaining a
great deal of knowledge both useful and useless without
the aid of the dialectic, they believe that they can continue
excellently through life without it. In reality they dispense
with the dialectic only to the extent they fail to check, to
polish, and to sharpen theoretically their tools of thought,
and to the extent that they fail to break practically from
the narrow circle of their daily relationships. When thrown
against great events they are easily lost and relapse again

into petty-bourgeois ways of thinking.

Appealing to "inconsistency" as justification for an un-principled theoretical bloc, signifies giving oneself bad cre-dentials as a Marxist. Inconsistency is not accidental, and in politics it does not appear solely as an individual symp-tom. Inconsistency usually serves a social function. There are social groupings which cannot be consistent. Petty-bourgeois elements who have not rid themselves of hoary petty-bourgeois tendencies are systematically compelled within a workers party to make theoretical compromises with their own conscience.

Comrade Shachtman's attitude toward the dialectic method, as manifested in the above-quoted argumentation, cannot be called anything but eclectical skepticism. It is clear that Shachtman became infected with this attitude not in the school of Marx but among the petty-bourgeois intellectu-als to whom all forms of skepticism are proper.

Warning and verification

The article astonished me to such an extent that I imme-diately wrote to Comrade Shachtman: "I have just read the article you and Burnham wrote on the intellectuals. Many parts are excellent. However, the section on the dialectic is the greatest blow that you, personally, as the editor of the *New International*, could have delivered to Marxist theory. Comrade Burnham says: 'I don't recognize the dialectic.' It is clear and everybody has to acknowledge it. But you say: 'I recognize the dialectic, but no matter; it does not have the slightest importance.' Reread what you wrote. This sec-tion is terribly misleading for the readers of the *New Inter-national* and the best of gifts to the Eastmans of all kinds. Good! We will speak about it publicly."

My letter was written January 20, some months before the present discussion. Shachtman did not reply until March 5, when he answered in effect that he couldn't understand why I was making such a stir about the matter. On March 9, I answered Shachtman in the following words: "I did not reject in the slightest degree the possibility of collaboration with the anti-dialecticians, but only the advisability of writing an article together where the question of the dialectic plays, or should play, a very important role. The polemic develops on two planes: political and theoretical. Your political criticism is OK. Your theoretical criticism is insufficient; it stops at the point at which it should just become aggressive. Namely, the task consists of showing that their mistakes (insofar as they are *theoretical* mistakes) are products of their incapacity and unwillingness to think the things through dialectically. This task could be accomplished with a very serious pedagogical success. Instead of this you declare that dialectics is a private matter and that one can be a very good fellow without dialectic thinking." By allying himself in *this* question with the anti-dialectician Burnham, Shachtman deprived himself of the possibility of showing why Eastman, Hook, and many others began with a philosophical struggle against the dialectic but finished with a political struggle against the socialist revolution. That is, however, the essence of the question.

The present political discussion in the party has confirmed my apprehensions and warning in an incomparably sharper form than I could have expected, or, more correctly, feared. Shachtman's methodological skepticism bore its deplorable fruits in the question of the nature of the Soviet state. Burnham began some time ago by constructing, purely empirically, on the basis of his immediate impressions, a nonproletarian and nonbourgeois state, liquidating in passing the Marxist theory of the state as the organ of class rule. Shachtman unexpectedly took an evasive position: "The question, you see, is subject to further consideration"; moreover, the sociological definition of the USSR does not possess any direct and immediate significance for our "political tasks" in which Shachtman agrees completely with Burnham. Let the reader again refer to what these comrades wrote concerning the dialectic. Burnham rejects the dialectic. Shachtman seems to accept, but . . . the divine gift of "inconsistency" permits them to meet on common political conclusions. *The attitude of each of them toward the nature of the Soviet state reproduces point for point their attitude toward the dialectic.*

In both cases Burnham takes the leading role. This is not surprising: he *possesses* a method—pragmatism. Shachtman has no method. He adapts himself to Burnham. Without assuming complete responsibility for the anti-Marxian conceptions of Burnham, he defends his bloc of aggression against the Marxian conceptions with Burnham in the sphere of philosophy as well as in the sphere of sociology. In both cases Burnham appears as a pragmatist and Shachtman as an eclectic. This example has this invaluable advantage that the complete parallelism between Burnham's and Shachtman's positions upon two different planes of thought and upon two questions of primary importance, will strike the eyes even of comrades who have had no experience in purely theoretical thinking. The method of thought can be dialectic or vulgar, conscious or unconscious, but it exists and makes itself known.

Last January we heard from our authors: "But it does not now, nor has anyone yet demonstrated that agreement or disagreement on the more abstract doctrines of dialectical materialism necessarily affects today's and tomorrow's concrete political issues. . . ." Nor has anyone yet demonstrated! Not more than a few months passed before Burnham and Shachtman themselves demonstrated that their attitude toward such an "abstraction" as dialectical materialism found its precise manifestation in their attitude toward the Soviet state.

To be sure it is necessary to mention that the difference between the two instances is rather important, but it is of a political and not a theoretical character. In both cases Burnham and Shachtman formed a bloc on the basis of rejection and semi-rejection of the dialectic. But in the first instance that bloc was directed against the opponents of the proletarian party. In the second instance the bloc was concluded against the Marxist wing of their own party. The front of military operations, so to speak, has changed but the weapon remains the same.

True enough, people are often inconsistent. Human consciousness nevertheless tends toward a certain homogeneity. Philosophy and logic are compelled to rely upon this homogeneity of human consciousness and not upon what this homogeneity lacks, that is, inconsistency. Burnham does not recognize the dialectic, but the dialectic recognizes Burnham, that is, extends its sway over him. Shachtman thinks that the dialectic has no importance in political conclusions, but in the political conclusions of Shachtman himself we see the deplorable fruits of his disdainful attitude toward the dialectic. We should include this example in the textbooks on dialectical materialism.

Last year I was visited by a young British professor of political economy, a sympathizer of the Fourth International. During our conversation on the ways and means of realizing socialism, he suddenly expressed the tendencies of British utilitarianism in the spirit of Keynes and others: "It is necessary to determine a clear economic end, to choose the most reasonable means for its realization," etc. I remarked: "I see that you are an adversary of dialectics." He replied, somewhat astonished: "Yes, I don't see any use in it." "However," I replied to him, "the dialectic enabled me on the basis of a few of your observations upon economic problems to determine what category of philosophical thought you belong to—this alone shows that there is an appreciable value in the dialectic." Although I have received no word about my visitor since then, I have no doubt that this anti-dialectic professor maintains the opinion that the USSR is not a workers state, that unconditional defense of the USSR is an "outmoded" opinion, that our organizational methods are bad, etc. If it is possible to place a given person's general type of thought on the basis of his relation to concrete practical problems, it is also possible to predict approximately, knowing his general type of thought, how a given individual will approach one or another practical question. That is the incomparable educational value of the dialectical method of thought.

The ABC of materialist dialectics

Gangrenous skeptics like Souvarine believe that "nobody knows" what the dialectic is. And there are "Marxists" who kowtow reverently before Souvarine and hope to learn something from him. And these Marxists hide not only in the *Modern Monthly*. Unfortunately a current of Souvarinism exists in the present opposition of the SWP. And here it is necessary to warn young comrades: Beware of this malignant infection!

The dialectic is neither fiction nor mysticism, but a science of the forms of our thinking insofar as it is not limited to the daily problems of life but attempts to arrive at an understanding of more complicated and drawn-out processes. The dialectic and formal logic bear a relationship similar to that between higher and lower mathematics.

I will here attempt to sketch the substance of the problem in a very concise form. The Aristotelian logic of the simple syllogism starts from the proposition that "A" is equal to

"A." This postulate is accepted as an axiom for a multitude of practical human actions and elementary generalizations. But in reality "A" is not equal to "A." This is easy to prove if we observe these two letters under a lens—they are quite different from each other. But, one can object, the question is not of the size or the form of the letters, since they are only symbols for equal quantities, for instance, a pound of sugar. The objection is beside the point; in reality a pound of sugar is never equal to a pound of sugar—a more delicate scale always discloses a difference. Again one can object: but a pound of sugar is equal to itself. Neither is this true— all bodies change uninterruptedly in size, weight, color, etc. They are never equal to themselves. A sophist will respond that a pound of sugar is equal to itself "at any given moment." Aside from the extremely dubious practical value of this "axiom," it does not withstand theoretical criticism either. How should we really conceive the word "moment"? If it is an infinitesimal interval of time, then a pound of sugar is subjected during the course of that "moment" to inevitable changes. Or is the "moment" a purely mathematical abstraction, that is, a zero of time? But everything exists in time; and existence itself is an uninterrupted process of transformation; time is consequently a fundamental element of existence. Thus the axiom "A" is equal to "A" signifies that a thing is equal to itself if it does not change, that is, if it does not exist.

At first glance it could seem that these "subtleties" are useless. In reality they are of decisive significance. The axiom "A" is equal to "A" appears on one hand to be the point of departure for all our knowledge, on the other hand the point of departure for all the errors in our knowledge. To make use of the axiom "A" is equal to "A" with impunity is possible only within certain *limits*. When quantitative changes in "A" are negligible for the task at hand then we can presume that "A" is equal to "A." This is, for example, the manner in which a buyer and a seller consider a pound of sugar. We consider the temperature of the sun likewise. Until recently we considered the buying power of the dollar in the same way. But quantitative changes beyond certain limits become converted into qualitative. A pound of sugar subjected to the action of water or kerosene ceases to be a pound of sugar. A dollar in the embrace of a president ceases to be a dollar. To determine at the right moment the critical point where quantity changes into quality is one of the most important and difficult tasks in all the spheres of knowledge including sociology.

Every worker knows that it is impossible to make two completely equal objects. In the elaboration of bearing-brass into cone bearings, a certain deviation is allowed for the cones which should not, however, go beyond certain limits (this is called tolerance). By observing the norms of tolerance, the cones are considered as being equal. ("A" is equal to "A.") When the tolerance is exceeded the quantity goes over into quality; in other words, the cone bearings become inferior or completely worthless.

Our scientific thinking is only a part of our general practice including techniques. For concepts there also exists "tolerance" which is established not by formal logic issuing from the axiom "A" is equal to "A," but by dialectical logic issuing from the axiom that everything is always changing. "Common sense" is characterized by the fact that it systematically exceeds dialectical "tolerance."

Vulgar thought operates with such concepts as capitalism, morals, freedom, workers state, etc. as fixed abstractions, presuming that capitalism is equal to capitalism, morals are equal to morals, etc. Dialectical thinking analyzes all things and phenomena in their continuous change, while determining in the material conditions of those changes that critical limit beyond which "A" ceases to be "A," a workers state ceases to be a workers state.

The fundamental flaw of vulgar thought lies in the fact that it wishes to content itself with motionless imprints of a reality which consists of eternal motion. Dialectical thinking gives to concepts, by means of closer approximations, corrections, concretizations, a richness of content and flexibility; I would even say a succulence which to a certain extent brings them close to living phenomena. Not capitalism in general, but a given capitalism at a given stage of development. Not a workers state in general, but a given workers state in a backward country in an imperialist encirclement, etc.

Dialectical thinking is related to vulgar thinking in the same way that a motion picture is related to a still photograph. The motion picture does not outlaw the still photograph but combines a series of them according to the laws of motion. Dialectics does not deny the syllogism, but teaches us to combine syllogisms in such a way as to bring our understanding closer to the eternally changing reality. Hegel in his *Logic* established a series of laws: change of quantity into quality, development through contradictions, conflict of content and form, interruption of continuity, change of possibility into inevitability, etc., which are just as important for theoretical thought as is the simple syllogism for more elementary tasks.

Hegel wrote before Darwin and before Marx. Thanks to the powerful impulse given to thought by the French Revolution, Hegel anticipated the general movement of science. But because it was only an *anticipation*, although by a genius, it received from Hegel an idealistic character. Hegel operated with ideological shadows as the ultimate reality. Marx demonstrated that the movement of these ideological shadows reflected nothing but the movement of material bodies.

We call our dialectic, materialist, since its roots are neither in heaven nor in the depths of our "free will," but in objective reality, in nature. Consciousness grew out of the unconscious, psychology out of physiology, the organic world out of the inorganic, the solar system out of nebulae. On all the rungs of this ladder of development, the quantitative changes were transformed into qualitative. Our thought, including dialectical thought, is only one of the forms of the expression of changing matter. There is place within this system for neither God, nor Devil, nor immortal soul, nor eternal norms of laws and morals. The dialectic of thinking, having grown out of the dialectic of nature, possesses consequently a thoroughly materialist character.

Darwinism, which explained the evolution of species through quantitative transformations passing into qualitative, was the highest triumph of the dialectic in the whole field of organic matter. Another great triumph was the discovery of the table of atomic weights of chemical elements and further the transformation of one element into another.

With these transformations (species, elements, etc.) is closely linked the question of classification, equally important in the natural as in the social sciences. Linnaeus' system (eighteenth century), utilizing as its starting point the immutability of species, was limited to the description and classification of plants according to their external characteristics. The infantile period of botany is analogous to the infantile period of logic, since the forms of our thought develop like everything that lives. Only decisive repudiation of the idea of fixed species, only the study of the history of the evolution of plants and their anatomy prepared the basis for a really scientific classification.

Marx, who in distinction from Darwin was a conscious dialectician, discovered a basis for the scientific classification of human societies in the development of their productive forces and the structure of the relations of ownership which constitute the anatomy of society. Marxism substituted for the vulgar descriptive classification of societies and states, which even up to now still flourishes in the universities, a materialistic dialectical classification. Only through using the method of Marx is it possible correctly to determine both the concept of a workers state and the moment of its downfall.

All this, as we see, contains nothing "metaphysical" or "scholastic," as conceited ignorance affirms. Dialectic logic expresses the laws of motion in contemporary scientific thought. The struggle against materialist dialectics on the contrary expresses a distant past, conservatism of the petty bourgeoisie, the self-conceit of university routinists and . . . a spark of hope for an afterlife.

The nature of the USSR

The definition of the USSR given by Comrade Burnham, "not a workers and not a bourgeois state," is purely negative, wrenched from the chain of historical development, left dangling in midair, void of a single particle of sociology, and represents simply a theoretical capitulation of pragmatism before a *contradictory* historical phenomenon.

If Burnham were a dialectical materialist, he would have probed the following three questions: (1) What is the historical origin of the USSR? (2) What changes has this state suffered during its existence? (3) Did these changes pass from the quantitative stage to the qualitative? That is, did they create a historically necessary domination by a new exploiting class? Answering these questions would have forced Burnham to draw the only possible conclusion—the USSR is still a degenerated workers state.

The dialectic is not a magic master key for all questions. It does not replace concrete scientific analysis. But it directs this analysis along the correct road, securing it against sterile wanderings in the desert of—subjectivism and scholasticism.

Bruno R. places both the Soviet and fascist regimes under the category of "bureaucratic collectivism," because the USSR, Italy, and Germany are all ruled by bureaucracies; here and there are the principles of planning; in one case private property is liquidated, in another limited, etc. Thus on the basis of the *relative* similarity of *certain* external characteristics of *different* origin, of *different* specific weight, of *different* class significance, a fundamental *identity* of social regimes is constructed, completely in the spirit of bourgeois professors who construct categories of "controlled economy," "centralized state," without taking into consideration whatsoever the class nature of one or the other. Bruno R. and his followers, or semi-followers like Burnham, at best remain in the sphere of social classification on the level of Linnaeus, in whose justification it should be remarked however that he lived before Hegel, Darwin, and Marx.

Even worse and more dangerous, perhaps, are those eclectics who express the idea that the class character of the Soviet state "does not matter," and that the direction of our policy is determined by "the character of the war." As if the war were an independent super-social substance; as if the character of the war were not determined by the character of the ruling class, that is, by the same social factor that also determines the character of the state. Astonishing how easily some comrades forget the ABC's of Marxism under the blows of events!

It is not surprising that the theoreticians of the opposition who reject dialectic thought capitulate lamentably before the contradictory nature of the USSR. However the contradiction between the social basis laid down by the revolution, and the character of the caste which arose out of the degeneration of the revolution is not only an irrefutable historical fact but also a motor force. In our struggle for the overthrow of the bureaucracy we base ourselves on this contradiction. Meanwhile some ultralefts have already reached the ultimate absurdity by affirming that it is necessary to sacrifice the social structure of the USSR in order to overthrow the Bonapartist oligarchy! They have no suspicion that the USSR minus the social structure founded by the October revolution would be a fascist regime.

Evolution and dialectics

Comrade Burnham will probably protest that as an evolutionist he is interested in the development of society and state forms not less than we dialecticians. We will not dispute this. Every educated person since Darwin has labeled himself an "evolutionist." But a real evolutionist must apply the idea of evolution to his own forms of thinking. Elementary logic, founded in the period when the idea of evolution itself did not yet exist, is evidently insufficient for the analysis of evolutionary processes. Hegel's logic is the logic of evolution.

Only one must not forget that the concept of "evolution" itself has been completely corrupted and emasculated by university professors and liberal writers to mean peaceful "progress." Whoever has come to understand that evolution proceeds through the struggle of antagonistic forces; that a slow accumulation of changes at a certain moment explodes the old shell and brings about a catastrophe, revolution; whoever has learned finally to apply the general laws of evolution to thinking itself, he is a dialectician, as distinguished from vulgar evolutionists. Dialectic training of the mind, as necessary to a revolutionary fighter as finger exercises to a pianist, demands approaching all problems as *processes* and not as *motionless categories*. Whereas vulgar evolutionists, who limit themselves generally to recognizing evolution in only certain spheres, content themselves in all other questions with the banalities of "common sense."

The American liberal, who has reconciled himself to the existence of the USSR, more precisely to the Moscow bureaucracy, believes, or at least believed until the Soviet-German pact, that the Soviet regime on the whole is a "progressive thing," that the repugnant features of the bureaucracy ("Well naturally they exist!") will progressively slough away and that peaceful and painless "progress" is thus assured.

A vulgar petty-bourgeois radical is similar to a liberal "progressive" in that he takes the USSR as a whole, failing to understand its internal contradictions and dynamics. When Stalin concluded an alliance with Hitler, invaded Poland, and now Finland, the vulgar radicals triumphed; the identity of the methods of Stalinism and fascism was proved! They found themselves in difficulties however when the new authorities invited the population to expropriate the landowners and capitalists—they had not foreseen this possibility at all! Meanwhile the social revolutionary measures, carried out via bureaucratic military means, not only did not disturb *our*, dialectic, definition of the USSR as a degenerated workers state, but gave it the most incontrovertible corroboration. Instead of utilizing this triumph of Marxian analysis for persevering agitation, the petty-bourgeois oppositionists began to shout with criminal lightmindedness that the events have refuted our prognosis, that our old formulas are no longer applicable, that new words are necessary. What words? They haven't decided yet themselves.

Defense of the USSR

We began with philosophy and then went to sociology. It became clear that in both spheres, of the two leading personalities of the opposition, one had taken an anti-Marxian, the other an eclectic position. If we now consider politics, particularly the question of the defense of the USSR, we will find that just as great surprises await us.

The opposition discovered that our formula of "unconditional defense of the USSR," the formula of our program, is "vague, abstract, and outmoded (!?)." Unfortunately they do not explain under what future "conditions" they are ready to defend the conquests of the revolution. In order to give at least an ounce of sense to their new formula, the opposition attempts to represent the matter as if up to now we had "unconditionally" defended the international policy of the Kremlin government with its Red Army and GPU. Everything is turned upside down! In reality for a long time we have not defended the Kremlin's international policy, not even conditionally, particularly since the time that we openly proclaimed the necessity of crushing the Kremlin oligarchy through insurrection! A wrong policy not only mutilates the current tasks but also compels one to represent his own past in a false light.

In the above-quoted article in the *New International*, Burnham and Shachtman cleverly labeled the group of disillusioned intellectuals "The League of Abandoned Hopes," and persistently asked what would be the position of this deplorable League in case of military conflict between a capitalistic country and the Soviet Union. "We take this occasion, therefore," they wrote, "to demand from Hook, Eastman, and Lyons *unambiguous* declarations on the question of defense of the Soviet Union from attack by Hitler or Japan—or for that matter by England. . . ." Burnham and Shachtman did not lay down any "conditions," they did not specify any "concrete" circumstances, and at the same time they demanded an "unambiguous" reply. ". . . Would the League (of Abandoned Hopes) also refrain from taking a position or would it declare itself neutral?" they continued; "In a word, is it for the defense of the Soviet Union from imperialist attack, *regardless and in spite of the Stalinist regime?*" (My emphasis.) A quotation to marvel at! And this is exactly what our program declares. Burnham and Shachtman in January 1939 stood in favor of unconditional defense of the Soviet Union and defined the significance of unconditional defense entirely correctly as "regardless and in spite of the Stalinist regime." And yet this article was written when the experience of the Spanish revolution had already been drained to completion. Comrade Cannon is absolutely right when he says that the role of Stalinism in Spain was incomparably more criminal than in Poland or Finland. In the first case the bureaucracy through hangman's methods strangled a socialist revolution. In the second case it gives an impulse to the socialist revolution through bureaucratic methods. Why did Burnham and Shachtman themselves so unexpectedly shift to the position of the "League of Abandoned Hopes"? Why? We cannot consider Shachtman's superabstract references to the "concreteness of events" as an explanation. Nevertheless, it is not difficult to find an explanation. The Kremlin's participation in the Republican camp in Spain was supported by the bourgeois democrats all over the world. Stalin's work in Poland and Finland is met with frantic condemnation from the same democrats. In spite of all its noisy formulas the opposition happens to be a reflection inside the Socialist Workers Party of the moods of the "left" petty bourgeoisie. This fact, unfortunately, is incontrovertible.

"Our subjects," wrote Burnham and Shachtman about the League of Abandoned Hopes, "take great pride in believing that they are contributing something 'fresh,' that they are 'reevaluating in the light of new experiences,' that they are 'not dogmatists' ('conservatives'?—L.T.) who refuse to reexamine their 'basic assumption,' etc. What a pathetic self-deception! None of them has brought to light any new

facts, given any new understanding of the present or future."
Astonishing quotation! Should we not add a new chapter
to their article, "Intellectuals in Retreat"? I offer Comrade
Shachtman my collaboration. . . .

How is it possible that outstanding individuals like Burnham and Shachtman, unconditionally devoted to the cause
of the proletariat, could become so frightened of the not so
frightening gentlemen of the League of Abandoned Hopes!
On the purely theoretical plane the explanation in respect
to Burnham rests in his incorrect method, in respect to
Shachtman in his disregard for method. Correct method
not only facilitates the attainment of a correct conclusion,
but, connecting every new conclusion with the preceding
conclusions in a consecutive chain, fixes the conclusions
in one's memory. If political conclusions are made empirically, if inconsistency is proclaimed as a kind of advantage,
then the Marxian system of politics is invariably replaced
by impressionism—in so many ways characteristic of petty-
bourgeois intellectuals. Every new turn of events catches the
empiricist-impressionist unawares, compels him to forget
what he himself wrote yesterday, and produces a consum-
ing desire for new formulas before new ideas have appeared
in his head.

The Soviet-Finnish war*

The resolution of the opposition upon the question of the
Soviet-Finnish war is a document which could be signed,
perhaps with slight changes, by the Bordigists, Vereecken,
Sneevliet, Fenner Brockway, Marceau Pivert, and the like,

---

* Soviet troops attacked Finland on November 30, 1939. The
invasion bogged down against heavy initial resistance. In March
1940 a treaty was signed ceding parts of southeastern Finland to
the Soviet Union.

but in no case by Bolshevik-Leninists. Based exclusively on features of the Soviet bureaucracy and on the mere fact of the "invasion," the resolution is void of the slightest social content. It places Finland and the USSR on the same level and unequivocally "condemns, rejects, and opposes *both* governments and their armies." Having noticed, however, that something was not in order, the resolution unexpectedly and without any connection with the text adds: "In the application (!) of this perspective, the Fourth International will, of course (how marvelous is this "of course"), take into account (!) the differing economic relations in Finland and Russia." Every word is a pearl. By "concrete" circumstances our lovers of the "concrete" mean the military situation, the needs of the masses, and in the third place the opposed economic regimes. As to just how these three "concrete" circumstances will be "taken into account," the resolution doesn't give the slightest inkling. If the opposition opposes equally "both governments and their armies" in relation to this war, how will it "take into account" the differences in the military situation and the social regimes? Definitely nothing of this is comprehensible.

In order to punish the Stalinists for their unquestionable crimes, the resolution, following the petty-bourgeois democrats of all shadings, does not mention by so much as a word that the Red Army in Finland expropriates large landowners and introduces workers control while preparing for the expropriation of the capitalists.

Tomorrow the Stalinists will strangle the Finnish workers. But now they are giving—they are compelled to give—a tremendous impulse to the class struggle in its sharpest form. The leaders of the opposition construct their policy not upon the "concrete" process that is taking place in Finland, but upon democratic abstractions and noble sentiments.

The Soviet-Finnish war is apparently beginning to be

supplemented by a civil war in which the Red Army finds itself at the given stage in the same camp as the Finnish petty peasants and the workers, while the Finnish army enjoys the support of the owning classes, the conservative labor bureaucracy, and the Anglo-Saxon imperialists. The hopes which the Red Army awakens among the Finnish poor will, unless international revolution intervenes, prove to be an illusion; the collaboration of the Red Army with the poor will be only temporary; the Kremlin will soon turn its weapons against the Finnish workers and peasants. We know all this now and we say it openly as a warning. But in this "concrete" civil war that is taking place on Finnish territory, what "concrete" position must the "concrete" partisans of the Fourth International take? If they fought in Spain in the Republican camp in spite of the fact that the Stalinists were strangling the socialist revolution, all the more must they participate in Finland in that camp where the Stalinists are compelled to support the expropriation of the capitalists.

Our innovators cover the holes in their position with violent phrases. They label the policy of the USSR "imperialist." Vast enrichment of the sciences! Beginning from now on both the foreign policy of finance capital and the policy of exterminating finance capital will be called imperialism. This will help significantly in the clarification and class education of the workers! But simultaneously—will shout the, let us say, very hasty Stanley—the Kremlin supports the policy of finance capital in Germany! This objection is based on the substitution of one problem for another, in the dissolving of the concrete into the abstract (the usual mistake of vulgar thought).

If Hitler tomorrow were forced to send arms to the insurrectionary Indians, must the revolutionary German workers oppose this concrete action by strikes or sabotage? On the contrary they must make sure that the insurrectionists receive the arms as soon as possible. We hope that *this* is clear to Stanley. But this example is purely hypothetical. We used it in order to show that even a fascist government of finance capital can under certain conditions be forced to support a national revolutionary movement (in order to attempt to strangle it the next day). Hitler would never under any circumstances support a proletarian revolution for instance in France. As for the Kremlin it is at the present time forced—and this is not a hypothetical but a real situation—to provoke a social revolutionary movement in Finland (in order to attempt to strangle it politically tomorrow). To cover a given social revolutionary movement with the all-embracing term of imperialism only because it is provoked, mutilated, and at the same time strangled by the Kremlin merely testifies to one's theoretical and political poverty.

It is necessary to add that the stretching of the concept of "imperialism" lacks even the attraction of novelty. At present not only the "democrats" but also the bourgeoisie of the democratic countries describe Soviet policy as imperialist. The aim of the bourgeoisie is transparent—to erase the social contradictions between capitalistic and Soviet expansion, to hide the problem of property, and in this way to help genuine imperialism. What is the aim of Shachtman and the others? They don't know themselves. Their terminological novelty objectively leads them away from the Marxian terminology of the Fourth International and brings them close to the terminology of the "democrats." This circumstance, alas, again testifies to the opposition's extreme sensitivity to the pressure of petty-bourgeois public opinion.

The 'organizational question'

From the ranks of the opposition one begins to hear more frequently: "The Russian question isn't of any decisive importance in and of itself; the most important task is to change the party regime." Change in regime, it is necessary to understand, means a change in leadership, or more precisely, the elimination of Cannon and his close collaborators from directing posts. These clamorous voices demonstrate that the tendency towards a struggle against "Cannon's faction" preceded that "concreteness of events" to which Shachtman and others refer in explaining their change of position. At the same time these voices remind us of a whole series of past oppositional groups who took up a struggle on different occasions; and who, when the principled basis began to crumble under their feet, shifted to the so-called "organizational question"—the case was identical with Molinier, Sneevliet, Vereecken, and many others. As disagreeable as these precedents may appear, it is impossible to pass over them.

It would be incorrect, however, to believe that the shifting of the struggle to the "organizational question" represents a simple "maneuver" in the factional struggle. No, the inner feelings of the opposition tell them, in truth, however confusedly, that the issue concerns not only the "Russian problem" but rather the entire approach to political problems in general, including also the methods of building the party. And this is in a certain sense correct.

We too have attempted above to prove that the issue concerns not only the Russian problem but even more the opposition's method of thought, which has its social roots. The opposition is under the sway of petty-bourgeois moods and tendencies. This is the essence of the whole matter.

We saw quite clearly the ideological influence of another class in the instances of Burnham (pragmatism) and Shachtman (eclecticism). We did not take into consideration other leaders such as Comrade Abern because he generally does not participate in principled discussions, limiting himself to the plane of the "organizational question." This does not mean, however, that Abern has no importance. On the contrary, it is possible to say that Burnham and Shachtman are the amateurs of the opposition, while Abern is the unquestionable professional. Abern, and only he, has his own traditional group which grew out of the old Communist Party and became bound together during the first period of the independent existence of the "Left Opposition." All the others who hold various reasons for criticism and discontent cling to this group.

Any serious factional fight in a party is always in the final analysis a reflection of the class struggle. The majority faction established from the beginning the ideological dependence of the opposition upon petty-bourgeois democracy. The opposition, on the contrary, precisely because of its petty-bourgeois character, does not even attempt to look for the social roots of the hostile camp.

The opposition opened up a severe factional fight which is now paralyzing the party at a very critical moment. That such a fight could be justified and not pitilessly condemned, very serious and deep foundations would be necessary. For a Marxist such foundations can have only a *class* character. Before they began their bitter struggle, the leaders of the opposition were obligated to ask themselves this question: What nonproletarian class influence is reflected in the majority of the National Committee? Nevertheless, the opposition has not made the slightest attempt at such a class evaluation of the divergences. It sees only "conservatism," "errors," "bad methods," and similar psychological, intellectual, and technical deficiencies. The opposition is not interested in the class nature of the opposition faction, just as it is not interested in the class nature of the USSR. This fact alone is sufficient to demonstrate the petty-bourgeois character of the opposition, with its tinge of academic pedantry and journalistic impressionism.

In order to understand what classes or strata are reflected in the factional fight, it is necessary to study the fight of both factions historically. Those members of the opposition who affirm that the present fight has "nothing in common" with the old factional struggles, demonstrate once again their superficial attitude toward the life of their own party. The fundamental core of the opposition is the same which three years ago grouped itself around Muste and Spector. The fundamental core of the majority is the same which grouped itself around Cannon. Of the leading figures only Shachtman and Burnham have shifted from one camp to the other. But these personal shifts, important though they might be, do not change the general character of the two groups. I will not go into the historical sequence of the faction fight, referring the reader to the in every respect excellent article by Joseph Hansen, "Organizational Methods and Political Principles."*

If we subtract everything accidental, personal, and episodical, if we reduce the present groupings in struggle to their fundamental political types, then indubitably the struggle of Comrade Abern against Comrade Cannon has been the most consistent. In this struggle Abern represents a propagandistic group, petty-bourgeois in its social composition, united by old personal ties, and having almost the character of a family. Cannon represents the proletarian party in process of formation. The historical right in this struggle— independent of what errors and mistakes might have been made—rests wholly on the side of Cannon.

When the representatives of the opposition raised the hue and cry that the "leadership is bankrupt," "the prognoses

---

* This article is contained in Joseph Hansen, *The Abern Clique* (New York: Pathfinder, 1972).

did not turn out to be correct," "the events caught us unawares," "it is necessary to change our slogans," all this
without the slightest effort to think the questions through
seriously, they appeared fundamentally as party defeatists.
This deplorable attitude is explained by the irritation and
fright of the old propagandistic circle before the new tasks
and the new party relations. The sentimentality of personal
ties does not want to yield to the sense of duty and discipline. The task that stands before the party is to break up
the old clique ties and to dissolve the best elements of the
propagandistic past in the proletarian party. It is necessary
to develop such a spirit of party patriotism that nobody dare
say: "The reality of the matter is not the Russian question
but that we feel more easy and comfortable under Abern's
leadership than under Cannon's."

I personally did not arrive at this conclusion yesterday. I
happened to have expressed it tens and hundreds of times
in conversations with members of Abern's group. I invariably emphasized the petty-bourgeois composition of this
group. I insistently and repeatedly proposed to transfer
from membership to candidacy such petty-bourgeois fellow travelers as proved incapable of recruiting workers for
the party. Private letters, conversations, and admonitions,
as has been shown by subsequent events, have not led to
anything—people rarely learn from someone else's experience. The antagonism between the two party layers and
the two periods of its development rose to the surface and
took on the character of bitter factional struggle. Nothing
remains but to give an opinion, clearly and definitely, to the
American section and the whole International. "Friendship
is friendship but duty is duty"—says a Russian proverb.

The following question can be posed: If the opposition is
a petty-bourgeois tendency, does that signify further unity
is impossible? Then how reconcile the petty-bourgeois ten-

dency with the proletarian? To pose the question like this means to judge one-sidedly, undialectically, and thus falsely. In the present discussion the opposition has clearly manifested its petty-bourgeois features. But this does not mean that the opposition has no other features. The majority of the members of the opposition are deeply devoted to the cause of the proletariat and are capable of learning. Tied today to a petty-bourgeois milieu they can tomorrow tie themselves to the proletariat. The inconsistent ones, under the influence of experience, can become more consistent. When the party embraces thousands of workers even the professional factionalists can reeducate themselves in the spirit of proletarian discipline. It is necessary to give them time for this. That is why Comrade Cannon's proposal to keep the discussion free from any threats of split, expulsions, etc., was absolutely correct and in place.

Nevertheless, it remains not less indubitable that if the party as a whole should take the road of the opposition it could suffer complete destruction. The present opposition is incapable of giving the party Marxian leadership. The majority of the present National Committee expresses more consistently, seriously, and profoundly the proletarian tasks of the party than the minority. Precisely because of this the majority can have no interest in directing the struggle toward split—correct ideas will win. Nor can the healthy elements of the opposition wish a split—the experience of the past demonstrates very clearly that all the different kinds of improvised groups who split from the Fourth International condemned themselves to sterility and decomposition. That is why it is possible to envisage the next party convention without any fear. It will reject the anti-Marxian novelties of the opposition and guarantee party unity.

11

Letter to John G. Wright‡

DECEMBER 19, 1939

Dear Friend,

I read your letter to Joe. I endorse completely your opinion about the necessity for a firm even implacable theoretical and political fight against the petty-bourgeois tendencies of the opposition. You will see from my last article, which will be airmailed to you tomorrow, that I characterize the divergences of the opposition even more sharply than has the majority. But at the same time, I believe that the implacable ideological fight should go parallel with very cautious and wise organizational tactics. You have not the slightest interest in a split, even if the opposition should become, accidentally, a majority at the next convention. You have not the slightest reason to give the heterogeneous and unbalanced army of the opposition a pretext for a split. Even as an eventual minority, you should in my opinion remain disciplined and loyal towards the party as a whole. It is extremely important for the education in genuine party patriotism, about the necessity of which Cannon wrote me one time very correctly.

A majority composed of this opposition would not last more than a few months. Then the proletarian tendency of the party will again become the majority with tremendously increased authority. Be extremely firm but don't lose your nerve—this applies now more than ever to the strategy of the proletarian wing of the party.

With best comradely greetings and wishes,

Yours,

Leon Trotsky
COYOACÁN, D.F.

P.S. The evils came from: (1) bad composition especially of the most important New York branch; (2) lack of experience especially by the members who came over from the Socialist Party (Youth). To overcome these difficulties inherited from the past is not possible by exceptional measures. Firmness and patience are necessary.

L.T.

Letter to Max Shachtman[‡]

DECEMBER 20, 1939

Dear Comrade Shachtman,

I am sending you a copy of my last article.[*] You will see from my polemics that I consider the divergences as of decisive character. I believe that you are on the wrong side of the barricades, my dear friend. By your position you give courage to all the petty-bourgeois and anti-Marxist elements to fight our doctrine, our program, and our tradition. I don't hope to convince you with these lines, but I do express the prognosis that if you refuse now to find a way towards collaboration with the Marxist wing against the petty-bourgeois revisionists, you will inevitably deplore for years and years the greatest error of your life.

If I had the possibility I would immediately take an airplane to New York City in order to discuss with you for 48 or 72 hours uninterruptedly. I regret very much that you don't feel in this situation the need to come here to discuss the questions with me. Or do you? I should be happy . . .

L. Trotsky
COYOACÁN, D.F.

---

[*] The article referred to is "A Petty-Bourgeois Opposition in the Socialist Workers Party."

Four letters to the National Committee majority[‡]

(1)   DECEMBER 26, 1939

Dear Friends,

I was previously disposed in favor of transmitting the discussion in the *Socialist Appeal* and the *New International*, but I must recognize that your arguments are very serious especially in connection with the arguments of Comrade Burnham.[*]

The *New International* and *Socialist Appeal* are not instruments of the discussion under the control of a special discussion committee, but rather instruments of the party and its National Committee. In the discussion bulletin the opposition can ask for equal rights with the majority, but the official party publications have the duty to defend the point of view of the party and the Fourth International until they are changed. A discussion on the pages of the official party publications can be conducted only within the limits established by the majority of the National Committee. It is so self-evident that arguments are not necessary.

---

[*] The minority of the National Committee demanded that the discussion be carried in the *Socialist Appeal*, the weekly newspaper of the SWP, and the *New International*, the party's monthly theoretical magazine. This was rejected by the majority.

The permanent juridical guarantees for the minority surely are not borrowed from the Bolshevik experience. But they are also not an invention of Comrade Burnham; the French Socialist Party has had for a long time such constitutional guarantees which correspond completely to the spirit of envious literary and parliamentary cliques, but never prevent the subjugation of the workers by the coalition of these cliques.

The organizational structure of the proletarian vanguard must be subordinated to the positive demands of the revolutionary fight and not to the negative guarantees against their degeneration. If the party is not fit for the needs of the socialist revolution, it would degenerate in spite of the wisest juridical stipulations. On the organizational field, Burnham shows a complete lack of revolutionary conception of the party, as he showed it on the political field in the small but very significant question of the Dies Committee.* In both cases he proposes a purely negative attitude, as, in the question of the Soviet state, he gave a purely negative definition. It is not sufficient to dislike the capitalist society (a negative attitude), it is necessary to accept all the practical conclusions of a social revolutionary conception. Alas, this is not the case of Comrade Burnham.

My practical conclusions?

First, it is necessary to officially condemn before the party

---

* The House Un-American Activities Committee (HUAC) was then headed by Rep. Martin Dies. In October 1939 Trotsky was invited to testify before the committee. Seeing it as an opportunity to present communist views to a broader audience, he accepted. Burnham had made a motion in the Political Committee urging Trotsky to reject the invitation, and calling for the SWP to publicly criticize him if he went ahead; the motion was defeated. See "Why I Consented to Appear before the Dies Committee," in *Writings of Leon Trotsky [1939–40]*, pp. 132–35.

the attempt to annihilate the party line by putting the party program on the same level with every innovation not accepted by the party.

Second, if the National Committee finds it necessary to devote one issue of the *New International* to the discussion (I don't propose it now), it should be done in such a way that the reader sees where the party position is and where the attempt at revision, and that the last word remain with the majority and not with the opposition.

Third, if the internal bulletins are not sufficient, it would be possible to publish a special symposium of articles devoted to the agenda of the convention.

The fullest loyalty in the discussion, but not the slightest concession to the petty-bourgeois, anarchistic spirit!

W. Rork [Leon Trotsky]
COYOACÁN, D.F.

(2)   DECEMBER 27, 1939

Dear Friends,

I must confess that your communication about the insistences of Comrades Burnham and Shachtman concerning the publication of the controversial articles in the *New International* and the *Socialist Appeal* in the first moment surprised me. What can be the reason, I asked myself. That they feel so sure of their position is completely excluded. Their arguments are of a very primitive nature, the contradictions between themselves are sharp and they cannot help but feel that the majority represents the tradition and the Marxist doctrine. They can't hope to issue victorious from a theoretical fight; not only Shachtman and Abern but

also Burnham must understand it. What is then the source
of their thirst for publicity? The explanation is very simple:
they are impatient to justify themselves before the democratic public opinion, to shout to all the Eastmans, Hooks,
and the others that they, the opposition, are not so bad as
we. This inner necessity must be especially imperative with
Burnham. It is the same kind of inner capitulation which
we observed in Zinoviev and Kamenev on the eve of the
October revolution and by many "internationalists" under
the pressure of the patriotic war wave. If we make abstractions from all the individual peculiarities, accidents, or
misunderstandings and errors, we have before us the first
social-patriotic sin-fall in our own party. You established
this fact correctly from the beginning, but it appears to me
in full clarity only now after they proclaimed their wish to
announce—as the POUMists, Pivertists, and many others—
that they are not so bad as the "Trotskyites."

This consideration is a supplementary argument against
any concession to them in this field. Under the given conditions, we have the full right to say to them: you must wait
for the verdict of the party and not appeal before the verdict
is pronounced to the democratic patriotic judges.

I considered the question previously too abstractly, namely,
only from the point of view of the theoretical fight, and from
this point of view I agree completely with Comrade Goldman
that we could only win. But the larger political criterion indi-
cates that we should eliminate the premature intervention of
the democratic patriotic factor in our inner-party fight and
that the opposition should reckon in the discussion only on
their own strength as the majority does. Under these conditions the test and the selection of different elements of the
opposition would have a more efficient character and the
results would be more favorable for the party.

Engels spoke one time about the mood of the enraged

petty bourgeois. It seems to me that a trace of this mood can be found in the ranks of the opposition. Yesterday many of them were hypnotized by the Bolshevik tradition. They never absorbed it innerly but didn't dare to challenge it openly. But Shachtman and Abern gave them this kind of courage and now they openly enjoy the mood of the enraged petty bourgeois. This is the impression, for example, which I received from the last articles and letters of Stanley. He has lost totally his self-criticism and believes sincerely that every inspiration which visits his brain is worthy of being proclaimed and printed if only it is directed against the program and tradition of the party. The crime of Shachtman and Abern consists especially in having provoked such an explosion of petty-bourgeois self-satisfaction.

W. Rork [Leon Trotsky]

P.S. It is absolutely sure that the Stalinist agents are working in our midst with the purpose to sharpen the discussion and provoke a split. It would be necessary to check many factional "fighters" from this special point of view.

W.R.

COYOACÁN, D.F.

(3)   JANUARY 3, 1940

Dear Friends,

I received the two documents of the opposition,* studied that on bureaucratic conservatism and am now studying the

---

* These documents were "The War and Bureaucratic Conservatism" and "What Is at Issue in the Dispute on the Russian Question."

second on the Russian question. What lamentable writings! It is difficult to find a sentence expressing a correct idea or placing a correct idea in the correct place. Intelligent and even talented people occupied an evidently false position and push themselves more and more into a blind alley.

The phrase of Abern about the "split" can have two senses: either he wishes to frighten you with a split as he did during the entry discussion* or he wishes really to commit political suicide. In the first case, he will of course not prevent our giving a Marxist appreciation of the opposition politics. In the second case, nothing can be done; if an adult person wishes to commit suicide it is difficult to hinder him.

The reaction of Burnham is a brutal challenge to all Marxists. If dialectics is a religion and if it is true that religion is the opium of the people, how can he refuse to fight for liberating his own party from this venom? I am now writing an open letter to Burnham on this question. I don't believe that the public opinion of the Fourth International would permit the editor of the theoretical Marxist magazine to limit himself to rather cynical aphorisms about the foundation of scientific socialism. In any case, I will not rest until the anti-Marxist conceptions of Burnham are unmasked to the end before the Party and the International. I hope to send the open letter, at least the Russian text, the day after tomorrow.

Simultaneously, I am writing an analysis of the two documents. Excellent is the explanation why they agree to disagree about the Russian question.

I grit my teeth upon losing my time in the reading of these absolutely stale documents. The errors are so elementary

---

* When the Workers Party of the U.S. was discussing entrance into the Socialist Party in the first months of 1936, Abern was bitterly opposed to the move.

that it is necessary to make an effort to remember the necessary argument from the ABC of Marxism. . . .

W. *Rork [Leon Trotsky]*
COYOACÁN, D.F.

(4)   JANUARY 4, 1940

Dear Friends,

I enclose a copy of my letter to Shachtman which I sent more than two weeks ago.* Shachtman didn't even answer me. It shows the mood into which he has pushed himself by his unprincipled fight. He makes a bloc with the anti-Marxist Burnham and he refuses to answer my letters concerning this bloc. The fact in itself is of course of doubtful importance but it has an indisputable symptomatic vein. This is my reason for sending you a copy of my letter to Shachtman.

With best wishes,

L. *Trotsky*
COYOACÁN, D.F.

---

* See page 138 of this volume.

14

Letter to Joseph Hansen[‡]

JANUARY 5, 1940

Dear Joe,

Thank you for your interesting information. In the case of necessity or of advisability, Jim could publish our correspondence and that with Wright concerning the split matter. This correspondence shows our firm desire to preserve the unity of the party in spite of the sharp factional struggle. I mentioned in my letter to Wright[*] that even as a minority the bolshevik wing of the party should in my opinion remain disciplined and Jim answered that he wholeheartedly agreed with that view. These two quotations are decisive for the matter.

Concerning my remarks about Finland in the article on the petty-bourgeois opposition, I will say here only a few words. Is there a principled difference between Finland and Poland— yes or no? Was the intervention of the Red Army in Poland accompanied by civil war—yes or no? The press of the Mensheviks who are very well informed thanks to their friendship with Bund and with PPS [Polish Socialist Party] émigrés says openly that a revolutionary wave surrounded the advance of the Red Army. And not only in Poland but also in Romania.

The Kremlin created the Kuusinen government with the

---

* See page 136 of this volume.

evident purpose of supplementing the war by civil war. There was information about the beginning of the creation of a Finnish Red Army, about "enthusiasm" of poor Finnish farmers in the occupied regions where the large land properties were confiscated, and so on. What is this if not the beginning of civil war?

The further development of the civil war depended completely upon the advance of the Red Army. The "enthusiasm" of the people was evidently not hot enough to produce independent insurrections of peasants and workers under the sword of the hangman Mannerheim. The retreat of the Red Army necessarily halted the elements of the civil war at the very beginning.

If the imperialists help the Finnish bourgeoisie efficiently in defending the capitalist regime, the civil war in Finland would become for the next period impossible. But if, as is more probable, the reinforced detachments of the Red Army more successfully penetrate into the country, we will inevitably observe the process of civil war paralleling the invasion.

We cannot foresee all the military episodes, the ups and downs of purely tactical interest, but they don't change the general "strategical" line of events. In this case as in all others, the opposition makes a purely conjunctural and impressionistic policy instead of a principled one.

(It is not necessary to repeat that the civil war in Finland as was the case in Poland would have a limited, semi-stifled nature and that it can, in the next stage, go over into a civil war between the Finnish masses and the Moscow bureaucracy. We know this at least as clearly as the opposition and we openly warn the masses. But we analyze the process as it is and we don't identify the first stage with the second one.)

With warm wishes and greetings for all friends,

L. Trotsky
COYOACÁN, D.F.

15

An open letter to Comrade Burnham

JANUARY 7, 1940

Dear Comrade:

You have expressed as your reaction to my article on the petty-bourgeois opposition, I have been informed, that you do not intend to argue over the dialectic with me and that you will discuss only the "concrete questions." "I stopped arguing about religion long ago," you added ironically. I once heard Max Eastman voice this same sentiment.

Is there logic in identifying logic with religion?

As I understand this, your words imply that the dialectic of Marx, Engels, and Lenin belongs to the sphere of religion. What does this assertion signify? The dialectic, permit me to recall once again, is the *logic of evolution*. Just as a machine shop in a plant supplies instruments for all departments, so logic is indispensable for all spheres of human knowledge. If you do not consider logic in general to be a religious prejudice (sad to say, the self-contradictory writings of the opposition incline one more and more toward this lamentable idea), then just which logic do you accept? I know of two systems of logic worthy of attention: the logic of Aristotle (formal logic) and the logic of Hegel (the dialectic). Aristotelian logic takes as its starting point immutable objects and phenomena.

The scientific thought of our epoch studies all phenomena in their origin, change, and disintegration. Do you hold that the progress of the sciences, including Darwinism, Marxism, modern physics, chemistry, etc., has not influenced in any way the forms of our thought? In other words, do you hold that in a world where everything changes, the syllogism alone remains unchanging and eternal? The Gospel according to St. John begins with the words: "In the beginning was the Word," i.e., in the beginning was Reason or the Word (reason expressed in the word, namely, the syllogism). To St. John the syllogism is one of the literary pseudonyms for God. If you consider that the syllogism is immutable, i.e., has neither origin nor development, then it signifies that to you it is the product of divine revelation. But if you acknowledge that the logical forms of our thought develop in the process of our adaptation to nature, then please take the trouble to inform us just who following Aristotle analyzed and systematized the subsequent progress of logic. So long as you do not clarify this point, I shall take the liberty of asserting that to identify logic (the dialectic) with religion reveals utter ignorance and superficiality in the basic questions of human thought.

Is the revolutionist not obliged to fight against religion?

Let us grant however that your more than presumptuous innuendo is correct. But this does not improve affairs to your advantage. Religion, as I hope you will agree, diverts attention away from real to fictitious knowledge, away from the struggle for a better life to false hopes for reward in the Hereafter. Religion is the opium of the people. Whoever fails to struggle against religion is unworthy of bearing the name of revolutionist. On what grounds then do you justify your refusal to fight against the dialectic if you deem it one of the varieties of religion?

You stopped bothering yourself long ago, as you say, about the question of religion. But you stopped only *for yourself*. In addition to you, there exist all the others. Quite a few of them. We revolutionists never "stop" bothering ourselves about religious questions, inasmuch as our task consists in emancipating from the influence of religion, not only ourselves but also the masses. If the dialectic is a religion, how is it possible to renounce the struggle against this opium within one's own party?

Or perhaps you intended to imply that religion is of no political importance? That it is possible to be religious and at the same time a consistent communist and revolutionary fighter? You will hardly venture so rash an assertion. Naturally, we maintain the most considerate attitude toward the religious prejudices of a backward worker. Should he desire to fight for our program, we would accept him as a party member; but at the same time, our party would persistently educate him in the spirit of materialism and atheism. If you agree with this, how can you refuse to struggle against a "religion," held, to my knowledge, by the overwhelming majority of those members of your own party who are interested in theoretical questions? You have obviously overlooked this most important aspect of the question.

Among the educated bourgeoisie there are not a few who have broken personally with religion, but whose atheism is solely for their own private consumption; they keep thoughts like these to themselves but in public often maintain that it is well the people have a religion. Is it possible that you hold such a point of view toward your own party? Is it possible that this explains your refusal to discuss with us the philosophic foundations of Marxism? If that is the case, under your scorn for the dialectic rings a note of contempt for the party.

Please do not make the objection that I have based myself

on a phrase expressed by you in private conversation, and that you are not concerned with publicly refuting dialectic materialism. This is not true. Your winged phrase serves only as an illustration. Whenever there has been an occasion, for various reasons you have proclaimed your negative attitude toward the doctrine which constitutes the theoretical foundation of our program. This is well known to everyone in the party. In the article "Intellectuals in Retreat," written by you in collaboration with Shachtman and published in the party's theoretical organ, it is categorically affirmed that you reject dialectic materialism. Doesn't the party have the right after all to know just why? Do you really assume that in the Fourth International an editor of a theoretical organ can confine himself to the bare declaration: "I decisively reject dialectical materialism"—as if it were a question of a proffered cigarette: "Thank you, I don't smoke." The question of a correct philosophical doctrine, that is, a correct method of thought, is of decisive significance to a revolutionary party just as a good machine shop is of decisive significance to production. It is still possible to defend the old society with the material and intellectual methods inherited from the past. It is absolutely unthinkable that this old society can be overthrown and a new one constructed without first critically analyzing the current methods. If the party errs in the very foundations of its thinking it is your elementary duty to point out the correct road. Otherwise your conduct will be interpreted inevitably as the cavalier attitude of an academician toward a proletarian organization which, after all, is incapable of grasping a real "scientific" doctrine. What could be worse than that?

Instructive examples

Anyone acquainted with the history of the struggles of tendencies within workers parties knows that desertions to

the camp of opportunism and even to the camp of bourgeois reaction began not infrequently with rejection of the
dialectic. Petty-bourgeois intellectuals consider the dialectic
the most vulnerable point in Marxism and at the same time
they take advantage of the fact that it is much more difficult
for workers to verify differences on the philosophical than
on the political plane. This long-known fact is backed by
all the evidence of experience. Again, it is impermissible to
discount an even more important fact, namely, that all the
great and outstanding revolutionists—first and foremost,
Marx, Engels, Lenin, Luxemburg, Franz Mehring—stood
on the ground of dialectic materialism. Can it be assumed
that all of them were incapable of distinguishing between
science and religion? Isn't there too much presumptuous-
ness on your part, Comrade Burnham? The examples of
Bernstein, Kautsky, and Franz Mehring are extremely instructive. Bernstein categorically rejected the dialectic as
"scholasticism" and "mysticism." Kautsky maintained indifference toward the question of the dialectic, somewhat like
Comrade Shachtman. Mehring was a tireless propagandist
and defender of dialectic materialism. For decades he followed all the innovations of philosophy and literature, inde-
fatigably exposing the reactionary essence of idealism, neo-
Kantianism, utilitarianism, all forms of mysticism, etc. The
political fate of these three individuals is very well known.
Bernstein ended his life as a smug petty-bourgeois democrat;
Kautsky, from a centrist, became a vulgar opportunist. As
for Mehring, he died a revolutionary communist.

In Russia three very prominent academic Marxists, Struve,
Bulgakov, and Berdyaev, began by rejecting the philosophic
doctrine of Marxism and ended in the camp of reaction and
the Orthodox Church. In the United States, Eastman, Sidney
Hook, and their friends utilized opposition to the dialectic
as cover for their transformation from fellow travelers of

the proletariat to fellow travelers of the bourgeoisie. Similar examples by the score could be cited from other countries. The example of Plekhanov, which appears to be an exception, in reality only proves the rule. Plekhanov was a remarkable propagandist of dialectic materialism, but during his whole life he never had the opportunity of participating in the actual class struggle. His thinking was divorced from practice. The revolution of 1905 and subsequently the World War flung him into the camp of petty-bourgeois democracy and forced him in actuality to renounce dialectic materialism. During the World War Plekhanov came forward openly as the protagonist of the Kantian categorical imperative in the sphere of international relations: "Do not do unto others as you would not have them do unto you." The example of Plekhanov only proves that dialectic materialism *in and of itself* still does not make a man a revolutionist.

Shachtman on the other hand argues that Liebknecht left a posthumous work against dialectic materialism which he had written in prison. Many ideas enter a person's mind while in prison which cannot be checked by association with other people. Liebknecht, whom nobody, least of all himself, considered a theoretician, became a symbol of heroism in the world labor movement. Should any of the American opponents of the dialectic display similar self-sacrifice and independence from patriotism during war, we shall render what is due him as a revolutionist. But that will not thereby resolve the question of the dialectic method.

It is impossible to say what Liebknecht's own final conclusions would have been had he remained at liberty. In any case before publishing his work, undoubtedly he would have shown it to his more competent friends, namely, Franz Mehring and Rosa Luxemburg. It is quite probable that on their advice he would have simply tossed the manuscript into the fire. Let us grant however that against the advice of

people far excelling him in the sphere of theory he nevertheless had decided to publish his work. Mehring, Luxemburg,
Lenin, and others would not of course have proposed that
he be expelled for this from the party; on the contrary, they
would have intervened decisively in his behalf had anyone
made such a foolish proposal. But at the same time they
would not have formed a philosophical bloc with him, but
rather would have differentiated themselves decisively from
his theoretical mistakes.

Comrade Shachtman's behavior, we note, is quite otherwise.
"You will observe," he says—and this to teach the youth!—
"that Plekhanov was an outstanding theoretician of dialectic
materialism but ended up an opportunist; Liebknecht was
a remarkable revolutionist but he had his doubts about dialectic materialism." This argument if it means anything at
all signifies that dialectic materialism is of no use whatsoever to a revolutionist. With these examples of Liebknecht
and Plekhanov, artificially torn out of history, Shachtman
reinforces and "deepens" the idea of his last year's article,
namely, that politics does not depend on method, inasmuch
as method is divorced from politics through the divine gift
of inconsistency. By falsely interpreting two "exceptions,"
Shachtman seeks to overthrow the rule. If this is the argument of a "supporter" of Marxism, what can we expect from
an opponent? The revision of Marxism passes here into its
downright liquidation; more than that, into the liquidation
of every doctrine and every method.

What do you propose instead?

Dialectic materialism is not of course an eternal and immutable philosophy. To think otherwise is to contradict
the spirit of the dialectic. Further development of scientific
thought will undoubtedly create a more profound doctrine
into which dialectic materialism will enter merely as struc-

tural material. However, there is no basis for expecting that this philosophic revolution will be accomplished under the decaying bourgeois regime, without mentioning the fact that a Marx is not born every year or every decade. The life-and-death task of the proletariat now consists not in *interpreting* the world anew but in *remaking* it from top to bottom. In the next epoch we can expect great revolutionists of action but hardly a new Marx. Only on the basis of socialist culture will mankind feel the need to review the ideological heritage of the past and undoubtedly will far surpass us not only in the sphere of economy but also in the sphere of intellectual creation. The regime of the Bonapartist bureaucracy in the USSR is criminal not only because it creates an ever-growing inequality in all spheres of life but also because it degrades the intellectual activity of the country to the depths of the unbridled blockheads of the GPU.

Let us grant however that contrary to our supposition the proletariat is so fortunate during the present epoch of wars and revolutions as to produce a new theoretician or a new constellation of theoreticians who will surpass Marxism and in particular advance logic beyond the materialist dialectics. It goes without saying that all advanced workers will learn from the new teachers and the old men will have to reeducate themselves again. But in the meantime this remains the music of the future. Or am I mistaken? Perhaps you will call my attention to those works which should supplant the system of dialectic materialism for the proletariat? Were these at hand surely you would not have refused to conduct a struggle against the opium of the dialectic. But none exist. While attempting to discredit the philosophy of Marxism you do not propose anything with which to replace it.

Picture to yourself a young amateur physician who proceeds to argue with a surgeon using a scalpel that modern anatomy, neurology, etc., are worthless, that much in them remains unclear and incomplete and that only "conservative bureaucrats" could set to work with a scalpel on the basis of these pseudosciences, etc. I believe that the surgeon would ask his irresponsible colleague to leave the operating room. We too, Comrade Burnham, cannot yield to cheap innuendoes about the philosophy of scientific socialism. On the contrary, since in the course of the factional struggle the question has been posed point-blank, we shall say, turning to all members of the party, especially the youth: Beware of the infiltration of bourgeois skepticism into your ranks. Remember that socialism to this day has not found higher scientific expression than Marxism. Bear in mind that the method of scientific socialism is dialectic materialism. Occupy yourselves with serious study! Study Marx, Engels, Plekhanov, Lenin, and Franz Mehring. This is a hundred times more important for you than the study of tendentious, sterile, and slightly ludicrous treatises on the conservatism of Cannon. Let the present discussion produce at least this positive result, that the youth attempt to imbed in their minds a serious theoretical foundation for revolutionary struggle!

False political 'realism'

In your case, however, the question is not confined to the dialectic. The remarks in your resolution to the effect that you do not now pose for the decision of the party the question of the nature of the Soviet state signify in reality that you *do pose* this question, if not juridically then theoretically and politically. Only infants can fail to understand this. This very statement likewise has another meaning, far more outrageous and pernicious. It means that you divorce politics from Marxist sociology. Yet for us the crux of the matter lies precisely in this. If it is possible to give a correct definition of the state without utilizing the method of dialectic materialism; if it is possible correctly to determine politics without giving a class analysis of the state, then the question arises: Is there any need whatsoever for Marxism?

Disagreeing among themselves on the class nature of the Soviet state, the leaders of the opposition agree on this, that the foreign policy of the Kremlin must be labeled "imperialist" and that the USSR cannot be supported "unconditionally." (Vastly substantial platform!) When the opposing "clique" raises the question of the nature of the Soviet state point-blank at the convention (what a crime!) you have in advance agreed . . . to disagree, i.e., to vote differently. In the British "national" government this precedent occurs of ministers who "agree to disagree," i.e., to vote differently. But His Majesty's ministers enjoy this advantage, that they are well aware of the nature of *their* state and can afford the luxury of disagreement on *secondary* questions. The leaders of the opposition are far less favorably situated. They permit themselves the luxury of differing on the fundamental question in order to solidarize on secondary questions. If this is Marxism and principled politics then I don't know what unprincipled combinationism means.

You seem to consider apparently that by refusing to discuss dialectic materialism and the class nature of the Soviet state and by sticking to "concrete" questions you are acting the part of a realistic politician. This self-deception is a result of your inadequate acquaintance with the history of the past fifty years of factional struggles in the labor movement. In every principled conflict, without a single exception, the Marxists invariably sought to face the party squarely with the fundamental problems of doctrine and program, considering that only under this condition could the "concrete" questions find their proper place and proportion. On the other hand the opportunists of every shade,

especially those who had already suffered a few defeats in
the sphere of principled discussion, invariably counterposed
to the Marxist class analysis "concrete" conjunctural appraisals which they, as is the custom, formulated under
the pressure of bourgeois democracy. Through decades of
factional struggle this division of roles has persisted. The
opposition, permit me to assure you, has invented nothing
new. It is continuing the tradition of revisionism in theory
and opportunism in politics.

Toward the close of the last century the revisionist attempts of Bernstein, who in England came under the influence of Anglo-Saxon empiricism and utilitarianism—the
most wretched of philosophies!—were mercilessly repulsed.
Whereupon the German opportunists suddenly recoiled
from philosophy and sociology. At conventions and in the
press they did not cease to berate the Marxist "pedants,"
who replaced the "concrete political questions" with general principled considerations. Read over the records of the
German Social Democracy toward the close of the last and
the beginning of the present century—and you will be astonished yourself at the degree to which, as the French say,
le mort saisit le vif (the dead grip the living)!

You are not unacquainted with the great role played by
Iskra in the development of Russian Marxism. *Iskra* began
with the struggle against so-called "Economism" in the
labor movement and against the Narodniki (Party of the
Social Revolutionists). The chief argument of the "Economists" was that *Iskra* floats in the sphere of theory while
they, the "Economists," propose leading the concrete labor
movement. The main argument of the Social Revolutionists
was as follows: *Iskra* wants to found a school of dialectic
materialism while we want to overthrow tsarist autocracy.
It must be said that the Narodnik terrorists took their own
words very seriously: bomb in hand they sacrificed their

lives. We argued with them: "Under certain circumstances a bomb is an excellent thing but we should first clarify our own minds." It is historical experience that the greatest revolution in all history was not led by the party which started out with bombs but by the party which started out with dialectic materialism.

When the Bolsheviks and the Mensheviks were still members of the same party, the preconvention periods and the convention itself invariably witnessed an embittered struggle over the agenda. Lenin used to propose as first on the agenda such questions as clarification of the nature of the tsarist monarchy, the analysis of the class character of the revolution, the appraisal of the stages of the revolution we were passing through, etc. Martov and Dan, the leaders of the Mensheviks, invariably objected: We are not a sociological club but a political party; we must come to an agreement not on the class nature of tsarist economy but on the "concrete political tasks." I cite this from memory but I do not run any risk of error since these disputes were repeated from year to year and became stereotyped in character. I might add that I personally committed not a few sins on this score myself. But I have learned something since then.

To those enamored with "concrete political questions" Lenin invariably explained that our politics is not of conjunctural but of principled character; that tactics are subordinate to strategy; that for us the primary concern of every political campaign is that it guide the workers from the particular questions to the general, that it teach them the nature of modern society and the character of its fundamental forces. The Mensheviks always felt the need urgently to slur over principled differences in their unstable conglomeration by means of evasions whereas Lenin on the contrary posed principled questions point-blank. The current arguments of the opposition against philosophy and sociology in favor

of "concrete political questions" is a belated repetition of
Dan's arguments. Not a single new word! How sad it is that
Shachtman respects the principled politics of Marxism only
when it has aged long enough for the archives.

Especially awkward and inappropriate does the appeal
to shift from Marxist theory to "concrete political questions" sound on your lips, Comrade Burnham, for it was
not I but you who raised the question of the character of
the USSR, thereby forcing me to pose the question of the
method through which the class character of the state is determined. True enough, you withdrew your resolution. But
this factional maneuver has no objective meaning whatsoever.
You draw your *political* conclusions from your *sociological*
premise, even if you have temporarily slipped it into your
briefcase. Shachtman draws exactly the same political conclusions without a sociological premise: he adapts himself
to you. Abern seeks to profit equally both from the hidden
premise and the absence of a premise for his "organizational" combinations. This is the real and not the diplomatic
situation in the camp of the opposition. You proceed as an
anti-Marxist; Shachtman and Abern—as *platonic* Marxists. Who is worse, it is not easy to determine.

The dialectic of the present discussion

When confronted with the diplomatic front covering the
hidden premises and lack of premises of our opponents, we,
the "conservatives," naturally reply: A fruitful dispute over
"concrete questions" is possible only if you clearly specify
what class premises you take as your starting point. We are
not compelled to confine ourselves to those topics in this
dispute which you have selected artificially. Should someone
propose that we discuss as "concrete" questions the invasion of Switzerland by the Soviet fleet or the length of a tail
of a Bronx witch, then I am justified in posing in advance

such questions as: Does Switzerland have a sea coast? Are there witches at all?

Every serious discussion develops from the particular and even the accidental to the general and fundamental. The immediate causes and motives of a discussion are of interest, in most cases, only symptomatically. Of actual political significance are only those problems which the discussion raises in its development. To certain intellectuals, anxious to indict "bureaucratic conservatism" and to display their "dynamic spirit," it might seem that questions concerning the dialectic, Marxism, the nature of the state, centralism are raised "artificially" and that the discussion has taken a "false" direction. The nub of the matter however consists in this, that discussion has its own objective logic which does not coincide at all with the subjective logic of individuals and groupings. The *dialectic* character of the discussion proceeds from the fact that its objective course is determined by the living conflict of opposing tendencies and not by a preconceived logical plan. The *materialist* basis of the discussion consists in its reflecting the pressure of different classes. Thus, the present discussion in the SWP, like the historic process as a whole, develops—with or without your permission, Comrade Burnham—according to the laws of dialectic materialism. There is no escape from these laws.

'Science' against Marxism and 'experiments' against program

Accusing your opponents of "bureaucratic conservatism" (a bare psychological abstraction insofar as no specific social interests are shown underlying this "conservatism"), you demand in your document that conservative politics be replaced by "critical and experimental politics—in a word, scientific politics." (p. 32.) This statement, at first glance so innocent and meaningless with all its pompousness, is in itself a complete exposure. You don't speak of Marxist

politics. You don't speak of proletarian politics. You speak
of "experimental," "critical," "scientific" politics. Why this
pretentious and deliberately abstruse terminology so unusual
in our ranks? I shall tell you. It is the product of your adaptation, Comrade Burnham, to bourgeois public opinion, and
the adaptation of Shachtman and Abern to your adaptation.
Marxism is no longer fashionable among the broad circles
of bourgeois intellectuals. Moreover if one should mention
Marxism, God forbid, he might be taken for a dialectic materialist. It is better to avoid this discredited word. What to
replace it with? Why, of course, with "science," even with
Science capitalized. And science, as everybody knows, is
based on "criticism" and "experiments." It has its own ring;
so solid, so tolerant, so unsectarian, so professorial! With
this formula one can enter any democratic salon.

Reread, please, your own statement once again: "In place
of conservative politics, we must put bold, flexible, critical,
and experimental politics—in a word, scientific politics."
You couldn't have improved it! But this is precisely the formula which all petty-bourgeois empiricists, all revisionists
and, last but not least, all political adventurers have counterposed to "narrow," "limited," "dogmatic," and "conservative" Marxism.

Buffon once said: The style is the man. Political terminology is not only the man but the party. Terminology is one
of the elements of the class struggle. Only lifeless pedants
can fail to understand this. In your document you painstakingly expunge—yes, no one else but you, Comrade Burnham—not only such terms as the dialectic and materialism
but also Marxism. You are above all this. You are a man
of "critical," "experimental" science. For exactly the same
reason you culled the label "imperialism" to describe the
foreign policy of the Kremlin. This innovation differentiates
you from the too-embarrassing terminology of the Fourth

International by creating less "sectarian," less "religious," less rigorous formulas, common to you and—oh happy coincidence!—bourgeois democracy.

You want to experiment? But permit me to remind you that the workers movement possesses a long history with no lack of experience and, if you prefer, experiments. This experience so dearly bought has been crystallized in the shape of a definite doctrine, the very Marxism whose name you so carefully avoid. Before giving you the right to experiment, the party has the right to ask: What method will you use? Henry Ford would scarcely permit a man to experiment in his plant who had not assimilated the requisite conclusions of the past development of industry and the innumerable experiments already carried out. Furthermore, experimental laboratories in factories are carefully segregated from mass production. Far more impermissible even are witch doctor experiments in the sphere of the labor movement— even though conducted under the banner of anonymous "science." For us the science of the workers movement is Marxism. Nameless social science, Science with a capital letter, we leave these completely at the disposal of Eastman and his ilk.

I know that you have engaged in disputes with Eastman and in some questions you have argued very well. But you debate with him as a representative of your own circle and not as an agent of the class enemy. You revealed this conspicuously in your joint article with Shachtman when you ended up with the unexpected invitation to Eastman, Hook, Lyons, and the rest that they take advantage of the pages of the *New International* to promulgate their views. It did not even concern you that they might pose the question of the dialectic and thus drive you out of your diplomatic silence.

On January 20 of last year, hence long prior to this discussion, in a letter to Comrade Shachtman I insisted on the urgent necessity of attentively following the internal developments of the Stalinist party. I wrote: "It would be a thousand times more important than inviting Eastman, Lyons and the others to present their personal sweatings. I was wondering a bit why you gave space to Eastman's last insignificant and arrogant article. He has at his disposal *Harper's Magazine, Modern Monthly, Common Sense*, etc. But I am absolutely perplexed that you personally *invited* these people to besmirch the not-so-numerous pages of the *New International*. The perpetuation of this polemic can interest some *petty-bourgeois intellectuals* but not the revolutionary elements. It is my firm conviction that a certain reorganization of the *New International* and the *Socialist Appeal* is necessary: more distance from Eastman, Lyons, etc.; and nearer to the workers and, in this sense, to the Stalinist party."

As always in such cases Shachtman replied inattentively and carelessly. In actuality, the question was resolved by the fact that the enemies of Marxism whom you invited refused to accept your invitation. This episode, however, deserves closer attention. On the one hand, you, Comrade Burnham, bolstered by Shachtman, invite bourgeois democrats to send in friendly explanations to be printed in the pages of our party organ. On the other hand, you, bolstered by this same Shachtman, refuse to engage in a debate with me over the dialectic and the class nature of the Soviet state. Doesn't this signify that you, together with your ally Shachtman, have turned your faces somewhat toward the bourgeois semi-opponents and your backs toward your own party? Abern long ago came to the conclusion that Marxism is a doctrine to be honored, but a good oppositional combination is something far more substantial. Meanwhile, Shachtman slips and slides downward, consoling himself with wisecracks. I feel, however, that his heart is a trifle heavy. Upon reaching a certain point, Shachtman will, I hope, pull himself together and begin the upward climb again. Here is the hope that his "experimental" factional politics will at least turn out to the profit of "Science."

'An unconscious dialectician'

Using as his text my remark concerning Darwin, Shachtman has stated, I have been informed, that you are an "unconscious dialectician." This ambiguous compliment contains an iota of truth. Every individual is a dialectician *to some extent or other*, in most cases, unconsciously. A housewife knows that a certain amount of salt flavors soup agreeably, but that added salt makes the soup unpalatable. Consequently, an illiterate peasant woman guides herself in cooking soup by the Hegelian law of the transformation of quantity into quality. Similar examples from daily life could be cited without end. Even animals arrive at their practical conclusions not only on the basis of the Aristotelian syllogism but also on the basis of the Hegelian dialectic. Thus a fox is aware that quadrupeds and birds are nutritious and tasty. On sighting a hare, a rabbit, or a hen, a fox concludes: this particular creature belongs to the tasty and nutritive type, and—chases after the prey. We have here a complete syllogism, although the fox, we may suppose, never read Aristotle. When the same fox, however, encounters the first animal which exceeds it in size, for example, a wolf, it quickly concludes that quantity passes into quality, and turns to flee. Clearly, the legs of a fox are equipped with Hegelian tendencies, even if not fully conscious ones. All this demonstrates, in passing, that our methods of thought, both formal logic and the dialectic, are not arbitrary constructions of our reason but rather expressions of the actual interrelationships in nature itself. In this sense, the universe throughout is permeated with "unconscious" dialectics. But nature did not stop there. No little development occurred before nature's inner relationships were converted into the language of the consciousness of foxes and men, and man was then enabled to generalize these forms of consciousness and transform them into logical (dialectical) categories, thus creating the possibility for probing more deeply into the world about us.

The most finished expression to date of the laws of the dialectic which prevail in nature and in society has been given by Hegel and Marx. Despite the fact that Darwin was not interested in verifying his logical methods, his empiricism—that of a genius—in the sphere of natural science reached the highest dialectic generalizations. In this sense, Darwin was, as I stated in my previous article, an "unconscious dialectician." We do not, however, value Darwin for his inability to rise to the dialectic, but for having, despite his philosophical backwardness, explained to us the origin of species. Engels was, it might be pointed out, exasperated by the narrow empiricism of the Darwinian method, although he, like Marx, immediately appreciated the greatness of the theory of natural selection. Darwin, on the contrary, remained, alas, ignorant of the meaning of Marx's sociology to the end of his life. Had Darwin come out in the press against the dialectic or materialism, Marx and Engels would have attacked him with redoubled force so as not to allow his authority to cloak ideological reaction.

In the attorney's plea of Shachtman to the effect that you are an "unconscious dialectician," the stress must be laid on the word *unconscious*. Shachtman's aim (also partly unconscious) is to defend his bloc with you by degrading dialectic materialism. For in reality, Shachtman is saying: The difference between a "conscious" and an "unconscious" dialectician is not so great that one must quarrel about it. Shachtman thus attempts to discredit the Marxist method.

But the evil goes beyond even this. Very many unconscious or semi-unconscious dialecticians exist in this world. Some of them apply the materialist dialectic excellently to politics, even though they have never concerned themselves with questions of method. It would obviously be pedantic blockheadedness to attack such comrades. But it is otherwise with you, Comrade Burnham. You are an editor of the theoretical organ whose task it is to educate the party in the spirit of the Marxist method. Yet you are a *conscious opponent of the dialectic* and not at all an *unconscious dialectician*. Even if you had, as Shachtman insists, successfully followed the dialectic in political questions, i.e., even if you were endowed with a dialectic "instinct," we would still be compelled to begin a struggle against you, because your dialectic instinct, like other individual qualities, cannot be transmitted to others, whereas the conscious dialectic method can, to one degree or another, be made accessible to the entire party.

The dialectic and Mr. Dies

Even if you have a dialectic instinct—and I do not undertake to judge this—it is well-nigh stifled by academic routine and intellectual hauteur. What we term the class instinct of the worker, accepts with relative ease the dialectic approach to questions. There can be no talk of such a class instinct in a bourgeois intellectual. Only by *consciously* surmounting his petty-bourgeois spirit can an intellectual divorced from the proletariat rise to Marxist politics. Unfortunately, Shachtman and Abern are doing everything in their power to bar this road to you. By their support they render you a very bad service, Comrade Burnham.

Bolstered by your bloc, which might be designated as the "League of Factional Abandon," you commit one blunder after another: in philosophy, in sociology, in politics, in the organizational sphere. Your errors are not accidental. You approach each question by isolating it, by splitting it away from its connection with other questions, away from its connection with social factors, and—independently of international experience. You lack the dialectic method. Despite all your education, in politics you proceed like a witch doctor.

In the question of the Dies Committee your mumbo jumbo manifested itself no less glaringly than in the question of Finland. To my arguments in favor of utilizing this parliamentary body, you replied that the question should be decided not by principled considerations but by some special circumstances known to you alone but which you refrained from specifying. Permit me to tell you what these circumstances were: your ideological dependence on bourgeois public opinion. Although bourgeois democracy, in all its sections, bears full responsibility for the capitalist regime, including the Dies Committee, it is compelled, in the interests of this very same capitalism, shamefacedly to distract attention away from the too-naked organs of the regime. A simple division of labor! An old fraud which still continues, however, to operate effectively! As for the workers, to whom you refer vaguely, a section of them, and a very considerable section, is like yourself under the influence of bourgeois democracy. But the average worker, not infected with the prejudices of the labor aristocracy, would joyfully welcome every bold revolutionary word thrown in the very face of the class enemy. And the more reactionary the institution which serves as the arena for the combat, all the more complete is the satisfaction of the worker. This has been proved by historical experience. Dies himself, becoming frightened and jumping back in time, demonstrated how false your position was. It is always better to compel the enemy to retreat than to hide oneself without a battle.

But at this point I see the irate figure of Shachtman rising to stop me with a gesture of protest: "The opposition bears no responsibility for Burnham's views on the Dies Committee. This question did not assume a factional character," and so forth and so on. I know all this. As if the only thing that lacked was for the entire opposition to express itself in favor of the tactic of boycott, so utterly senseless in this instance! It is sufficient that the leader of the opposition, who has views and openly expressed them, came out in favor of boycott. If you happened to have outgrown the age when one argues about "religion," then, let me confess, I had considered that the entire Fourth International had outgrown the age when abstentionism is accounted the most revolutionary of policies. Aside from your lack of method, you revealed in this instance an obvious lack of political sagacity. In the given situation, a revolutionist would not have needed to discuss long before springing through a door flung open by the enemy and making the most of the opportunity. For those members of the opposition who together with you spoke against participation in the Dies Committee—and their number is not so small—it is necessary in my opinion to arrange special elementary courses in order to explain to them the elementary truths of revolutionary tactics, which have nothing in common with the pseudoradical abstentionism of the intellectual circles.

'Concrete political questions'

The opposition is weakest precisely in the sphere where it imagines itself especially strong—the sphere of day-to-day revolutionary politics. This applies above all to you, Comrade Burnham. Impotence in the face of great events manifested itself in you as well as in the entire opposition most glaringly in the questions of Poland, the Baltic states, and Finland.

Shachtman began by discovering a philosopher's stone: the achievement of a simultaneous insurrection against Hitler and Stalin in occupied Poland. The idea was splendid; it is only too bad that Shachtman was deprived of the opportunity of putting it into practise. The advanced workers in eastern Poland could justifiably say: "A simultaneous insurrection against Hitler and Stalin in a country occupied by troops might perhaps be arranged very conveniently from the Bronx;* but here, locally, it is more difficult. We should like to hear Burnham's and Shachtman's answer to a 'concrete political question': What shall we do between now and the coming insurrection?" In the meantime, the commanding staff of the Soviet army called upon the peasants and workers to seize the land and the factories. This call, supported by armed force, played an enormous role in the life of the occupied country. Moscow papers were filled to overflowing with reports of the boundless "enthusiasm" of workers and poor peasants. We should and must approach these reports with justifiable distrust: there is no lack of lies. But it is nevertheless impermissible to close one's eyes to facts. The call to settle accounts with the landlords and to drive out the capitalists could not have failed to rouse the spirit of the hounded and crushed Ukrainian and Byelorussian peasants and workers who saw in the Polish landlord a double enemy.

In the Parisian organ of the Mensheviks, who are in solidarity with the bourgeois democracy of France and not the Fourth International, it was stated categorically that the advance of the Red Army was accompanied by a wave of revolutionary upsurge, echoes of which penetrated even the peasant masses of Romania. What adds special weight to the dispatches of this organ is the close connection with the

---

* Shachtman was a member of the SWP's Bronx branch.

Mensheviks and the leaders of the Jewish Bund, the Polish Socialist Party, and other organizations who are hostile to the Kremlin and who fled from Poland. We were therefore completely correct when we said to the Bolsheviks in eastern Poland: "Together with the workers and peasants, and in the forefront, you must conduct a struggle against the landlords and the capitalists; do not tear yourself away from the masses, despite all their illusions, just as the Russian revolutionists did not tear themselves away from the masses who had not yet freed themselves from their hopes in the tsar (Bloody Sunday, January 22, 1905); educate the masses in the course of the struggle, warn them against naive hopes in Moscow, but do not tear yourself away from them, fight in their camp, try to extend and deepen their struggle, and to give it the greatest possible independence. Only in this way will you prepare the coming insurrection against Stalin." The course of events in Poland has completely confirmed this directive, which was a continuation and a development of all our previous policies, particularly in Spain.

Since there is no principled difference between the Polish and Finnish situations, we can have no grounds for changing our directive. But the opposition, who failed to understand the meaning of the Polish events, now tries to clutch at Finland as a new anchor of salvation. "Where is the civil war in Finland? Trotsky talks of a civil war. We have seen nothing about it in the press," and so on. The question of Finland appears to the opposition as in principle different from the question of western Ukraine and Byelorussia. Each question is isolated and viewed aside and apart from the general course of development. Confounded by the course of events, the opposition seeks each time to support itself on some accidental, secondary, temporary, and conjunctural circumstances.

Do these cries about the absence of civil war in Finland

signify that the opposition would adopt our policy if civil war were actually to unfold in Finland? Yes or no? If yes, then the opposition thereby condemns its own policy in relation to Poland, since there, despite the civil war, they limited themselves to refusal to participate in the events, while they waited for a simultaneous uprising against Stalin and Hitler. It is obvious, Comrade Burnham, that you and your allies have not thought this question through to the end.

What about my assertion concerning a civil war in Finland? At the very inception of military hostilities, one might have conjectured that Moscow was seeking through a "small" punitive expedition to bring about a change of government in Helsingfors and to establish the same relations with Finland as with the other Baltic states. But the appointment of the Kuusinen government in Terrijoki demonstrated that Moscow had other plans and aims. Dispatches then reported the creation of a Finnish "Red Army." Naturally, it was only a question of small formations set up from above. The program of Kuusinen was issued. Next the dispatches appeared of the division of large estates among poor peasants. In their totality, these dispatches signified an attempt on the part of Moscow to organize a civil war. Naturally, this is a civil war of a special type. It does not arise spontaneously from the depths of the popular masses. It is not conducted under the leadership of the Finnish revolutionary party based on mass support. It is introduced on bayonets from without. It is controlled by the Moscow bureaucracy. All this we know, and we dealt with all this in discussing Poland. Nevertheless, it is precisely a question of civil war, of an appeal to the lowly, to the poor, a call to them to expropriate the rich, drive them out, arrest them, etc. I know of no other name for these actions except civil war.

"But, after all, the civil war in Finland did not unfold," object the leaders of the opposition. "This means that your predictions did not materialize." With the defeat and the retreat of the Red Army, I reply, the civil war in Finland cannot, of course, unfold under the bayonets of Mannerheim. This fact is an argument not against me but against Shachtman; since it demonstrates that in the first stages of war, at a time when discipline in armies is still strong, it is much easier to organize insurrection, and on two fronts to boot, from the Bronx than from Terrijoki.

We did not foresee the defeats of the first detachments of the Red Army. We could not have foreseen the extent to which stupidity and demoralization reign in the Kremlin and in the tops of the army beheaded by the Kremlin. Nevertheless, what is involved is only a military episode, which cannot determine our political line. Should Moscow, after its first unsuccessful attempt, refrain entirely from any further offensive against Finland, then the very question which today obscures the entire world situation to the eyes of the opposition would be removed from the order of the day. But there is little chance for this. On the other hand, if England, France, and the United States, basing themselves on Scandinavia, were to aid Finland with military force, then the Finnish question would be submerged in a war between the USSR and the imperialist countries. In this case, we must assume that even a majority of the oppositionists would remind themselves of the program of the Fourth International.

At the present time, however, the opposition is not interested in these two variants: either the suspension of the offensive on the part of the USSR, or the outbreak of hostilities between the USSR and the imperialist democracies. The opposition is interested only in the isolated question of the USSR's invasion of Finland. Very well, let us take this as our starting point. If the second offensive, as may be assumed, is better prepared and conducted, then the advance of the Red Army into the country will again place the question of civil war on the order of the day, and moreover on a much broader scale than during the first and ignominiously unsuccessful attempt. Our directive, consequently, remains completely valid so long as the question itself remains on the agenda. But what does the opposition propose in the event the Red Army successfully advances into Finland and civil war unfolds there? The opposition apparently doesn't think about this at all, for they live from one day to the next, from one incident to another, clutching at episodes, clinging to isolated phrases in an editorial, feeding on sympathies and antipathies, and thus creating for themselves the semblance of a platform. The weakness of empiricists and impressionists is always revealed most glaringly in their approach to "concrete political questions."

Theoretical bewilderment and political abstentionism

Throughout all the vacillations and convulsions of the opposition, contradictory though they may be, two general features run like a guiding thread from the pinnacles of theory down to the most trifling political episodes. The first general feature is the absence of a unified conception. The opposition leaders split sociology from dialectic materialism. They split politics from sociology. In the sphere of politics they split our tasks in Poland from our experience in Spain— our tasks in Finland from our position on Poland. History becomes transformed into a series of exceptional incidents; politics becomes transformed into a series of improvisations. We have here, in the full sense of the term, the disintegration of Marxism, the disintegration of theoretical thought, the disintegration of politics into its constituent elements. Empiricism and its foster brother, impressionism, dominate from top to bottom. That is why the ideological leadership, Comrade Burnham, rests with you as an opponent of the dialectic, as an empiricist, unabashed by his empiricism.

Throughout the vacillations and convulsions of the opposition, there is a second general feature intimately bound to the first, namely, a tendency to refrain from active participation, a tendency to self-elimination, to abstentionism, naturally under cover of ultraradical phrases. You are in favor of overthrowing Hitler and Stalin in Poland; Stalin and Mannerheim in Finland. And until then, you reject both sides *equally*, in other words, you withdraw from the struggle, including the civil war. Your citing the absence of civil war in Finland is only an accidental conjunctural argument. Should the civil war unfold, the opposition will attempt not to notice it, as they tried not to notice it in Poland, or they will declare that inasmuch as the policy of the Moscow bureaucracy is "imperialist" in character "we" do not take part in this filthy business. Hot on the trail of "concrete" political tasks in words, the opposition actually places itself outside the historical process. Your position, Comrade Burnham, in relation to the Dies Committee merits attention precisely because it is a graphic expression of this same tendency of abstentionism and bewilderment. Your guiding principle still remains the same: "Thank you, I don't smoke."

Naturally, any man, any party, and even any class can become bewildered. But with the petty bourgeoisie, bewilderment, especially in the face of great events, is an inescapable and, so to speak, congenital condition. The intellectuals attempt to express their state of bewilderment in the language of "science." The contradictory platform of the opposition reflects petty-bourgeois bewilderment expressed in the bombastic language of the intellectuals. There is nothing proletarian about it.

The petty bourgeoisie and centralism

In the organizational sphere, your views are just as schematic, empiric, nonrevolutionary as in the sphere of theory and politics. A Stolberg, lantern in hand, chases after an ideal revolution, unaccompanied by any excesses, and guaranteed against Thermidor and counterrevolution; you, likewise, seek an ideal party democracy which would secure forever and for everybody the possibility of saying and doing whatever popped into his head, and which would ensure the party against bureaucratic degeneration. You overlook a trifle, namely, that the party is not an arena for the assertion of free individuality, but an instrument of the proletarian revolution; that only a victorious revolution is capable of preventing the degeneration not only of the party but of the proletariat itself and of modern civilization as a whole. You do not see that our American section is not sick from too much centralism—it is laughable even to talk about it— but from a monstrous abuse and distortion of democracy on the part of petty-bourgeois elements. This is at the root of the present crisis.

A worker spends his day at the factory. He has comparatively few hours left for the party. At the meetings he is interested in learning the most important things: the correct evaluation of the situation and the political conclusions. He values those leaders who do this in the clearest and the most precise form and who keep in step with events. Petty-bourgeois, and especially declassed elements, divorced from the proletariat, vegetate in an artificial and shut-in environment. They have ample time to dabble in politics or its substitute. They pick out faults, exchange all sorts of tidbits and gossip concerning happenings among the party "tops." They always locate a leader who initiates them into all the "secrets." Discussion is their native element. No amount of democracy is ever enough for them. For their war of words they seek the fourth dimension. They become jittery, they revolve in a vicious circle, and they quench their thirst with salt water. Do you want to know the organizational program of the opposition? It consists of a mad hunt for the fourth dimension of party democracy. In practice this means burying politics beneath discussion; and burying centralism beneath the anarchy of the intellectual circles. When a few thousand workers join the party, they will call the petty-bourgeois anarchists severely to order. The sooner, the better.

Conclusions

Why do I address you and not the other leaders of the opposition? Because you are the ideological leader of the bloc. Comrade Abern's faction, destitute of a program and a banner, is ever in need of cover. At one time Shachtman served as cover, then came Muste with Spector, and now you, with Shachtman adapting himself to you. Your ideology I consider the expression of bourgeois influence in the proletariat.

To some comrades, the tone of this letter may perhaps seem too sharp. Yet, let me confess, I did everything in my power to restrain myself. For, after all, it is a question of nothing more or less than an attempt to reject, disqualify, and overthrow the theoretical foundations, the political principles, and organizational methods of our movement.

In reaction to my previous article, Comrade Abern, it has been reported, remarked: "This means split." Such a response merely demonstrates that Abern lacks devotion to the party and the Fourth International; he is a circle man. In any case, threats of split will not deter us from presenting a Marxist analysis of the differences. For us Marxists, it is a question not of split but of educating the party. It is my firm hope that the coming convention will ruthlessly repulse the revisionists.

The convention, in my opinion, must declare categorically that in their attempts to divorce sociology from dialectic materialism and politics from sociology, the leaders of the opposition have broken from Marxism and become the transmitting mechanism for petty-bourgeois empiricism. While reaffirming, decisively and completely, its loyalty to the Marxist doctrine and the political and organizational methods of bolshevism, while binding the editorial boards of its official publications to promulgate and defend this doctrine and these methods, the party will, of course, extend the pages of its publications in the future to those of its members who consider themselves capable of adding something new to the doctrine of Marxism. But it will not permit a game of hide-and-seek with Marxism and light-minded gibes concerning it.

The politics of a party has a class character. Without a class analysis of the state, the parties, and ideological tendencies, it is impossible to arrive at a correct political orientation. The party must condemn as vulgar opportunism the attempt to determine policies in relation to the USSR from incident to incident and independently of the class nature of the Soviet state.

The disintegration of capitalism, which engenders sharp dissatisfaction among the petty bourgeoisie and drives its bottom layers to the left, opens up broad possibilities but it also contains grave dangers. The Fourth International needs only those emigrants from the petty bourgeoisie who have broken completely with their social past and who have come over decisively to the standpoint of the proletariat.

This theoretical and political transit must be accompanied by an actual break with the old environment and the establishment of intimate ties with workers, in particular, by participation in the recruitment and education of proletarians for their party. Emigrants from the petty-bourgeois milieu who prove incapable of settling in the proletarian milieu must after the lapse of a certain period of time be transferred from membership in the party to the status of sympathizers.

Members of the party untested in the class struggle must not be placed in responsible positions. No matter how talented and devoted to socialism an emigrant from the bourgeois milieu may be, before becoming a teacher, he must first go to school in the working class. Young intellectuals must not be placed at the head of the intellectual youth but sent out into the provinces for a few years, into the purely proletarian centers, for hard practical work.

The class composition of the party must correspond to its class program. The American section of the Fourth International will either become proletarian or it will cease to exist.

Comrade Burnham! If we can arrive at an agreement with you on the basis of these principles, then without difficulty we shall find a correct policy in relation to Poland, Finland, and even India. At the same time, I pledge myself to help you conduct a struggle against any manifestations whatsoever of bureaucratism and conservatism. These in my opinion are the conditions necessary to end the present crisis.

With Bolshevik greetings,

L. Trotsky
COYOACÁN, D.F.

Letter to James P. Cannon‡

JANUARY 9, 1940

Dear Friend,

Yesterday I sent the Russian text of my new article written in the form of a letter to Burnham. Not all comrades possibly are content with the fact that I give the predominant place in the discussion to the matter of dialectics. But I am sure it is now the only way to begin the theoretical education of the party, especially of the youth and to inject an aversion to empiricism and eclectics.

W. Rork [Leon Trotsky]

Letter to Farrell Dobbs‡

JANUARY 10, 1940

Dear Friend,

In my article sent for translation to Wright I don't mention at all two questions:

First, that of bureaucratic conservatism. I believe we discussed the matter a bit with you here. As a political tendency, bureaucratic conservatism represents the material interests of a certain social stratum, namely of the privileged workers bureaucracy in the capitalist, especially in the imperialist states and in an incomparably higher degree in the USSR. It would be fantastic, not to say stupid to search for such roots of the "bureaucratic conservatism" of the majority. If bureaucratism and conservatism are not determined by social conditions then they represent traits in the personal characters of some leaders. Such things occur. But how explain in this case the formation of a faction? Is it a selection of conservative individualities? We have here a psychological and not a political explanation. If we admit (I personally don't do it) that Cannon for example has bureaucratic tendencies, then we must inevitably reach the conclusion that the majority supports Cannon *in spite* of this trait and not *because* of it. It signifies that the question of the social foundations of the factional fight isn't even touched by the minority leaders.

Second, in order to compromise my "defense" of Cannon they insist that I falsely defended Molinier. I am the last to deny that I can commit mistakes of political nature as well as of personal appreciations. But in spite of all, the argument is not very profound. I never supported the false theories of Molinier. It was namely a question of his personal character: brutality, lack of discipline, and his private financial affairs. Some comrades, among them Vereecken, insisted upon immediate separation from Molinier. I insisted upon the necessity for the organization to try to discipline Molinier. But in 1934 when Molinier tried to replace the party program by "four slogans" and created a paper on this basis, I was among those who proposed his expulsion. This is the whole story. One can be of different opinion about the wisdom of my patient conduct in regard to Molinier, however I was guided of course not by the personal interests of Molinier, but by the interests of the education of the party: our own sections inherited some Comintern venom in the sense that many comrades are inclined to the abuse of such measures as expulsion, split, or threats of expulsions and splits. In the case of Molinier as in the case of some American comrades (Field, Weisbord, and some others), I was for a more patient attitude. In several cases I succeeded, in several others it was a failure. But I don't regret at all my more patient attitude towards some doubtful figures in our movement. In any case, my "defense" of them was never a bloc at the expense of principles. If somebody should propose, for example, to expel Comrade Burnham, I would oppose it energetically. But at the same time, I find it necessary to conduct the most strenuous ideological fight against his anti-Marxist conceptions.

Yours fraternally,

L. Trotsky
COYOACÁN, D.F.

Letter to John G. Wright[‡]

JANUARY 13, 1940

Dear Comrade Wright,

I agree completely with your appreciation of the pamphlet of Comrade Shachtman.* It is the *weak* Shachtman multiplied by factional passion. He lacks a small thing which is called the proletarian point of view. He lives in the realm of literary shadows: when he stands with his face toward the proletariat and Marxism, his shadows are useful because they correspond more or less with reality; now he turns his back to the proletarian majority of the party and to Marxism and as a result every word he writes is a fantastic misinterpretation of facts and ideas. I am obliged now to lose again a couple of days to submit his absolutely extravagant document to a more attentative analysis. I hope to show to the party members including the majority of the minority that Shachtman's document is in every line a pathetic rupture with Marxism and with bolshevism.

Yours fraternally,

L. Trotsky

---

* The pamphlet referred to is "The Crisis in the American Party—An Open letter to Comrade Leon Trotsky" published in *Internal Bulletin*, vol. 2, no. 7, dated January 1, 1940.

Letter to James P. Cannon[‡]

JANUARY 16, 1940

Dear Friend,

What miserable writing is Shachtman's open letter. Its only merit is that it obliged me to tell him the full truth about his politics. My answer is already dictated, I have only to polish it. Unfortunately it will not be shorter than my letter to Burnham.

L.T.

Letter to George Novack[‡]

JANUARY 16, 1940

Dear Comrade Warde,

. . . You are one of the comparatively few comrades who are seriously interested in the methodological questions of our movement. Don't you believe that your intervention in the discussion from *this* point of view would be very useful?

Friends write me that the interest for dialectical materialism in our party, especially in the youth, is becoming very acute. Don't you believe that comrades who could orientate this interest should now create some purely theoretical association with the purpose of promoting in the party the doctrines of dialectical materialism? Yourself, Comrade Wright, Comrade Gerland (very well acquainted with the matter) could possibly form the first nucleus of such an association, of course, under the control of the propaganda department of the National Committee. It is, certainly, only a vague suggestion from afar which should be discussed with the responsible party institutions. . . .

Yours comradely,

Leon Trotsky
COYOACÁN, D.F.

Letter to Joseph Hansen[‡]

JANUARY 18, 1940

Dear Joe,

. . . My article against Shachtman is already written. I need now to polish it for two days, and I will try to use some of your quotations.

But I wish to speak here about another more important question. Some of the leaders of the opposition are preparing a split; whereby they represent the opposition in the future as a persecuted minority. It is very characteristic of their state of mind. I believe we must answer them approximately as follows:

"You are already afraid of our future repressions? We propose to you mutual guarantees for the future minority, independently of who might be this minority, you or we. These guarantees could be formulated in four points: (1) No prohibition of factions; (2) no other restrictions on factional activity than those dictated by the necessity for common action; (3) the official publications must represent, of course, the line established by the new convention; (4) the future minority can have, if it wishes, an internal bulletin destined for party members, or a common discussion bulletin with the majority."

The continuation of discussion bulletins immediately after

a long discussion and a convention is, of course, not a rule but an exception, a rather deplorable one. But we are not bureaucrats at all. We don't have immutable rules. We are dialecticians also in the organizational field. If we have in the party an important minority which is dissatisfied with the decisions of the convention, it is incomparably more preferable to legalize the discussion after the convention than to have a split.

We can go, if necessary, even further and propose to them to publish, under the supervision of the new National Committee, special discussion symposiums, not only for party members, but for the public in general. We should go as far as possible in this respect in order to disarm their at least premature complaints and handicap them in provoking a split.

For my part I believe that the prolongation of the discussion, if it is channelized by the good will of both sides, can only serve in the present conditions the education of the party.

I believe that the majority should make these propositions officially in the National Committee in a written form. Whatever might be their answer, the party could only win.

With best greetings,

Cornell [Leon Trotsky]
COYOACÁN, D.F.

22

From a scratch—to the danger of gangrene

JANUARY 24, 1940

The discussion is developing in accordance with its own internal logic. Each camp, corresponding to its social character and political physiognomy, seeks to strike at those points where its opponent is weakest and most vulnerable. It is precisely this that determines the course of the discussion and not a priori plans of the leaders of the opposition. It is belated and sterile to lament now over the flaring up of the discussion. It is necessary only to keep a sharp eye on the role played by Stalinist provocateurs who are unquestionably in the party and who are under orders to poison the atmosphere of the discussion and to head the ideological struggle toward split. It is not so very difficult to recognize these gentlemen; their zeal is excessive and of course artificial; they replace ideas and arguments with gossip and slander. They must be exposed and thrown out through the joint efforts of both factions. But the principled struggle must be carried through to the end, that is, to serious clarification of the more important questions that have been posed. It is necessary to so utilize the discussion that it raises the theoretical level of the party.

A considerable proportion of the membership of the American section as well as our entire young International, came to us either from the Comintern in its period of decline or from the Second International. These are bad schools. The discussion has revealed that wide circles of the party lack a sound theoretical education. It is sufficient, for instance, to refer to the circumstance that the New York local of the party did not respond with a vigorous defensive reflex to the attempts at light-minded revision of Marxist doctrine and program but on the contrary gave support in the majority to the revisionists. This is unfortunate but remediable to the degree that our American section and the entire International consist of honest individuals sincerely seeking their way to the revolutionary road. They have the desire and the will to learn. But there is no time to lose. It is precisely the party's penetration into the trade unions, and into the workers' milieu in general, that demands heightening the theoretical qualification of our cadres. I do not mean by cadres the "apparatus" but the party as a whole. Every party member should and must consider himself an officer in the proletarian army.

"Since when have you become specialists in the question of philosophy?" the oppositionists now ironically ask the majority representatives. Irony here is completely out of place. Scientific socialism is the conscious expression of the unconscious historical process; namely, the instinctive and elemental drive of the proletariat to reconstruct society on communist beginnings. These organic tendencies in the psychology of workers spring to life with utmost rapidity today in the epoch of crises and wars. The discussion has revealed beyond all question a clash in the party between a petty-bourgeois tendency and a proletarian tendency. The petty-bourgeois tendency reveals its confusion in its attempt to reduce the program of the party to the small coin of "concrete" questions. The proletarian tendency on the contrary strives to correlate all the partial questions

into theoretical unity. At stake at the present time is not
the extent to which individual members of the majority
consciously apply the dialectic method. What is important
is the fact that the majority as a whole pushes toward the
proletarian posing of the questions and by very reason of
this tends to assimilate the dialectic, which is the "algebra
of the revolution." The oppositionists, I am informed, greet
with bursts of laughter the very mention of "dialectics." In
vain. This unworthy method will not help. The dialectic of
the historic process has more than once cruelly punished
those who tried to jeer at it.

Comrade Shachtman's latest article, "An Open Letter
to Leon Trotsky," is an alarming symptom. It reveals that
Shachtman refuses to learn from the discussion and persists
instead in deepening his mistakes, exploiting thereby not
only the inadequate theoretical level of the party, but also
the specific prejudices of its petty-bourgeois wing. Everybody is aware of the facility with which Shachtman is able
to weave various historical episodes around one or another
axis. This ability makes Shachtman a talented journalist. Unfortunately, this by itself is not enough. The main question
is what axis to select. Shachtman is absorbed always by the
reflection of politics in literature and in the press. He lacks
interest in the actual processes of the class struggle, the life
of the masses, the interrelationships between the different
layers within the working class itself, etc. I have read not a
few excellent and even brilliant articles by Shachtman, but
I have never seen a single commentary of his which actually probed into the life of the American working class or
its vanguard.

A qualification must be made to this extent—that not
only Shachtman's personal failing is embodied therein, but
the fate of a whole revolutionary generation which because
of a special conjuncture of historical conditions grew up

outside the labor movement. More than once in the past I have had occasion to speak and write about the danger of these valuable elements degenerating *despite* their devotion to the revolution. What was an inescapable characteristic of adolescence in its day has become a weakness. Weakness invites disease. If neglected, the disease can become fatal. To escape this danger it is necessary to open a new chapter consciously in the development of the party. The propagandists and journalists of the Fourth International must begin a new chapter in their own consciousness. It is necessary to rearm. It is necessary to make an about-face on one's own axis: to turn one's back to the petty-bourgeois intellectuals, and to face toward the workers.

To view as the cause of the present party crisis—the conservatism of its worker section; to seek a solution to the crisis through the victory of the petty-bourgeois bloc—it would be difficult to conceive a mistake more dangerous to the party. As a matter of fact, the gist of the present crisis consists in the conservatism of the petty-bourgeois elements who have passed through a purely propagandistic school and who have not yet found a pathway to the road of the class struggle. The present crisis is the final battle of these elements for self-preservation. Every oppositionist as an individual can, if he firmly desires, find a worthy place for himself in the revolutionary movement. As a faction they are doomed. In the struggle that is developing, Shachtman is not in the camp where he ought to be. As always in such cases, his strong sides have receded into the background while his weak traits on the other hand have assumed an especially finished expression. His "Open Letter" represents, so to speak, a crystallization of his weak traits.

Shachtman has left out a trifle: his class position. Hence his extraordinary zigzags, his improvisations and leaps. He

replaces class analysis with disconnected historical anecdotes for the sole purpose of covering up his own shift, for
camouflaging the contradiction between his yesterday and
today. This is Shachtman's procedure with the history of
Marxism, the history of his own party, and the history of
the Russian opposition. In carrying this out, he heaps mistakes upon mistakes. All the historical analogies to which
he resorts, speak, as we shall see, against him.

It is much more difficult to correct mistakes than to commit them. I must ask patience from the reader in following
with me step by step all the zigzags of Shachtman's mental
operations. For my part I promise not to confine myself
merely to exposing mistakes and contradictions, but to
counterpose from beginning to end the proletarian position
against the petty-bourgeois, the Marxist position against
the eclectic. In this way all of us perhaps may learn something from the discussion.

'Precedents'

"How did we, irreconcilable revolutionists, so suddenly
become a petty-bourgeois tendency?" Shachtman demands
indignantly. Where are the proofs? "Wherein (has) this tendency manifested itself in the last year (!) or two among
the representative spokesmen of the Minority?" (*Internal
Bulletin*, vol. 2, no. 7, Jan. 1940, p. 11.) Why didn't we
yield in the past to the influence of the petty-bourgeois
democracy? Why during the Spanish civil war did we . . .
and so forth and so on. This is Shachtman's trump argument in beginning his polemic against me and the one on
which he plays variations in all keys, apparently investing
it with exceptional importance. It does not so much as enter Shachtman's mind that I can turn this very argument
against him.

The opposition document, "War and Bureaucratic

Conservatism,"* concedes that Trotsky is right nine times out of ten, perhaps ninety-nine times out of a hundred. I understand only too well the qualified and extremely magnanimous character of this concession. The proportion of my mistakes is in reality considerably greater. How explain then the fact that two or three weeks after this document was written, Shachtman suddenly decided that Trotsky:

(a) Is incapable of a critical attitude toward information supplied him although one of his informants for ten years has been Shachtman himself.

(b) Is incapable of distinguishing a proletarian tendency from a petty-bourgeois tendency—a bolshevik tendency from a menshevik tendency.

(c) Is champion of the absurd conception of "bureaucratic revolution" in place of revolution by the masses.

(d) Is incapable of working out a correct answer to concrete questions in Poland, Finland, etc.

(e) Is manifesting a tendency to capitulate to Stalinism.

(f) Is unable to comprehend the meaning of democratic centralism—and so on ad infinitum.

In a word, during the space of two or three weeks Shachtman has discovered that I make mistakes ninety-nine times out of a hundred, especially where Shachtman himself happens to become involved. It occurs to me that the latest percentage also suffers from slight exaggeration—but this time in the opposite direction. In any event Shachtman discovered my tendency to replace revolution by the masses with "bureaucratic revolution" far more abruptly than I discovered his petty-bourgeois deviation.

Comrade Shachtman invites me to present proof of the existence of a "petty-bourgeois tendency" in the party dur-

---

* Published as an appendix to James P. Cannon, *The Struggle for a Proletarian Party* (New York: Pathfinder, 1972), pp. 257–93.

ing the past year; or even two-three years. Shachtman is completely justified in not wishing to refer to the more distant past. But in accordance with Shachtman's invitation, I shall confine myself to the last three years. Please pay attention. To the rhetorical questions of my unsparing critic I shall reply with a few exact documents.

(I) On May 25, 1937, I wrote to New York concerning the policy of the Bolshevik-Leninist faction in the Socialist Party:

". . . I must cite two recent documents: (a) the private letter of 'Max' about the convention, and (b) Shachtman's article, 'Towards a Revolutionary Socialist Party.' The title of this article alone characterizes a false perspective. It seems to me established by the developments, including the last convention, that the party is evolving, not into a 'revolutionary' party, but into a kind of ILP, that is, a miserable centrist political abortion without any perspective.

"The affirmation that the American Socialist Party is now 'closer to the position of revolutionary Marxism than any party of the Second or Third Internationals' is an absolutely unmerited compliment: the American Socialist Party is only more backward than the analogous formations in Europe—the POUM, ILP, SAP, etc. . . . Our duty is to unmask this negative advantage of Norman Thomas and Co., and not to speak about the 'superiority (of the war resolution) over any resolution ever adopted before by the party. . . .' This is a *purely literary appreciation*, because every resolution must be taken in connection with historical events, with the political situation and its imperative needs. . . ."

In both of the documents mentioned in the above letter, Shachtman revealed excessive adaptability toward the left wing of the petty-bourgeois democrats—political mimicry—a very dangerous symptom in a revolutionary politician! It is extremely important to take note of his high appraisal of the "radical" position of Norman Thomas in relation to war . . . in Europe. Opportunists, as is well known, tend to all the greater radicalism the further removed they are from events. With this law in mind it is not difficult to appraise at its true value the fact that Shachtman and his allies accuse us of a tendency to "capitulate to Stalinism." Alas, sitting in the Bronx, it is much easier to display irreconcilability toward the Kremlin than toward the American petty bourgeoisie.

(II) To believe Comrade Shachtman, I dragged the question of the class composition of the factions into the dispute by the hair. Here too, let us refer to the recent past.

On October 3, 1937, I wrote to New York:

"I have remarked hundreds of times that the worker who remains unnoticed in the 'normal' conditions of party life reveals remarkable qualities in a change of the situation when general formulas and fluent pens are not sufficient, where acquaintance with the life of workers and practical capacities are necessary. Under such conditions a gifted worker reveals a sureness of himself and reveals also his general political capabilities.

"Predominance in the organization of intellectuals is inevitable in the first period of the development of the organization. It is at the same time a big handicap to the political education of the more gifted workers. . . . It is absolutely necessary at the next convention to introduce in the local and central committees as many workers as possible. To a worker, activity in the leading party body is at the same time a high political school. . . .

"The difficulty is that in every organization there are traditional committee members and that different secondary, factional and personal considerations play a too great role in the composition of the list of candidates."

I have never met either attention or interest from Comrade Shachtman in questions of this kind.

(III) To believe Comrade Shachtman, I injected the question of Comrade Abern's faction as a concentration of petty-bourgeois individuals artificially and without any basis in fact. Yet on October 10, 1937, at a time when Shachtman marched shoulder to shoulder with Cannon and it was considered officially that Abern had no faction, I wrote to Cannon:

"The party has only a minority of genuine factory workers. . . . The nonproletarian elements represent a very necessary yeast, and I believe that we can be proud of the good quality of these elements. . . . But . . . Our party can be inundated by nonproletarian elements and can even lose its revolutionary character. The task is naturally not to prevent the influx of intellectuals by artificial methods, . . . but to orient practically all the organization toward the factories, the strikes, the unions. . . .

"A concrete example: We cannot devote enough or equal forces to all the factories. Our local organization can choose for its activity in the next period one, two, or three factories in its area and concentrate all its forces upon these factories. If we have in one of them two or three workers we can create a special help commission of five nonworkers with the purpose of enlarging our influence in these factories.

"The same can be done among the trade unions. We cannot introduce nonworker members in workers' unions. But we can with success build up help commissions for oral and literary action in connection with our comrades in the union. The unbreakable conditions should be: *not to command the workers but only to help them*, to give them suggestions, to arm them with the facts, ideas, factory papers, special leaflets, and so on.

"Such collaboration would have a tremendous educational importance from one side for the worker comrades, from the other side for the nonworkers who need a solid reeducation.

"You have for example an important number of Jewish nonworker elements in your ranks. They can be a very valuable yeast *if the party succeeds by and by in extracting them from a closed milieu* and ties them to the factory workers by daily activity. I believe *such an orientation would also assure a more healthy atmosphere inside the party.* . . .

"One general rule we can establish immediately: a party member who doesn't win during three or six months a new worker for the party is not a good party member.

"If we established seriously such a general orientation and if we verified every week the practical results, we will avoid a *great danger*; namely, that the intellectuals and white collar workers might suppress the worker minority, condemn it to silence, *transform the party into a very intelligent discussion club but absolutely not habitable for workers.*

"The same rules should be in a corresponding form elaborated for the working and recruiting of the *youth organization, otherwise we run the danger of educating good young elements into revolutionary dilettantes and not revolutionary fighters.*"

From this letter it is obvious, I trust, that I did not mention the danger of a petty-bourgeois deviation the day following the Stalin-Hitler pact or the day following the dismemberment of Poland, but brought it forward persistently two years ago and more. Furthermore, as I then pointed out, bearing in mind primarily the "nonexistent" Abern faction, it was absolutely requisite in order to cleanse the atmosphere of the party, that the Jewish petty-bourgeois elements of the New York local be shifted from their ha-

bitual conservative milieu and dissolved in the real labor
movement. It is precisely because of this that the above letter (not the first of its kind), written more than two years
before the present discussion began, is of far greater weight
as evidence than all the writings of the opposition leaders
on the motives which impelled me to come out in defense
of the "Cannon clique."

(IV) Shachtman's inclination to yield to petty-bourgeois
influence, especially the academic and literary, has never
been a secret to me. During the time of the Dewey Commission I wrote, on October 14, 1937, to Cannon, Shachtman, and Warde [Novack].

". . . I insisted upon the necessity to surround the Committee
by delegates of workers' groups in order to create channels
from the Committee in the masses. . . . Comrades Warde,
Shachtman, and others declared themselves in agreement
with me on this point. Together we analyzed the practical
possibilities to realize this plan. . . . But later, in spite of repeated questions from me, I never could have information
about the matter and only accidentally I heard that Comrade
Shachtman was opposed to it. Why? I don't know."

Shachtman never did divulge his reasons to me. In my
letter I expressed myself with the utmost diplomacy but I
did not have the slightest doubt that while agreeing with
me in words Shachtman in reality was afraid of wounding
the excessive political sensibilities of our temporary liberal
allies: in *this* direction Shachtman demonstrates exceptional
"delicacy."

(V) On April 15, 1938, I wrote to New York:
"I am a bit astonished about the kind of publicity given to
Eastman's letter in the *New International*. The publication
of the letter is all right, but the prominence given it on the

cover, combined with the silence about Eastman's article in *Harper's*, seems to me a bit compromising for the *New International*. Many people will interpret this fact as our willingness to close our eyes on principles when friendship is concerned."

(VI) On June 1, 1938, I wrote Comrade Shachtman:
"It is difficult to understand here why you are so tolerant and even friendly toward Mr. Eugene Lyons. He speaks, it seems, at your banquets; at the same time he speaks at the banquets of the White Guards."

This letter continued the struggle for a more independent and resolute policy toward the so-called "liberals," who, while waging a struggle against the revolution, wish to maintain "friendly relations" with the proletariat, for this doubles their market value in the eyes of bourgeois public opinion.

(VII) On October 6, 1938, almost a year before the discussion began, I wrote about the necessity of our party press turning its face decisively toward the workers:
"Very important in this respect is the attitude of the *Socialist Appeal*. It is undoubtedly a very good Marxist paper, but it is not a genuine instrument of political action. I tried to interest the editorial board of the *Socialist Appeal* in this question, but without success."

A note of complaint is evident in these words. And it is not accidental. Comrade Shachtman as has been mentioned already displays far more interest in isolated literary episodes of long-ago-concluded struggles than in the social composition of his own party or the readers of his own paper.

(VIII) On January 20, 1939, in a letter which I have already cited in connection with dialectic materialism, I once again touched on the question of Comrade Shachtman's gravitation toward the milieu of the petty-bourgeois literary fraternity.

"I cannot understand why the *Socialist Appeal* is almost neglecting the Stalinist party. This party now represents a mass of contradictions. Splits are inevitable. The next important acquisitions will surely come from the Stalinist party. Our political attention should be concentrated on it. We should follow the development of its contradictions day by day and hour by hour. Someone on the staff ought to devote the bulk of his time to the Stalinists' ideas and actions. We could provoke a discussion and, if possible, publish the letters of hesitating Stalinists.

"It would be a thousand times more important than inviting Eastman, Lyons, and the others to present their individual sweatings. I was wondering a bit at why you gave place to Eastman's last insignificant and arrogant article. . . . But I am absolutely perplexed that you, personally, *invite* these people to besmirch the not-so-numerous pages of the *New International*. The perpetuation of this polemic can interest some *petty-bourgeois intellectuals*, but not the revolutionary elements.

"It is my firm conviction that a certain reorganization of the *New International* and the *Socialist Appeal* is necessary: more distance from Eastman, Lyons, and so on; and nearer the workers and, in this sense, to the Stalinist party."

Recent events have demonstrated, sad to say, that Shachtman did not turn away from Eastman and Co. but on the contrary drew closer to them.

(IX) On May 27, 1939, I again wrote concerning the character of the *Socialist Appeal* in connection with the social composition of the party:

"From the minutes I see that you are having difficulty with

the *Socialist Appeal*. The paper is very well done from the journalistic point of view; but it is a paper for the workers and not a workers' paper. . . .

"As it is, the paper is divided among various writers, each of whom is very good, but collectively they do not permit the workers to penetrate to the pages of the *Appeal*. Each of them speaks for the workers (and speaks very well) but nobody will hear the workers. In spite of its literary brilliance, to a certain degree the paper becomes a victim of journalistic routine. You do not hear at all how the workers live, fight, clash with the police, or drink whiskey. It is very dangerous for the paper as a revolutionary instrument of the party. The task is not to make a paper through the joint forces of a skilled editorial board but to encourage the workers to speak for themselves.

"A radical and courageous change is necessary as a condition of success. . . .

"Of course it is not only a question of the paper, but of the whole course of policy. I continue to be of the opinion that you have *too many petty-bourgeois boys and girls* who are very good and devoted to the party, but who do not fully realize that their duty is not to discuss among themselves, but to penetrate into the fresh milieu of workers. I repeat my proposition: Every petty-bourgeois member of the party who, during a certain time, let us say three or six months, does not win a worker for the party, should be demoted to the rank of candidate and after another three months expelled from the party. In some cases it might be unjust, but the party as a whole would receive a salutary shock which it needs very much. A very radical change is necessary."

In proposing such draconian measures as the expulsion of those petty-bourgeois elements incapable of linking themselves to the workers, I had in mind not the "defense" of Cannon's faction but the rescue of the party from degeneration.

(**X**) Commenting on skeptical voices from the Socialist Workers Party which had reached my ears, I wrote Comrade Cannon on June 16, 1939:

"The prewar situation, the aggravation of nationalism and so on is a natural hindrance to our development and the profound cause of the depression in our ranks. But it must now be underlined that *the more the party is petty-bourgeois in its composition, the more it is dependent upon the changes in the official public opinion*. It is a supplementary argument for the necessity for a courageous and active reorientation toward the masses.

"The pessimistic reasonings you mention in your article are, of course, a reflection of the patriotic, nationalistic pressure of the official public opinion. 'If fascism is victorious in France, . . .' 'If fascism is victorious in England. . . .' And so on. The victories of fascism are important, but the death agony of capitalism is more important."

The question of the dependence of the petty-bourgeois wing of the party upon official public opinion consequently was posed several months before the present discussion began and was not at all dragged in artificially in order to discredit the opposition.

Comrade Shachtman demanded that I furnish "precedents" of petty-bourgeois tendencies among the leaders of the opposition during the past period. I went so far in answering this demand as to single out from the leaders of the opposition Comrade Shachtman himself. I am far from having exhausted the material at my disposal. Two letters—one of Shachtman's, the other mine—which are perhaps still more interesting as "precedents," I shall cite presently in another connection. Let Shachtman not object that the lapses and mistakes in which the correspondence is concerned likewise can be brought against other comrades, including representatives of the present majority. Possibly. Probably. But Shachtman's name is not repeated in this correspondence accidentally. Where others have committed episodic mistakes, Shachtman has evinced a tendency.

In any event, completely opposite to what Shachtman now claims concerning my alleged "sudden" and "unexpected" appraisals, I am able, documents in hand, to prove—and I believe have proved—that my article on the "Petty-Bourgeois Opposition" did no more than summarize my correspondence with New York during the last three years. (In reality the past ten.) Shachtman has very demonstratively asked for "precedents." I have given him "precedents." They speak entirely against Shachtman.

The philosophic bloc against Marxism

The opposition circles consider it possible to assert that the question of dialectic materialism was introduced by me only because I lacked an answer to the "concrete" questions of Finland, Latvia, India, Afghanistan, Baluchistan, and so on. This argument, void of all merit in itself, is of interest however in that it characterizes the level of certain individuals in the opposition, their attitude toward theory and toward elementary ideological loyalty. It would not be amiss, therefore, to refer to the fact that my first serious conversation with Comrades Shachtman and Warde, in the train immediately after my arrival in Mexico in January 1937, was devoted to the necessity of persistently propagating dialectic materialism. After our American section split from the Socialist Party I insisted most strongly on the earliest possible publication of a theoretical organ, having again in mind the need to educate the party, first and foremost its new members, in the spirit of dialectic material-

ism. In the United States, I wrote at that time, where the
bourgeoisie systematically instills vulgar empiricism in the
workers, more than anywhere else is it necessary to speed
the elevation of the movement to a proper theoretical level.
On January 20, 1939, I wrote to Comrade Shachtman concerning his joint article with Comrade Burnham, "Intellectuals in Retreat":

"The section on the dialectic is the greatest blow that you,
personally, as the editor of the *New International* could
have delivered to Marxist theory. . . . Good! We will speak
about it publicly."

Thus a year ago I gave open notice in advance to Shachtman that I intended to wage a public struggle against his
eclectic tendencies. At that time there was no talk whatever of the coming opposition; in any case furthest from my
mind was the supposition that the philosophic bloc against
Marxism prepared the ground for a political bloc against
the program of the Fourth International.

The character of the differences which have risen to the
surface has only confirmed my former fears both in regard
to the social composition of the party and in regard to the
theoretical education of the cadres. There was nothing that
required a change of mind or "artificial" introduction. This
is how matters stand in actuality. Let me also add that I feel
somewhat abashed over the fact that it is almost necessary
to justify coming out in defense of Marxism within one of
the sections of the Fourth International!

In his "Open Letter," Shachtman refers particularly to the
fact that Comrade Vincent Dunne expressed satisfaction over
the article on the intellectuals. But I too praised it: "Many
parts are excellent." However, as the Russian proverb puts it,
a spoonful of tar can spoil a barrel of honey. It is precisely
this spoonful of tar that is involved. The section devoted
to dialectic materialism expresses a number of conceptions

monstrous from the Marxist standpoint, whose aim, it is now clear, was to prepare the ground for a political bloc. In view of the stubbornness with which Shachtman persists that I seized upon the article as a pretext, let me once again quote the central passage in the section of interest to us: ". . . nor has anyone yet demonstrated that agreement or disagreement on the more abstract doctrines of dialectic materialism necessarily affects (!) today's and tomorrow's concrete political issues—and political parties, programs, and struggles are based on such concrete issues." (The *New International*, January 1939, p. 7.) Isn't this alone sufficient? What is above all astonishing is this formula, unworthy of revolutionists: ". . . political parties, programs, and struggles are based on such concrete issues." What parties? What programs? What struggles? All parties and all programs are here lumped together. The party of the proletariat is a party unlike all the rest. It is not at all based upon "such concrete issues." In its very foundation it is diametrically opposed to the parties of bourgeois horsetraders and petty-bourgeois rag patchers. Its task is the preparation of a social revolution and the regeneration of mankind on new material and moral foundations. In order not to give way under the pressure of bourgeois public opinion and police repression, the proletarian revolutionist, a leader all the more, requires a clear, far-sighted, completely thought-out world outlook. Only upon the basis of a unified Marxist conception is it possible to correctly approach "concrete" questions.

Precisely here begins Shachtman's betrayal—not a mere mistake as I wished to believe last year; but, it is now clear, an outright theoretical betrayal. Following in the footsteps of Burnham, Shachtman teaches the young revolutionary party that "no one has yet demonstrated" presumably that dialectic materialism affects the political activity of the party. "No one has yet demonstrated," in other words, that Marxism is of any use in the struggle of the proletariat. The party consequently does not have the least motive for acquiring and defending dialectic materialism. This is nothing else than renunciation of Marxism, of scientific method in general, a wretched capitulation to empiricism. Precisely this constitutes the philosophic bloc of Shachtman with Burnham and through Burnham with the priests of bourgeois "Science." It is precisely this and only this to which I referred in my January 20 letter of last year.

On March 5, Shachtman replied: "I have reread the January article of Burnham and Shachtman to which you referred, and while in the light of which you have written I might have proposed a different formulation here (!) and there (!) if the article were to be done over again, I cannot agree with the substance of your criticism."

This reply, as is always the case with Shachtman in a serious situation, in reality expresses nothing whatsoever; but it still gives the impression that Shachtman has left a bridge open for retreat. Today, seized with factional frenzy, he promises to "do it again and again tomorrow." Do what? Capitulate to bourgeois "Science"? Renounce Marxism?

Shachtman explains at length to me (we shall see presently with what foundation) the utility of this or that *political bloc*. I am speaking about the deadliness of *theoretical betrayal*. A bloc can be justified or not depending upon its content and the circumstances. Theoretical betrayal cannot be justified by any bloc. Shachtman refers to the fact that his article is of purely political character. I do not speak of the article but of that section which renounces Marxism. If a textbook on physics contained only two lines on God as the first cause it would be my right to conclude the author is an obscurantist.

Shachtman does not reply to the accusation but tries to distract attention by turning to irrelevant matters. "Wherein does what you call my 'bloc with Burnham in the sphere of philosophy' differ," he asks, "from Lenin's bloc with Bogdanov? Why was the latter principled and ours unprincipled? I should be very much interested to know the answer to this question." I shall deal presently with the political difference, or rather the political polar opposite between the two blocs. We are here interested in the question of Marxist method. Wherein is the difference you ask? In this, that Lenin never declaimed for Bogdanov's profit that dialectic materialism is superfluous in solving "concrete political questions." In this, that Lenin never theoretically confounded the Bolshevik Party with parties in general. He was organically incapable of uttering such abominations. And not he alone but not a single one of the serious Bolsheviks. That is the difference. Do you understand? Shachtman sarcastically promised me that he would be "interested" in a clear answer. The answer, I trust, has been given. I don't demand the "interest."

The abstract and the concrete; economics and politics

The most lamentable section of Shachtman's lamentable opus is the chapter, "The State and the Character of the War." "What then is our position?" asks the author. "Simply this: It is impossible to deduce *directly* our policy towards a *specific* war from an *abstract* characterization of the class character of the state involved in the war, more particularly, from the property forms prevailing in that state. Our policy must flow from a *concrete* examination of the character of the war in relation to the interests of the international socialist revolution." (Loc. cit., p. 13. My emphasis.) What a muddle! What a tangle of sophistry! If it is impossible to deduce our policy *directly* from the class character of a state, then why can't this be done *nondirectly*? Why must the analysis of the character of the state be *abstract* whereas the analysis of the character of the war is *concrete*? Formally speaking,

one can say with equal, in fact with much more right, that
our policy in relation to the USSR can be deduced not from
an *abstract* characterization of war as "imperialist," but
only from a *concrete* analysis of the character of the state
in the given historical situation. The fundamental sophistry upon which Shachtman constructs everything else is
simple enough: Inasmuch as the economic basis determines
events in the superstructure not *immediately*; inasmuch as
the mere class characterization of the state is *not enough* to
solve the practical tasks, therefore . . . therefore we can get
along without examining economics and the class nature
of the state; by replacing them, as Shachtman phrases it in
his journalistic jargon, with the "realities of living events."
(Loc. cit., p. 14.)

The very same artifice circulated by Shachtman to justify
his philosophic bloc with Burnham (dialectic materialism
determines our politics not immediately, consequently . . .
it does not *in general* affect the "concrete political tasks"),
is repeated here word for word in relation to Marxist sociology: Inasmuch as property forms determine the policy
of a state not immediately it is possible therefore to throw
Marxist sociology overboard in general in determining
"concrete political tasks."

But why stop there? Since the law of labor value determines prices not "directly" and not "immediately"; since
the laws of natural selection determine not "directly" and
not "immediately" the birth of a suckling pig; since the laws
of gravity determine not "directly" and not "immediately"
the tumble of a drunken policeman down a flight of stairs,
therefore . . . therefore let us leave Marx, Darwin, Newton,
and all the other lovers of "abstractions" to collect dust on a
shelf. This is nothing less than the solemn burial of science
for, after all, the entire course of the development of science
proceeds from "direct" and "immediate" causes to the more

remote and profound ones, from multiple varieties and ka-
leidoscopic events—to the unity of the driving forces.

The law of labor value determines prices not "immediately," but it nevertheless does determine them. Such "concrete"
phenomena as the bankruptcy of the New Deal find their
explanation in the final analysis in the "abstract" law of
value. Roosevelt does not know this, but a Marxist dare not
proceed without knowing it. Not immediately but through
a whole series of intermediate factors and their reciprocal
interaction, property forms determine not only politics but
also morality. A proletarian politician seeking to ignore the
class nature of the state would invariably end up like the
policeman who ignores the laws of gravitation; that is, by
smashing his nose.

Shachtman obviously does not take into account the
distinction between the abstract and the concrete. Striving
toward concreteness, our mind operates with abstractions.
Even "this," "given," "concrete" dog is an abstraction because it proceeds to change, for example, by dropping its
tail the "moment" we point a finger at it. Concreteness is a
relative concept and not an absolute one: what is concrete
in one case turns out to be abstract in another: that is, in-
sufficiently defined for a given purpose. In order to obtain
a concept "concrete" enough *for a given need* it is necessary to correlate several abstractions into one—just as in
reproducing a segment of life upon the screen, which is a
picture in movement, it is necessary to combine a number
of still photographs.

The concrete is a combination of abstractions—not an
arbitrary or subjective combination but one that corresponds
to the laws of the movement of a given phenomenon.

"The interests of the international socialist revolution," to
which Shachtman appeals against the class nature of the state,
represent in this given instance the vaguest of all abstrac-

tions. After all, the question which occupies us is precisely this, in what concrete way can we further the interests of the revolution? Nor would it be amiss to remember, too, that the task of the socialist revolution is to create a workers state. Before talking about the socialist revolution it is necessary consequently to learn how to distinguish between such "abstractions" as the bourgeoisie and the proletariat, the capitalist state and the workers state.

Shachtman indeed squanders his own time and that of others in proving that nationalized property does not determine "in and of itself," "automatically," "directly," "immediately" the policies of the Kremlin. On the question as to how the economic "base" determines the political, juridical, philosophical, artistic, and so on "superstructure" there exists a rich Marxist literature. The opinion that economics presumably determines directly and immediately the creativeness of a composer or even the verdict of a judge, represents a hoary caricature of Marxism which the bourgeois professordom of all countries has circulated time out of end to mask their intellectual impotence.*

As for the question which immediately concerns us, the interrelationship between the social foundations of the Soviet state and the policy of the Kremlin, let me remind the absent-minded Shachtman that for seventeen years we have already been establishing, publicly, the growing *contradiction* between the foundation laid down by the October revolution and the tendencies of the state "superstructure." We have followed step by step the increasing independence of the bureaucracy from the Soviet proletariat and the growth of its dependence upon other classes and groups both inside

---

* To young comrades I recommend that they study on this question the works of Engels (*Anti-Dühring*), Plekhanov, and Antonio Labriola.—L.T.

and outside the country. Just what does Shachtman wish to add in this sphere to the analysis already made?

However, although economics determines politics not directly or immediately, but only in the last analysis, *nevertheless economics does determine politics.* The Marxists affirm precisely this in contrast to the bourgeois professors and their disciples. While analyzing and exposing the growing political independence of the bureaucracy from the proletariat, we have never lost sight of the objective social boundaries of this "independence"; namely, nationalized property supplemented by the monopoly of foreign trade.

It is astonishing! Shachtman continues to support the slogan for a political revolution against the Soviet bureaucracy. Has he ever seriously thought out the meaning of this slogan? If we hold that the social foundations laid down by the October revolution were "automatically" reflected in the policy of the state, then why would a *revolution* against the bureaucracy be necessary? If the USSR, on the other hand, has completely ceased being a workers state, not a *political* revolution would be required but a *social* revolution. Shachtman consequently continues to defend the slogan which follows: (1) from the character of the USSR as a workers state; and (2) from the irreconcilable antagonism between the social foundations of the state and the bureaucracy. But as he repeats this slogan, he tries to undermine its theoretical foundation. Is it perhaps in order to demonstrate once again the independence of his politics from scientific "abstractions"?

Under the guise of waging a struggle against the bourgeois caricature of dialectic materialism, Shachtman throws the doors wide open to historical idealism. Property forms and the class character of the state are a matter of *indifference* to him in analyzing the policy of a government. The state itself appears to him an animal of indiscriminate sex.

Both feet planted firmly on this bed of chicken feathers, Shachtman pompously explains to us—today in the year 1940!—that in addition to the nationalized property there is also the Bonapartist filth and their reactionary politics. How new! Did Shachtman perchance think that he was speaking in a nursery?

Shachtman makes a bloc—also with Lenin

To camouflage his failure to understand the essence of the problem of the nature of the Soviet state, Shachtman leaped upon the words of Lenin directed against me on December 30, 1920, during the so-called trade union discussion. "Comrade Trotsky speaks of the workers' state. Permit me, this is an abstraction. . . . Our state is in reality not a workers' state but a workers' and peasants' state. . . . Our present state is such that the inclusively-organized proletariat must defend itself, and we must utilize these workers' organizations for the defense of the workers against their state and for the defense of our state by the workers." Pointing to this quotation and hastening to proclaim that I have repeated my "mistake" of 1920, Shachtman in his precipitance failed to notice a major error in the quotation concerning the definition of the nature of the Soviet state. On January 19, Lenin himself wrote the following about his speech of December 30: "I stated, 'our state is in reality not a workers' state but a workers' and peasants' state.' . . . On reading the report of the discussion, I now see that I was wrong. . . . I should have said: 'the workers' state is an abstraction. In reality we have a workers' state with the following peculiar features, (1) it is the peasants and not the workers who predominate in the population and (2) it is a workers' state with bureaucratic deformations.' " From this episode two conclusions follow: Lenin placed such great importance upon the precise sociological definition of the state that he considered it necessary to correct himself in the very heat of a polemic! But Shachtman is so little interested in the class nature of the Soviet state that twenty years later he noticed neither Lenin's mistake nor Lenin's correction!

I shall not dwell here on the question as to just how correctly Lenin aimed his argument against me. I believe he did so incorrectly—there was no difference of opinion between us on the definition of the state. But that is not the question now. The theoretical formulation on the question of the state, made by Lenin in the above-cited quotation—in conjunction with the major correction which he himself introduced a few days later—is absolutely correct. But let us hear what incredible use Shachtman makes of Lenin's definition: "Just as it was possible twenty years ago," he writes, "to speak of the term 'workers' state' as an abstraction, so is it possible to speak of the term 'degenerated workers' state' as an abstraction." (Loc. cit., p. 14.) It is self-evident that Shachtman fails completely to understand Lenin. Twenty years ago the term "workers' state" could not be considered in any way an abstraction *in general*: that is, something not real or not existing. The definition "workers' state," while correct in and of itself, was *inadequate* in relation to the *particular* task; namely, the defense of the workers through their trade unions, and only in this sense was it abstract. However, in relation to the defense of the USSR against imperialism this selfsame definition was in 1920, just as it still is today, unshakably concrete, making it obligatory for workers to defend the given state.

Shachtman does not agree. He writes: "Just as it was once necessary in connection with the trade union problem to speak concretely of what *kind* of workers' state exists in the Soviet Union, so it is necessary to establish in connection with the present war, the *degree* of degeneration of the Soviet state. . . . And the *degree* of the degeneration of the

regime cannot be established by abstract reference to the
existence of nationalized property, but only by observing
the realities (!) of living (!) events (!)." From this it is completely incomprehensible why in 1920 the question of the
character of the USSR was brought up in connection with
the trade unions, i.e., particular internal questions of the
regime, while today it is brought up in connection with the
defense of the USSR, that is, in connection with the entire
fate of the state. In the former case the workers state was
counterposed to the workers, in the latter case—to the imperialists. Small wonder that the analogy limps on both legs;
what Lenin counterposed, Shachtman identifies.

Nevertheless even if we take Shachtman's words at face
value, it follows that the question over which he is concerned
is only the *degree of the degeneration* (of what? a workers
state?); that is, of quantitative differences in the evaluation.
Let us grant that Shachtman has worked out (where?) the
"degree" more precisely than we have. But in what way can
purely quantitative differences in the evaluation of the degeneration of the *workers* state affect our decision as to the
defense of the USSR? It is impossible to make head or tail
out of this. As a matter of fact, Shachtman, remaining true
to eclecticism, that is, to himself, dragged in the question
of "degree" only in an effort to maintain his equilibrium
between Abern and Burnham. What is in dispute actually
is not at all the *degree* determined by "the realities of living events" (what a precise, "scientific," "concrete," "experimental" terminology!) but whether these *quantitative*
changes have been transformed into *qualitative* changes;
i.e., whether the USSR is still a workers state, even though
degenerated, or whether it has been transformed into a new
type of exploitive state.

To this basic question Shachtman has no answer; feels
no need for an answer. His argument is merely verbal

mimicry of Lenin's words which were spoken in a different connection, which had a different content and included an outright error. Lenin in his corrected version declares: "The given state is not merely a workers' state but a workers' state with bureaucratic deformations." Shachtman declares: "The given state is not merely a degenerated workers' state but . . ." . . . but? Shachtman has nothing further to say. Both the orator and the audience stare at each other, mouths wide open.

What does "degenerated workers state" signify in our program? To this question our program responds with a degree of concreteness which is wholly adequate for solving the question of the defense of the USSR; namely: (1) those traits which in 1920 were a "bureaucratic deformation" of the soviet system have now become an independent bureaucratic regime which has devoured the soviets; (2) the dictatorship of the bureaucracy, incompatible with the internal and international tasks of socialism, has introduced and continues to introduce profound deformations in the economic life of the country as well; (3) basically, however, the system of planned economy, on the foundation of state ownership of the means of production, has been preserved and continues to remain a colossal conquest of mankind. The defeat of the USSR in a war with imperialism would signify not solely the liquidation of the bureaucratic dictatorship, but of the planned state economy; and the dismemberment of the country into spheres of influence; and a new stabilization of imperialism; and a new weakening of the world proletariat.

From the circumstance that the "bureaucratic" deformation has grown into a regime of bureaucratic autocracy we draw the conclusion that the defense of the workers through their trade unions (which have undergone the selfsame degeneration as the state) is today in contrast to 1920

completely unrealistic; it is necessary to overthrow the bureaucracy; this task can be carried out only by creating an
illegal bolshevik party in the USSR.

From the circumstance that the degeneration of the political system has not yet led to the destruction of planned
state economy, we draw the conclusion that it is still the
duty of the world proletariat to defend the USSR against
imperialism and to aid the Soviet proletariat in its struggle
against the bureaucracy.

Just what in our definition of the USSR does Shachtman
find abstract? What concrete amendments does he propose? If the dialectic teaches us that "truth is always concrete" then this law applies with equal force to criticism. It
is not enough to label a definition abstract. It is necessary
to point out exactly what it lacks. Otherwise criticism itself becomes sterile. Instead of concretizing or changing the
definition which he claims is abstract, Shachtman replaces
it with a vacuum. That's not enough. A vacuum, even the
most pretentious vacuum, must be recognized as the worst
of all abstractions—it can be filled with any content. Small
wonder that the theoretical vacuum, in displacing the class
analysis, has sucked in the politics of impressionism and
adventurism.

'Concentrated economics'

Shachtman goes on to quote Lenin's words that "politics
is concentrated economics" and that in this sense "politics
cannot but take primacy over economics." From Lenin's
words Shachtman directs at me the moral that I, if you please,
am interested only in "economics" (nationalized means of
production) and skip over "politics." This second effort to
exploit Lenin is not superior to the first. Shachtman's mistake here assumes truly vast proportions! Lenin meant: when
economic processes, tasks, and interests acquire a *conscious*

and *generalized* ("concentrated") character, they enter the sphere of politics by virtue of this very fact, and constitute the essence of politics. In this sense politics as concentrated economics rises above the day-to-day atomized, unconscious, and ungeneralized economic activity.

The correctness of politics from the Marxist standpoint is determined precisely to the extent that it profoundly and all-sidedly "concentrates" economics, that is, expresses the progressive tendencies of its development. That is why we base our politics first and foremost upon our analysis of property forms and class relationships. A more detailed and concrete analysis of the factors in the "superstructure" is possible for us only on this theoretical basis. Thus, for example, were we to accuse an opposing faction of "bureaucratic conservatism" we would immediately seek the social, i.e., class roots of this phenomenon. Any other procedure would brand us as "platonic" Marxists, if not simply noisy mimics.

"Politics is concentrated economics." This proposition one should think applies to the Kremlin too. Or, in exception to the general law, is the policy of the Moscow government not "concentrated economics" but a manifestation of the bureaucracy's free will? Our attempt to reduce the politics of the Kremlin to nationalized economy, refracted through the interests of the bureaucracy, provokes frantic resistance from Shachtman. He takes his guidance in relation to the USSR not from the conscious generalization of economics but from "observing the realities of living events"; i.e., from rule of thumb, improvisations, sympathies and antipathies. He counterposes this impressionistic policy to our sociologically grounded policy and accuses us at the same time of . . . ignoring politics. Incredible but true! To be sure, in the final analysis Shachtman's weak-kneed and capricious politics is likewise the "concentrated" expression of economics but, alas, it is the economics of the declassed petty bourgeoisie.

Comparison with bourgeois wars

Shachtman reminds us that bourgeois wars were at one time progressive and that in another period they became reactionary and that therefore it is not enough to give the class definition of a state engaged in war. This proposition does not clarify the question but muddles it. Bourgeois wars could be progressive only at a time when the entire bourgeois regime was progressive; in other words, at a time when *bourgeois property* in contradistinction to feudal property was a progressive and constructive factor. Bourgeois wars became reactionary when bourgeois property became a brake on development. Does Shachtman wish to say in relation to the USSR that the state ownership of the means of production has become a brake upon development and that the extension of this form of property to other countries constitutes economic reaction? Shachtman obviously does not want to say this. He simply does not draw the logical conclusion to his own thoughts.

The example of national bourgeois wars does indeed offer a very instructive lesson, but Shachtman passes it by unconcernedly. Marx and Engels were striving for a unified German republic. In the war of 1870–71 they stood on the side of the Germans despite the fact that the struggle for unification was exploited and distorted by the dynastic parasites.

Shachtman refers to the fact that Marx and Engels immediately turned against Prussia upon the annexation of Alsace-Lorraine. But this turn only illustrates our standpoint all the more lucidly. It is impermissible to forget for a moment that what was in question was a war between two *bourgeois* states. Thus both camps had a common class denominator. To decide which of the two sides was the "lesser evil"—insofar as history generally left any room for choice—was possible only on the basis of supplementary factors. On the German side it was a question of creating a *national* bourgeois state as an economic and cultural arena. The *national* state during that period was a progressive historical factor. To that extent Marx and Engels stood on the side of the Germans despite Hohenzollern and his junkers. The annexation of Alsace-Lorraine violated the principle of the national state in regard to France as well as Germany and laid the basis for a war of revenge. Marx and Engels, naturally, turned sharply against Prussia. They did not thereby at all incur the risk of rendering service to an inferior system of economy as against a superior one since in both camps, we repeat, bourgeois relations prevailed. If France had been a workers state in 1870, then Marx and Engels would have been for France from the very beginning, inasmuch as they—one feels abashed again that this must be mentioned—guided themselves in all their activity by the class criterion.

Today in the old capitalist countries the solving of national tasks is no longer at stake at all. On the contrary mankind is suffering from the contradiction between the productive forces and the too-narrow framework of the national state. Planned economy on the basis of socialized property freed from national boundaries is the task of the international proletariat, above all—in Europe. It is precisely this task which is expressed in our slogan, "For the Socialist United States of Europe!" The expropriation of the property owners in Poland as in Finland is a progressive factor in and of itself. The bureaucratic methods of the Kremlin occupy the very same place in this process as did the dynastic methods of Hohenzollern—in the unification of Germany. Whenever we are confronted with the necessity of choosing be-

tween the defense of reactionary property forms through
reactionary measures and the introduction of progressive
property forms through bureaucratic measures, we do not
at all place both sides on the same plane, but choose the
lesser evil. In this there is no more "capitulation" to Stalinism than there was capitulation to Hohenzollern in the
policy of Marx and Engels. It is scarcely necessary to add
that the role of Hohenzollern in the war of 1870–71 justified neither the general historical role of the dynasty nor so
much as its existence.

Conjunctural defeatism, or Columbus and the egg

Let us now check up on how Shachtman, aided by a theoretical vacuum, operates with the "realities of living events"
in an especially vital question. He writes: "We have never
supported the Kremlin's international policy . . . but what
is war? War is the continuation of politics by other means.
Then why should we support the war which is the continuation of the international policy which we *did not* and do
not support?" (Loc. cit., p. 15.) The completeness of this
argument cannot be denied; in the shape of a naked syllogism we are presented here with a rounded-out theory of
defeatism. It is as simple as Columbus and the egg! Since
we have never supported the Kremlin's international policy,
therefore we ought *never* to support the USSR. Then why
not say it?

We rejected the internal and international policies of the
Kremlin prior to the German-Soviet pact and prior to the
invasion of Poland by the Red Army. This means that the
"realities of living events" of last year do not have the slightest bearing on the case. If we were defensists in the past in
connection with the USSR, it was only out of inconsistency.
Shachtman revises not only the present policy of the Fourth
International but also the past. Since we are against Stalin

we must therefore be against the USSR too. Stalin has long held this opinion. Shachtman has arrived at it only recently. From his rejection of the Kremlin's politics flows complete and indivisible defeatism. Then why not say so!

But Shachtman can't bring himself to say so. In a previous passage he writes: "We said—the minority continues to say it—that if the imperialists assail the Soviet Union with the aim of crushing the last conquest of the October revolution and reducing Russia to a bunch of colonies we will support the Soviet Union unconditionally." (Loc. cit., p. 15.) Permit me, permit me, permit me! The Kremlin's international policy is reactionary; the war is the continuation of its reactionary politics; we cannot support a reactionary war. How then does it unexpectedly turn out that if the pernicious imperialists "assail" the USSR and if the pernicious imperialists pursue the uncommendable aim of transforming it into a colony, that under these exceptional "conditions," Shachtman will defend the USSR . . ." "unconditionally"? How does this make sense? Where is the logic? Or has Shachtman, following Burnham's example, also relegated logic to the sphere of religion and other museum exhibits?

The key to this tangle of confusion rests in the fact that the statement, "We have never supported the Kremlin's international policy," is an abstraction. It must be dissected and concretized. In its present foreign as well as domestic policy, the bureaucracy places first and foremost for defense its own parasitic interests. To that extent we wage mortal struggle against it, but in the final analysis, through the interests of the bureaucracy, in a very distorted form the interests of the workers state are reflected. These interests we defend—with our own methods. Thus we do not at all wage a struggle against the fact that the bureaucracy safeguards (in its own way!) state property, the monopoly of foreign trade, or refuses to pay tsarist debts. Yet in a war between the USSR and the capitalist world—independently of the incidents leading up to that war or the "aims" of this or that government—what is involved is the fate of precisely those historical conquests which we defend unconditionally, i.e., despite the reactionary policy of the bureaucracy. The question consequently boils down—*in the last and decisive instance*—to the class nature of the USSR.

Lenin deduced the policy of defeatism from the imperialist character of the war; but he did not stop there. He deduced the imperialist character of the war from a specific stage in the development of the capitalist regime and its ruling class. Since the character of the war is determined precisely by the class character of society and the state, Lenin recommended that in determining our policy in regard to imperialist war we abstract ourselves from such "concrete" circumstances as democracy and monarchy, as aggression and national defense. In opposition to this Shachtman proposes that we deduce defeatism from conjunctural conditions. This defeatism is indifferent to the class character of the USSR and of Finland. Enough for it are the reactionary features of the bureaucracy and the "aggression." If France, England, or the United States sends airplanes and guns to Finland, this has no bearing in the determination of Shachtman's politics. But if British troops land in Finland, then Shachtman will place a thermometer under Chamberlain's tongue and determine Chamberlain's intentions—whether he aims only to save Finland from the Kremlin's imperialistic politics or whether in addition he aims to overthrow the "last conquest of the October revolution." Strictly in accordance with the readings of the thermometer, Shachtman, the defeatist, is ready to change himself into a defensist. This is what it means to replace abstract principles with the "realities of living events."

Shachtman, as we have already seen, persistently demands

the citation of precedents: when and where in the past have the leaders of the opposition manifested petty-bourgeois opportunism? The reply which I have already given him on this score must be supplemented here with two letters which we sent each other on the question of defensism and methods of defensism in connection with the events of the Spanish revolution. On September 18, 1937, Shachtman wrote me: ". . . You say, 'If we would have a member in the Cortes he would vote *against* the military budget of Negrín.' Unless this is a typographical error it seems to us to be a non sequitur. If, as we all contend, *the element of an imperialist war* is not dominant at the present time in the Spanish struggle, and if instead the decisive element is still the struggle between the decaying bourgeois democracy, with all that it involves, on the one side, and fascism on the other, and further if we are obliged to give military assistance to the struggle against fascism, we don't see how it would be possible to vote in the Cortes against the military budget. . . . If a Bolshevik-Leninist on the Huesca front were asked by a Socialist comrade why his representative in the Cortes voted against the proposal by Negrín to devote a million pesetas to the purchase of rifles for the front, what would this Bolshevik-Leninist reply? It doesn't seem to us that he would have an effective answer. . . ." (My emphasis.)

This letter astounded me. Shachtman was willing to express confidence in the perfidious Negrín government on the purely negative basis that the "element of an imperialist war" was not dominant in Spain.

On September 20, 1937, I replied to Shachtman:

"To vote the military budget of the Negrín government signifies to vote him *political* confidence. . . . To do it would be a crime. How do we explain our vote to the anarchist workers? Very simply: We have not the slightest confidence in the capacity of this government to conduct the war and assure victory. We accuse this government of protecting the rich and starving the poor. This government must be smashed. So long as we are not strong enough to replace it, we are fighting under its command. But on every occasion we express openly our nonconfidence in it: it is the only one possibility to mobilize the masses *politically* against this government and to prepare its overthrow. Any other politics would be a betrayal of the revolution."

The tone of my reply only feebly reflects the . . . amazement which Shachtman's opportunist position produced in me. Isolated mistakes are of course unavoidable but today, two and a half years later, this correspondence is illuminated with new light. Since we defend bourgeois democracy against fascism, Shachtman reasons, we therefore cannot refuse confidence to the bourgeois government. In applying this very theorem to the USSR it is transformed into its converse—since we place no confidence in the Kremlin government, we cannot, therefore, defend the workers state. Pseudoradicalism in this instance, too, is only the obverse side of opportunism.

Renunciation of the class criterion

Let us return once more to the ABC's. In Marxist sociology the initial point of analysis is the *class* definition of a given phenomenon, e.g., state, party, philosophic trend, literary school, etc. In most cases, however, the mere class definition is inadequate, for a class consists of different strata, passes through different stages of development, comes under different conditions, is subjected to the influence of other classes. It becomes necessary to bring up these second- and third-rate factors in order to round out the analysis, and they are taken either partially or completely, depending upon the specific aim. But for a Marxist, analysis is impossible without a class characterization of the phenomenon under consideration.

The skeletal and muscular systems do not exhaust the anatomy of an animal; nevertheless an anatomical treatise which attempted to "abstract" itself from bones and muscles would dangle in midair. War is not an organ but a function of society, i.e., its ruling class. It is impossible to define and study a function without understanding the organ, i.e., the state; it is impossible to gain scientific understanding of the organ without understanding the general structure of the organism, i.e., society. The bones and muscles of society consist of the productive forces and the class (property) relations. Shachtman holds it possible that a function, namely, war, can be studied "concretely" independently of the organ to which it pertains, i.e., the state. Isn't this monstrous?

This fundamental error is supplemented by another equally glaring. After splitting function away from organ, Shachtman in studying the function itself, contrary to all his promises, proceeds not from the abstract to the concrete but on the contrary dissolves the concrete in the abstract. *Imperialist* war is one of the functions of finance capital, i.e., the bourgeoisie at a certain stage of development resting upon capitalism of a specific structure, namely, monopoly capital. This definition is sufficiently concrete for our basic political conclusions. But by extending the term *imperialist* war to cover the Soviet state too, Shachtman cuts the ground away from under his own feet. In order to reach even a superficial justification for applying one and the same designation to the expansion of finance capital and the expansion of the workers state, Shachtman is compelled to detach himself from the social structure of both states altogether by proclaiming it to be—an abstraction. Thus playing hide and seek with Marxism, Shachtman labels the concrete as abstract and palms off the abstract as concrete!

This outrageous toying with theory is not accidental. Every petty bourgeois in the United States without exception is ready to call every seizure of territory "imperialist," especially today when the United States does not happen to be occupied with acquiring territories. But if this very same petty bourgeois is told that the entire foreign policy of finance capital is imperialist regardless of whether it be occupied at the given moment in carrying out an annexation or in "defending" Finland against annexation—then our petty bourgeois jumps back in pious indignation. Naturally the leaders of the opposition differ considerably from an average petty bourgeois in their aim and in their political level. But alas they have common roots of thought. A petty bourgeois invariably seeks to tear political events away from their social foundation, since there is an organic conflict between a class approach to facts and the social position and education of the petty bourgeoisie.

Once again: Poland

My remark that the Kremlin with its bureaucratic methods gave an impulse to the socialist revolution in Poland, is converted by Shachtman into an assertion that in my opinion a "bureaucratic revolution" of the proletariat is presumably possible. This is not only incorrect but disloyal. My expression was rigidly limited. It is not the question of "bureaucratic revolution" but only a bureaucratic impulse. To deny this impulse is to deny reality. The popular masses in western Ukraine and Byelorussia, in any event, felt this impulse, understood its meaning, and used it to accomplish a drastic overturn in property relations. A revolutionary party which failed to notice this impulse in time and refused to utilize it would be fit for nothing but the ash can.

This impulse in the direction of socialist revolution was possible only because the bureaucracy of the USSR straddles and has its roots in the economy of a workers state. The revolutionary utilization of this "impulse" by the Ukrainians and Byelorussians was possible only through the class struggle in the occupied territories and through the power of the example of the October revolution. Finally, the swift strangulation or semistrangulation of this revolutionary mass movement was made possible through the isolation of this movement and the might of the Moscow bureaucracy. Whoever failed to understand the dialectic interaction of these three factors: the workers state, the oppressed masses, and the Bonapartist bureaucracy, had best restrain himself from idle talk about events in Poland.

At the elections for the National Assembly of western Ukraine and western Byelorussia the electoral program, dictated of course by the Kremlin, included three extremely important points: inclusion of both provinces in the federation of the USSR; confiscation of landlords' estates in favor of the peasants; nationalization of large industry and the banks. The Ukrainian democrats, judging from their conduct, deem it a lesser evil to be unified under the rule of a single state. And from the standpoint of the future struggle for independence, they are correct. As for the other two points in the program, one would think that there could be no doubt in our midst as to their progressiveness. Seeking to get around reality, namely that nothing else but the social foundations of the USSR forced a social revolutionary program upon the Kremlin, Shachtman refers to Lithuania, Estonia, and Latvia where everything has remained as of old. An incredible argument! No one has said that the Soviet bureaucracy *always* and *everywhere* either wishes or is able to accomplish the expropriation of the bourgeoisie. We only say that no other government could have accomplished that social overturn which the Kremlin bureaucracy, notwithstanding its alliance with Hitler, found itself compelled to sanction in eastern Poland. Failing this, it could not include the territory in the federation of the USSR.

Shachtman is aware of the overturn itself. He cannot deny it. He is incapable of explaining it. But he nevertheless attempts to save face. He writes: "In the Polish Ukraine and White Russia, where class exploitation was intensified by national oppression . . . the peasants began to take over the land themselves, to drive off the landlords who were already half-in-flight," etc. (Loc. cit., p. 16.) The Red Army, it turns out, had no connection whatever with all this. It came into Poland only as a "counterrevolutionary force" in order to suppress the movement. But why didn't the workers and peasants in western Poland seized by Hitler arrange a revolution? Why was it chiefly revolutionists, "democrats," and Jews who fled from there, while in eastern Poland—it was chiefly the landlords and capitalists who fled? Shachtman lacks the time to think this out—he is in a hurry to explain to me that the conception of "bureaucratic revolution" is absurd, for the emancipation of the workers can be carried out only by the workers themselves. Am I not justified in repeating that Shachtman obviously feels he is standing in a nursery?

In the Parisian organ of the Mensheviks—who, if that is possible, are even more "irreconcilable" in their attitude toward the Kremlin's foreign policy than Shachtman—it is reported that "in the villages—very frequently at the very approach of the Soviet troops (i.e., even prior to their entering a given district—L.T.)—peasant committees sprang up everywhere, the elementary organs of revolutionary peasant self-rule. . . .". The military authorities hastened of course to subordinate these committees to the bureaucratic organs established by them in the urban centers. Nevertheless they were compelled to rest upon the peasant committees since without them it was impossible to carry out the agrarian revolution.

The leader of the Mensheviks, Dan, wrote on October 19:

"*According to the unanimous testimony of all observers* the appearance of the Soviet army and the Soviet bureaucracy provides not only in the territory occupied by them but beyond its confines—an impulse (!!!) to social turmoil and social transformations." The "impulse," it will be observed, was invented not by me but by "the unanimous testimony of all observers" who possessed eyes and ears. Dan goes even further and expresses the supposition that "the waves engendered by this impulse will not only hit Germany powerfully in a comparatively short period of time but also to one degree or another roll on to other states."

Another Menshevik author writes: "However they may have attempted in the Kremlin to avoid anything which might smack of the great revolution, the very fact of the entry of Soviet troops into the territories of eastern Poland with its long-outlived semifeudal agrarian relations, had to provoke a stormy agrarian movement. With the approach of Soviet troops the peasants began to seize landlords' estates and to form peasant committees." You will observe: with the *approach* of Soviet troops and not at all with their *withdrawal* as should follow in accordance with Shachtman's words. I cite the testimony of the Mensheviks because they are very well informed, their sources of information coming through Polish and Jewish émigrés friendly to them who have gathered in France, and also because having capitulated to the French bourgeoisie, these gentlemen cannot possibly be suspected of capitulation to Stalinism.

The testimony of the Mensheviks furthermore is confirmed by the reports of the bourgeois press:

"The agrarian revolution in Soviet Poland has had the force of a spontaneous movement. As soon as the report spread that the Red Army had crossed the river Zbrucz the peasants began to share out amongst themselves the landlords' acres. Land was given first to small holders and in this way

about 30 percent of agricultural land was expropriated."
(*New York Times*, January 17, 1940.)

   Under the guise of a new argument Shachtman hands me
my own words to the effect that the expropriation of property owners in eastern Poland cannot alter our appraisal
of the *general* policies of the Kremlin. Of course it cannot!
No one has proposed this. With the aid of the Comintern
the Kremlin has disoriented and demoralized the working
class so that it has not only facilitated the outbreak of a new
imperialist war but has also made extremely difficult the
utilization of this war for revolution. Compared with those
crimes the social overturn in the two provinces, which was
paid for moreover by the enslavement of Poland, is of course
of secondary importance and does not alter the general reactionary character of the Kremlin's policy. But upon the
initiative of the opposition itself, the question now posed is
not one of general policy but of its concrete refraction under specific conditions of time and place. To the peasants
of Galicia and western Byelorussia the agrarian overturn
was of highest importance. The Fourth International could
not have boycotted this overturn on the ground that the
initiative was taken by the reactionary bureaucracy. Our
outright duty was to participate in the overturn on the side
of the workers and peasants and *to that extent* on the side
of the Red Army. At the same time it was indispensable
to warn the masses tirelessly of the generally reactionary
character of the Kremlin's policy and of those dangers it
bears for the occupied territories. To know how to combine
these two tasks or more precisely two sides of one and the
same task—just this is bolshevik politics.

Once again: Finland

   Having revealed such odd perspicacity in understanding
the events in Poland, Shachtman descends upon me with

redoubled authority in connection with events in Finland. In my article "A Petty-Bourgeois Opposition," I wrote that "the Soviet-Finnish War is *apparently beginning* to be *supplemented* by a civil war in which the Red Army finds itself at a given stage in the same camp as the Finnish petty peasants and the workers. . . ." This extremely cautious formula did not meet with the approval of my unsparing judge. My evaluation of events in Poland had already taken him off balance. "I find even less (proof) for your—how shall I put it?—astonishing remarks about Finland," writes Shachtman on page 16 of his "Letter." I am very sorry that Shachtman chooses to become astonished rather than think things out.

In the Baltic states the Kremlin confined its tasks to making strategical gains with the unquestionable calculation that in the future these strategic military bases will permit the sovietization of these former sections of the tsarist empire too. These successes in the Baltic, achieved by diplomatic threat, met with resistance, however, from Finland. To reconcile itself to this resistance would have meant that the Kremlin placed in jeopardy its "prestige" and thereby its successes in Estonia, Latvia, and Lithuania. Thus contrary to its initial plans the Kremlin felt compelled to resort to armed force. From this fact every thinking person posed to himself the following question: Does the Kremlin wish only to frighten the Finnish bourgeoisie and force them to make concessions or must it now go further? To this question naturally there could be no "automatic" answer. It was necessary—in the light of general tendencies—to orient oneself upon concrete symptoms. The leaders of the opposition are incapable of this.

Military operations began on November 30. That very same day the Central Committee of the Finnish Communist Party, undoubtedly located in either Leningrad or Moscow, issued a radio manifesto to the toiling people of Finland. This manifesto proclaimed: "For the second time in the history of Finland the Finnish working class is beginning a struggle against the yoke of the plutocracy. The first experience of the workers and peasants in 1918 terminated in the victory of the capitalists and the landlords. But this time . . . the toiling people must win!" This manifesto alone clearly indicated that not an attempt to scare the bourgeois government of Finland was involved, but a plan to provoke insurrection in the country and to supplement the invasion of the Red Army with civil war.

The declaration of the so-called People's Government published on December 2 states: "In different parts of the country the people have already risen and proclaimed the creation of a democratic republic." This assertion is obviously a fabrication, otherwise the manifesto would have mentioned the places where the attempts at insurrection took place. It is possible, however, that isolated attempts, prepared from without, ended in failure and that precisely because of this it was deemed best not to go into details. In any case, the news concerning "insurrections" constituted a call to insurrection. Moreover, the declaration carried information concerning the formation of "the first Finnish corps which in the course of coming battles will be enlarged by volunteers from the ranks of revolutionary workers and peasants." Whether there were one thousand men in this "corps" or only one hundred, the meaning of the "corps" in determining the policies of the Kremlin was incontestable. At the same time cable dispatches reported the expropriation of large landholders in the border regions. There is not the slightest ground to doubt that this is just what took place during the first advance of the Red Army. But even if these dispatches are considered fabrications, they completely preserve their meaning as a call for an agrarian revolution. Thus I had every justification to declare that "The Soviet-Finnish War is apparently beginning to be supplemented by a civil war." At the beginning of December, true enough, I had at my disposal only a part of these facts. But against the background of the general situation, and I take the liberty to add, with the aid of an understanding of its internal logic, the isolated symptoms enabled me to draw the necessary conclusions concerning the direction of the entire struggle. Without such semi-a priori conclusions one can be a rationalizing observer but in no case an active participant in events.

But why did the appeal of the "People's Government" fail to bring immediate mass response? For three reasons: first, Finland is dominated completely by a reactionary military machine which is supported not only by the bourgeoisie but by the top layers of the peasantry and the labor bureaucracy; secondly, the policy of the Kremlin succeeded in transforming the Finnish Communist Party into an insignificant factor; thirdly, the regime of the USSR is in no way capable of arousing enthusiasm among the Finnish toiling masses. Even in the Ukraine from 1918 to 1920 the peasants responded very slowly to appeals to seize the estates of the landlords because the local soviet power was still weak and every success of the Whites brought about ruthless punitive expeditions. All the less reason is there for surprise that the Finnish poor peasants delay in responding to an appeal for an agrarian revolution. To set the peasants in motion, serious successes of the Red Army are required. But during the first badly prepared advance the Red Army suffered only failures. Under such conditions there could not even be talk of the peasants rising. It was impossible to expect an independent civil war in Finland at the given stage: my calculations spoke quite

precisely of *supplementing* military operations by measures of civil war. I have in mind—at least until the Finnish army is annihilated—only the occupied territory and
the nearby regions. Today on January 17 as I write these
lines dispatches from a Finnish source report that one of
the border provinces has been invaded by detachments of
Finnish émigrés and that brother is literally killing brother
there. What is this if not an episode in a civil war? In any
case there can be no doubt that a new advance of the Red
Army into Finland will confirm at every step our general
appraisal of the war. Shachtman has neither an analysis of
the events nor the hint of a prognosis. He confines himself
to noble indignation and for this reason at every step he
sinks deeper into the mire.

The appeal of the "People's Government" calls for workers
control. What can this mean! exclaims Shachtman. There
is no workers control in the USSR; whence will it come in
Finland? Sad to say, Shachtman reveals complete lack of understanding of the situation. In the USSR workers control is a
stage long ago completed. From control over the bourgeoisie
there they passed to management of nationalized production. From the management of workers—to the command
of the bureaucracy. New workers control would now signify
control over the bureaucracy. This cannot be established
except as the result of a successful uprising against the bureaucracy. In Finland, workers control still signifies nothing
more than crowding out the native bourgeoisie, whose place
the bureaucracy proposes to take. Furthermore one should
not think that the Kremlin is so stupid as to attempt ruling
eastern Poland or Finland by means of imported commissars. Of greatest urgency to the Kremlin is the extraction
of a new administrative apparatus from among the toiling
population of the occupied areas. This task can be solved
only in several stages. The first stage is the peasant com-

mittees and the committees of workers control.*

Shachtman clutches eagerly even at the fact that Kuusinen's program "is, formally, the program of a bourgeois 'democracy.' " Does he mean to say by this that the Kremlin is more interested in establishing bourgeois democracy in Finland than in drawing Finland into the framework of the USSR? Shachtman himself doesn't know what he wants to say. In Spain, which Moscow did not prepare for union with the USSR, it was actually a question of demonstrating the ability of the Kremlin to safeguard bourgeois democracy against proletarian revolution. This task flowed from the interests of the Kremlin bureaucracy in that particular international situation. Today the situation is a different one. The Kremlin is not preparing to demonstrate its usefulness to France, England, and the United States. As its actions have proved, it has firmly decided to sovietize Finland—at once or in two stages. The program of the Kuusinen government, even if approached from a "formal" point of view does not differ

---

* This article was already written when I read in the *New York Times* of January 17 the following lines relating to former eastern Poland: "In industry, drastic acts of expropriation have not yet been carried out on a large scale. The main centers of the banking system, the railway system, and a number of large industrial undertakings were state-owned for years before the Russian occupation. In small and medium-sized industries workmen now exercise control over production.

"The industrialists nominally retain a full right of ownership in their own establishments, but they are compelled to submit statements of costs of production, and so on, for the consideration of the workmen's delegates. The latter, jointly, with the employers, fix wages, conditions of work, and a 'just rate of profit' for the industrialist."

Thus we see that "the realities of living events" do not at all submit themselves to the pedantic and lifeless patterns of the leaders of the opposition. Meanwhile our "abstractions" are becoming transformed into flesh and blood.—L.T.

from the program of the Bolsheviks in November 1917. True enough, Shachtman makes much of the fact that I generally place significance on the manifesto of the "idiot" Kuusinen. However, I shall take the liberty of considering that the "idiot" Kuusinen acting on the ukase of the Kremlin and with the support of the Red Army represents a far more serious political factor than scores of superficial wiseacres who refuse to think through the internal logic (dialectics) of events.

As a result of his remarkable analysis, Shachtman this time openly proposes a *defeatist* policy in relation to the USSR, adding (for emergency use) that he does not at all cease to be a "patriot of his class." We are happy to get the information. But the trouble is that Dan, the leader of the Mensheviks, as far back as November 12 wrote that in the event the Soviet Union invaded Finland the world proletariat "must take a definitive defeatist position in relation to this violation." (*Sozialisticheski Vestnik*, no. 19–20, p. 43.) It is necessary to add that throughout the Kerensky regime, Dan was a rabid defensist; he failed to be a defeatist even under the tsar. Only the invasion of Finland by the Red Army has turned Dan into a defeatist. Naturally he does not thereby cease to be a "patriot of his class." What class? This question is not an uninteresting one. So far as the analysis of events is concerned Shachtman disagrees with Dan, who is closer to the theater of action and cannot replace facts with fiction; by way of compensation, where the "concrete political conclusions" are concerned, Shachtman has turned out to be a "patriot" of the very same class as Dan. In Marxist sociology this class, if the opposition will permit me, this class is called the *petty bourgeoisie*.

The theory of 'blocs'

To justify his bloc with Burnham and Abern—against the proletarian wing of the party, against the program of the

Fourth International, and against the Marxist method—
Shachtman has not spared the history of the revolutionary
movement which he—according to his own words—studied
especially in order to transmit great traditions to the young-
er generation. The goal itself is of course excellent. But it
demands a scientific method. Meanwhile, Shachtman has
begun by sacrificing scientific method for the sake of a bloc.
His historical examples are arbitrary, not thought out, and
downright false.

Not every collaboration is a bloc in the proper sense
of the term. By no means infrequent are episodic agreements which are not at all transformed and do not seek to
be transformed into a protracted bloc. On the other hand
membership in one and the same party can hardly be
called a bloc. We together with Comrade Burnham have
belonged (and I hope will continue to belong to the end) to
one and the same international party; but this is still not a
bloc. Two parties can conclude a long-term bloc with each
other against a common enemy: such was the policy of the
"People's Front." Within one and the same party close but
not congruent tendencies can conclude a bloc against a
third faction.

For the evaluation of inner-party blocs two questions are
of decisive significance: (1) First and foremost against whom
or what is the bloc directed? (2) What is the relationship of
forces within the bloc? Thus for a struggle against chauvin-
ism within one's own party, a bloc between internationalists
and centrists is wholly permissible. The result of the bloc
would in this case depend upon the clarity of the program
of the internationalists, upon their cohesiveness and discipline, for these traits are not infrequently more important
in determining the relationship of forces than their numeri-
cal strength.

Shachtman, as we said before, appeals to Lenin's bloc with

Bogdanov. I have already stated that Lenin did not make
the slightest theoretical concessions to Bogdanov. Now we
shall examine the political side of the "bloc." It is first of
all necessary to state that what was actually in question
was not a bloc but a collaboration in a common organization. The Bolshevik faction led an independent existence.
Lenin did not form a "bloc" with Bogdanov against other
tendencies within his own organization. On the contrary
he formed a bloc even with the Bolshevik-conciliators (Dubrovinsky, Rykov, and others) against the theoretical her-
esies of Bogdanov. In essence, the question so far as Lenin
was concerned was whether it was possible to remain with
Bogdanov in one and the same organization which although
called a "faction" bore all the traits of a party. If Shachtman does not look upon the opposition as an independent
organization, then his reference to the Lenin-Bogdanov
"bloc" falls to pieces.

But the mistake in the analogy is not restricted to this.
The Bolshevik faction-party carried on a struggle against
menshevism, which at that time had already revealed itself
completely as a petty-bourgeois agency of the liberal bourgeoisie. This was far more serious than the accusation of
so-called "bureaucratic conservatism," the class roots of
which Shachtman does not even attempt to define. Lenin's
collaboration with Bogdanov was collaboration between
a proletarian tendency and a sectarian centrist tendency
against petty-bourgeois opportunism. The class lines are
clear. The "bloc" (if one uses this term in the given instance)
was justified.

The subsequent history of the "bloc" is not lacking in significance. In the letter to Gorky cited by Shachtman, Lenin
expressed the hope that it would be possible to separate the
political questions from the purely philosophic ones. Shachtman forgets to add that Lenin's hope did not at all materi-

alize. Differences developed from the heights of philosophy down the line of all the other questions, including the most current ones. If the "bloc" did not discredit bolshevism it was only because Lenin had a finished program, a correct method, a firmly welded faction in which Bogdanov's group composed a small unstable minority.

Shachtman concluded a bloc with Burnham and Abern against the proletarian wing of his own party. It is impossible to evade this. The relationship of forces within the bloc is completely against Shachtman. Abern has his own faction. Burnham with Shachtman's assistance can create the semblance of a faction constituting intellectuals disillusioned with bolshevism. Shachtman has no independent program, no independent method, no independent faction. The eclectic character of the opposition "program" is determined by the contradictory tendencies within the bloc. In the event the bloc collapses—and the collapse is inevitable—Shachtman will emerge from the struggle with nothing but injury to the party and to himself.

Shachtman further appeals to the fact that in 1917 Lenin and Trotsky united after a long struggle and it would therefore be incorrect to remind them of their past differences. This example is slightly compromised by the fact that Shachtman has already utilized it once before to explain his bloc with—Cannon against Abern. But aside from this unpleasant circumstance the historical analogy is false to the core. Upon joining the Bolshevik Party, Trotsky recognized completely and wholeheartedly the correctness of the Leninist methods of building the party. At the same time the irreconcilable class tendency of bolshevism had corrected an incorrect prognosis. If I did not again raise the question of "permanent revolution" in 1917 it was because it had already been decided for both sides by the march of events. The basis for joint work was constituted not by subjective or episodic combinations but by the proletarian revolution. This is a solid basis. Furthermore, in question here was not a "bloc" but unification in a single party— against the bourgeoisie and its petty-bourgeois agents. Inside the party the October bloc of Lenin and Trotsky was directed against petty-bourgeois vacillations on the question of insurrection.

Equally superficial is Shachtman's reference to Trotsky's bloc with Zinoviev in 1926. The struggle at that time was conducted not against "bureaucratic conservatism" as the psychological trait of a few unsympathetic individuals but against the mightiest bureaucracy in the world, its privileges, its arbitrary rule, and its reactionary policy. The scope of permissible differences in a bloc is determined by the character of the adversary.

The relationship of elements within the bloc was likewise altogether different. The opposition of 1923 had its own program and its own cadres composed not at all of intellectuals as Shachtman asserts, echoing the Stalinists, but primarily workers. The Zinoviev-Kamenev opposition on our demand acknowledged in a special document that the 1923 opposition was correct on all fundamental questions. Nevertheless since we had different traditions and since we were far from agreeing in everything, the merger never did take place; both groups remained independent factions. In certain important questions, it is true, the 1923 opposition made principled concessions to the opposition in 1926—against my vote—concessions which I considered and still consider impermissible. The circumstance that I did not protest openly against these concessions was rather a mistake. But there was generally not much room for open protests—we were working illegally. In any event, both sides were very well acquainted with my views on the controversial questions. Within the 1923 opposition, nine

hundred and ninety-nine out of a thousand if not more
stood on my point of view and not on the point of view of
Zinoviev or Radek. With such a relation between the two
groups in the bloc there might have been these or other
partial mistakes but there was not so much as a semblance
of adventurism.

With Shachtman the case is completely different. Who
was right in the past and just when and where? Why did
Shachtman stand first with Abern, then with Cannon, and
now back again with Abern? Shachtman's own explanation
concerning the past bitter factional struggles is worthy not
of a responsible political figure but of a nursemaid: Johnny
was a little wrong, Max a little, all were a little wrong, and
now we are all a little right. Who was in the wrong and in
what, not a word of this. There is no tradition. Yesterday
is expunged from the calculations—and what is the reason
for all this? Because in the organism of the party Comrade
Shachtman plays the role of a floating kidney.

Seeking historical analogies, Shachtman avoids one example to which his present bloc does actually bear a resemblance. I have in mind the so-called August Bloc of 1912. I
participated actively in this bloc. In a certain sense I created
it. Politically I differed with the Mensheviks on all fundamental questions. I also differed with the ultraleft Bolsheviks, the *Vperyodists*. In the general tendency of politics I
stood far more closely to the Bolsheviks. But I was against
the Leninist "regime" because I had not yet learned to understand that in order to realize the revolutionary goal a
firmly welded centralized party is indispensable. And so I
formed this episodic bloc consisting of heterogeneous elements which was directed against the proletarian wing of
the party.

In the August Bloc the liquidators had their own faction,
the *Vperyodists* also had something resembling a faction.

I stood isolated, having co-thinkers but no faction. Most of the documents were written by me and through avoiding principled differences had as their aim the creation of a semblance of unanimity upon "concrete political questions." Not a word about the past! Lenin subjected the August Bloc to merciless criticism and the harshest blows fell to my lot. Lenin proved that inasmuch as I did not agree politically with either the Mensheviks or the *Vperyodists* my policy was adventurism. This was severe but it was true.

As "mitigating circumstances" let me mention the fact that I had set as my task not to support the right or ultra-left factions against the Bolsheviks but to unite the party as a whole. The Bolsheviks too were invited to the August conference. But since Lenin flatly refused to unite with the Mensheviks (in which he was completely correct) I was left in an unnatural bloc with the Mensheviks and the *Vperyo-dists*. The second mitigating circumstance is this, that the very phenomenon of bolshevism as the genuine revolutionary party was then developing for the first time—in the practice of the Second International there were no precedents. But I do not thereby seek in the least to absolve myself from guilt. Notwithstanding the conception of permanent revolution which undoubtedly disclosed the correct perspective, I had not freed myself at that period, especially in the organizational sphere, from the traits of a petty-bourgeois revolutionist. I was sick with the disease of conciliationism toward menshevism and with a distrustful attitude toward Leninist centralism. Immediately after the August conference the bloc began to disintegrate into its component parts. Within a few months I was not only in principle but organizationally outside the bloc.

I address Shachtman today with the very same rebuke which Lenin addressed to me twenty-seven years ago: "Your bloc is unprincipled." "Your policy is adventurism." With all my heart I express the hope that from these accusations Shachtman will draw the same conclusions which I once drew.

The factions in the struggle

Shachtman expresses surprise over the fact that Trotsky, "the leader of the 1923 opposition," is capable of supporting the bureaucratic faction of Cannon. In this as in the question of workers control Shachtman again reveals his lack of feeling for historical perspective. True, in justifying their dictatorship the Soviet bureaucracy exploited the principles of Bolshevik centralism but in the very process it transformed them into their exact opposite. But this does not discredit in the least the methods of bolshevism. Over a period of many years Lenin educated the party in the spirit of proletarian discipline and severe centralism. In so doing he suffered scores of times the attack of petty-bourgeois factions and cliques. Bolshevik centralism was a profoundly progressive factor and in the end secured the triumph of the revolution. It is not difficult to understand that the struggle of the present opposition in the Socialist Workers Party has nothing in common with the struggle of the Russian opposition of 1923 against the privileged bureaucratic caste, but it does instead bear great resemblance to the struggle of the Mensheviks against Bolshevik centralism.

Cannon and his group are according to the opposition "an expression of a type of politics which can be best described as bureaucratic conservatism." What does this mean? The domination of a conservative labor bureaucracy, shareholder in the profits of the national bourgeoisie, would be unthinkable without direct or indirect support of the capitalist state. The rule of the Stalinist bureaucracy would be unthinkable without the GPU, the army, the courts, etc. The Soviet bureaucracy supports Stalin precisely because he is the bureaucrat who defends their interests better than anybody else. The trade union bureaucracy supports Green and Lewis precisely because their vices, as able and dexterous bureaucrats, safeguard the material interests of the labor aristocracy. But upon what base does "bureaucratic conservatism" rest in the SWP? Obviously not on material interests but on a selection of bureaucratic types in contrast to another camp where innovators, initiators, and dynamic spirits have been gathered together. The opposition does not point to any objective, i.e., social basis for "bureaucratic conservatism." Everything is reduced to pure psychology. Under such conditions every thinking worker will say: It is possible that Comrade Cannon actually does sin in the line of bureaucratic tendencies—it is hard for me to judge at a distance—but if the majority of the National Committee and of the entire party who are not at all interested in bureaucratic "privileges" support Cannon they do so not because of his bureaucratic tendencies but in spite of them. This means that he has some other virtues which far outweigh his personal failing. That is what a serious party member will say. And in my opinion he would be correct.

To substantiate their complaints and accusations the leaders of the opposition bring up disjointed episodes and anecdotes which can be counted by the hundred and the thousand in every party and which moreover are impossible to verify objectively in most instances. Furthest from my mind is indulgence in a criticism of the story-telling section of the opposition documents. But there is one episode about which I wish to express myself as a participant and a witness. The leaders of the opposition very superciliously relate how easily, presumably without criticism and without deliberation, Cannon and his group accepted the program of transitional demands.* Here is what I wrote on April 15, 1938, to Comrade Cannon concerning the elaboration of this program:

"We have sent you the transitional program draft and a short statement about the labor party. Without your visit to Mexico I could never have written the program draft because I learned during the discussions many important things which permitted me to be more explicit and concrete. . . ."

Shachtman is thoroughly acquainted with these circumstances since he was one of those who took part in the discussion.

Rumors, personal speculations, and simple gossip cannot help but occupy an important place in petty-bourgeois circles where people are bound together not by party ties but by personal relationships and where no habit has been acquired of a class approach to events. It is passed from ear to ear that I have been visited exclusively by representatives of the majority and that I have been led astray from the path of truth. Dear comrades, don't believe this nonsense! I collect political information through the very same methods that I use in my work generally. A critical attitude toward information is an organic part of the political physiognomy of every politician. If I were incapable of distinguishing false communications from true ones, what value could my judgments have in general?

I am personally acquainted with no less than twenty members of Abern's faction. To several of them I am obligated for their friendly help in my work and I consider all of them,

---

* "The Death Agony of Capitalism and the Tasks of the Fourth International," known also as the Transitional Program. Contained in Trotsky, *The Transitional Program for Socialist Revolution* (New York: Pathfinder, 1977), pp. 109–52.

or almost all, as valuable party members. But at the same
time I must say that what distinguishes each of them to one
degree or another is the aura of a petty-bourgeois milieu,
lack of experience in the class struggle, and to a certain extent lack of the requisite connection with the proletarian
movement. Their positive features link them to the Fourth
International. Their negative features bind them to the most
conservative of all factions.

"An 'anti-intellectual' and 'anti-intellectuals' attitude is
drummed into the minds of party members," complains the
document on "Bureaucratic Conservatism." (*Internal Bulletin*, vol. 2, no. 6, January 1940, p. 12.) This argument is
dragged in by the hair. It is not those intellectuals who have
completely gone over to the side of the proletariat who are
in question, but those elements who are seeking to shift our
party to the position of petty-bourgeois eclecticism. This
same document declares: "An anti-New York propaganda
is spread which is at bottom a catering to prejudices that
are not always healthy" (idem). What prejudices are referred
to here? Apparently anti-Semitism. If anti-Semitic or other
race prejudices exist in our party, it is necessary to wage a
ruthless struggle against them through open blows and not
through vague insinuations. But the question of the Jewish
intellectuals and semi-intellectuals of New York is a *social*
not a *national* question. In New York there are a great many
Jewish proletarians, but Abern's faction is not built up of
them. The petty-bourgeois elements of this faction have
proved incapable to this day of finding a road to the Jewish
workers. They are contented with their own milieu.

There has been more than one instance in history—more
precisely it does not happen otherwise in history—that with
the transition of the party from one period to the next those
elements which played a progressive role in the past but who
proved incapable of adapting themselves with timeliness to

new tasks have drawn closer together in the face of danger and revealed not their positive but almost exclusively their negative traits. That is precisely the role today of Abern's faction, in which Shachtman plays the role of journalist and Burnham the role of theoretical brain trust. "Cannon knows," persists Shachtman, "how spurious it is to inject in the present discussion the 'Abern question.' He knows what every informed party leader, and many members know, namely, that for the past several years at least there has been no such thing as an 'Abern Group.' " I take the liberty of remarking that if anybody is here distorting reality it is none other than Shachtman himself. I have been following the development of the internal relations in the American section for about ten years. The specific composition and the special role played by the New York organization became clear to me before anything else. Shachtman will perhaps recall that while I was still in Prinkipo I advised the National Committee to move away from New York and its atmosphere of petty-bourgeois squabbles for a while to some industrial center in the provinces. Upon arriving in Mexico I gained the opportunity of becoming better acquainted with the English language and thanks to many visits from my northern friends, of arriving at a more vivid picture of the social composition and the political psychology of the various groupings. On the basis of my own personal and immediate observations during the past three years I assert that the Abern faction has existed uninterruptedly, statically if not "dynamically."

The members of the Abern faction, given a modicum of political experience, are easily recognizable not only by their social traits but by their approach to all questions. These comrades have always formally denied the existence of their faction. There was a period when some of them actually did try to dissolve themselves into the party. But they attempted this by doing violence to themselves, and on all critical questions they came out in relation to the party as a group. They were far less interested in principled questions, in particular the question of changing the social composition of the party, than in combinations at the top, personal conflicts, and generally occurrences in the "general staff." This is the Abern school. I persistently warned many of these comrades that soaking in this artificial existence would unfailingly bring them sooner or later to a new factional explosion.

The leaders of the opposition speak ironically and disparagingly of the proletarian composition of the Cannon faction; in their eyes this incidental "detail" carries no importance. What is this if not petty-bourgeois disdain combined with blindness? At the Second Congress of the Russian Social Democrats in 1903, where the split took place between the Bolsheviks and the Mensheviks, there were only three workers among several scores of delegates. All three of them turned up with the majority. The Mensheviks jeered at Lenin for investing this fact with great symptomatic significance. The Mensheviks themselves explained the position the three workers took by their lack of "maturity." But as is well known it was Lenin who proved correct.

If the proletarian section of our American party is "politically backward," then the first task of those who are "advanced" should have consisted in raising the workers to a higher level. But why has the present opposition failed to find its way to these workers? Why did they leave this work to the "Cannon clique"? What is involved here? Aren't the workers good enough for the opposition? Or is the opposition unsuitable for workers?

It would be asinine to think that the workers section of the party is perfect. The workers are only gradually reaching clear class consciousness. The trade unions always create a culture medium for opportunist deviations. Inevitably we will run up against this question in one of the next stages. More than once the party will have to remind its own trade unionists that a *pedagogical adaptation to the more backward layers of the proletariat must not become transformed into a political adaptation to the conservative bureaucracy of the trade unions.* Every new stage of development, every increase in the party ranks and the complication of the methods of its work open up not only new possibilities but also new dangers. Workers in the trade unions, even those trained in the most revolutionary school, often display a tendency to free themselves from party control. At the present time, however, this is not at all in question. At the present time the nonproletarian opposition, dragging behind it the majority of the nonproletarian youth, is attempting to revise our theory, our program, our tradition—and it does all this light-mindedly, in passing, for greater convenience in the struggle against the "Cannon clique." At the present time disrespect for the party is shown not by the trade unionists but by the petty-bourgeois oppositionists. It is precisely in order to prevent the trade unionists from turning their backs to the party in the future that it is necessary to decisively repulse these petty-bourgeois oppositionists.

It is moreover impermissible to forget that the actual or possible mistakes of those comrades working in the trade unions reflect the pressure of the American proletariat as it is today. This is our class. We are not preparing to capitulate to its pressure. But this pressure at the same time shows us our main historic road. The mistakes of the opposition on the other hand reflect the pressure of another and alien class. An ideological break with that class is the elementary condition for our future successes.

The reasonings of the opposition in regard to the youth are false in the extreme. Assuredly, without the conquest of the proletarian youth the revolutionary party cannot

develop. But the trouble is that we have almost an entirely
petty-bourgeois youth, to a considerable degree with a social democratic, i.e., opportunist past. The leaders of this
youth have indubitable virtues and ability but, alas, they
have been educated in the spirit of petty-bourgeois combinationism and if they are not wrenched out of their habitual
milieu, if they are not sent without high-sounding titles into
working-class districts for day-to-day dirty work among
the proletariat, they can forever perish for the revolutionary movement. In relation to the youth as in all the other
questions, Shachtman unfortunately has taken a position
that is false to the core.

It is time to halt!

To what extent Shachtman's thought, from a false starting point, has become debased is to be seen from the fact
that he depicts my position as a defense of the "Cannon
clique" and he harps several times on the fact that in France
I supported just as mistakenly the "Molinier clique." Everything is reduced to my supporting isolated individuals
or groups entirely independently of their program. The
example of Molinier only thickens the fog. I shall attempt
to dispel it. Molinier was accused not of retreating from
our program but of being undisciplined, arbitrary, and of
venturing into all sorts of financial adventures to support
the party and his faction. Since Molinier is a very energetic
man and has unquestionable practical capacities I found it
necessary—not only in the interests of Molinier but above
all in the interests of the organization itself—to exhaust all
the possibilities of convincing and reeducating him in the
spirit of proletarian discipline. Since many of his adversaries possessed all of his failings but none of his virtues I did
everything to convince them not to hasten a split but to test
Molinier over and over again. It was this that constituted

my "defense" of Molinier in the adolescent period of the existence of our French section.

Considering a patient attitude toward blundering or undisciplined comrades and repeated efforts to reeducate them in the revolutionary spirit as absolutely compulsory I applied these methods by no means solely to Molinier. I made attempts to draw closer into the party and save Kurt Landau, Field, Weisbord, the Austrian Frey, the Frenchman Treint, and a number of others. In many cases my efforts proved fruitless; in a few cases it was possible to rescue valuable comrades.

In any case I did not make the slightest principled concession to Molinier. When he decided to found a paper on the basis of "four slogans" instead of our program, and set out independently to execute this plan, I was among those who insisted upon his immediate expulsion. But I will not hide the fact that at the founding congress of the Fourth International I was in favor of once again testing Molinier and his group within the framework of the International to see if they had become convinced of the erroneousness of their policy. This time, too, the attempt led to nothing. But I do not renounce repeating it under suitable conditions once again. It is most curious that among the bitterest opponents of Molinier there were people like Vereecken and Sneevliet, who after they had broken with the Fourth International successfully united with him.

A number of comrades upon acquainting themselves with my archives have reproached me in a friendly way with having wasted and still continuing to waste so much time on convincing "hopeless people." I replied that many times I have had the occasion to observe how people change with circumstances and that I am therefore not ready to pronounce people as "hopeless" on the basis of a few even though serious mistakes.

When it became clear to me that Shachtman was driving himself and a certain section of the party into a blind alley I wrote him that if the opportunity were mine I would immediately take an airplane and fly to New York in order to discuss with him for seventy-two-hour stretches at a time. I asked him if he didn't wish to make it possible somehow for us to get together. Shachtman did not reply. This is wholly within his right. It is quite possible that those comrades who may become acquainted with my archives in the future will say in this case too that my letter to Shachtman was a false step on my part and they will cite this "mistake" of mine in connection with my over-persistent "defense" of Molinier. They will not convince me. It is an extremely difficult task to form an international proletarian vanguard under present conditions. To chase after individuals at the expense of principles would of course be a crime. But to do everything possible to bring back outstanding yet mistaken comrades to our program I have considered and still consider my duty.

From that very trade union discussion which Shachtman utilized with such glaring irrelevance, I quote the words of Lenin which Shachtman should engrave on his mind: "A mistake always begins by being small and growing greater. Differences always begin with trifles. Everyone has at times suffered a tiny wound but should this tiny wound become infected, a mortal disease may follow." Thus spoke Lenin on January 23, 1921. It is impossible not to make mistakes; some err more frequently, others less frequently. The duty of a proletarian revolutionist is not to persist in mistakes, not to place ambition above the interests of the cause but to call a halt in time. It is time for Comrade Shachtman to call a halt! Otherwise the scratch which has already developed into an ulcer can lead to gangrene.

COYOACÁN, D.F.

23

Letter to Martin Abern[‡]

JANUARY 29, 1940

Dear Comrade Abern:

I received the communication about your alleged expression "This means split" from Comrade Cannon. He wrote on December 28, 1939:

"Your document has already been widely distributed in the party. So far I have heard only two definite comments from leaders of the minority. Abern, after he had read the title and the first few paragraphs, remarked to Goldman, 'This means a split.'"

I know Cannon as a trustworthy comrade and I didn't have the slightest reason to doubt the veracity of his communication.

You say this report "is a lie." I know by a long experience that during the sharp fight, misunderstandings of such a kind are very often without bad will from one side or the other.

You ask me whether I made any effort to check the veracity of this report. None at all. If I had spread it in private correspondence as a fact known to me, it would not have been loyal. But I published it with a remark "it has been reported" and so gave you the full possibility to confirm or deny the report. I believe this to be the best checking possible in a party discussion.

You say in the beginning of your letter: "I have disregarded in the past a number of false statements, but I note among other things, in your open letter . . ." etc. What signifies here the phrase, "a number of false statements"? From whom? What signifies the expression, "among other things"? What kind of things? Don't you believe that your expressions can be understood by inexperienced comrades as vague insinuations? If, in my article, there are "a number of false statements" and "other things," it would be better to enumerate them exactly. If the false statements are not from me, I don't understand why you introduce them in your letter to me. I can also hardly understand how one can "disregard" a number of false statements if they have any political importance: it could be interpreted as a lack of attention toward the party.

In any case I note with satisfaction that you categorically deny the sentence "this means split." I interpret the energetic tone of your letter in this sense, that your denial is not a formal one, that is, that you deny not only the quotation, but that you consider as I do, the idea of split itself as a despicable betrayal of the Fourth International.

Fraternally yours,

Leon Trotsky
COYOACÁN, D.F.

Copy to Cannon

24

Two letters to Albert Goldman[‡]

Dear Comrade Goldman,

I agree completely with your letter of February 5. If I published Abern's remark about the split, it was with the purpose of provoking a clear and unambiguous statement from Comrade Abern and other leaders of the opposition—not about the alleged hidden intentions of the majority leaders in this respect but about their own.

I have already heard the aphorism about the "second-class citizens." I would ask the leaders of the opposition: when they call the opposing group, "Cannon's clique" or "conservative bureaucrats" and so on, do they wish to make second-class citizens of them? I can only add that extreme sensitiveness is one of the most salient features of every petty-bourgeois faction. I don't know if Shachtman, for example, wishes by his "Open Letter" to make me a second-class citizen. I am interested only in his ideas, not in his psychoanalytical guessing.

I am a bit under the impression that, unnerved by a series of mistakes, the leaders of the opposition push each other into a hysterical mood and then in order to justify their factional hysteria in their own eyes, they attribute to their adversaries the darkest and most incredible designs. When they say my exchange of letters with Cannon was a camouflage, I can only shrug my shoulders.

The best treatment for petty-bourgeois hysteria is Marxist objectivism. We will continue to discuss dialectics, Marxian sociology, the class nature of the Soviet state, the character of the war, not with the absurd and criminal purpose of provoking a split, but with the more reasonable purpose of convincing an important part of the party and of helping it pass over from a petty-bourgeois position to a proletarian one.

With warmest comradely greetings,

                                                              L. Trotsky

(2)   FEBRUARY 19, 1940

Dear Comrade Goldman,

A convention of the minority is only a caucus on a national scale.* This is why it does not signify, in itself, a principled change of the situation. It is only a new step on the same road, a bad step on the road of split, but not necessarily the split itself. Possibly, even surely, there are two or three tendencies inside the opposition in respect to the split question

---

* The minority convoked a conference of their group in Cleveland on February 24–25, 1940. This conference resolved that there existed two politically irreconcilable tendencies in the party and that "*the party must extend to whichever group is the minority at the convention the right to publish a public political journal of its own* defending the general program of the Fourth International [and which] would at the same time present in an objective manner the special position of its tendency on the disputed Russian question." The majority rejected the demands of the minority.

and the aim of the convention is to unify them. On what basis? Probably some leaders don't see in their desperation any other way than a split.

Under these conditions a vigorous intervention in favor of unity by the majority could possibly make more difficult the task of the conscious splitters. Could not your caucus or possibly even better, the official majority of the NC or the PC address the Cleveland convention with a message concerning one question only, namely the unity of the party. In such a letter I wouldn't introduce the question of the character of the Soviet Union or of the mixed war, otherwise it could be understood that their position on these questions must be abandoned as a precondition for remaining in the party. Not at all. You accept them as they are, if they have a real devotion to the party and the Fourth International and are ready to accept discipline in action.

With best greetings,

Leon Trotsky

Back to the party!‡

FEBRUARY 21, 1940

Dear Comrades,

The leaders of the minority have not as yet answered any theoretical or political argument from our part. The inconsistency of their own arguments was unmasked in the writings of the majority. Now the opposition leaders seem to have passed over to guerrilla warfare: It is the fate of many other defeated armies. Comrade A. Goldman characterized aptly the new method of the opposition in his circular letter of February 12. One of the most curious examples of this new warfare is the more valiant than sensible attack of Comrade Macdonald in connection with my *Liberty* article.* He didn't find, you see, in this article an analysis of the contradictory character of the Soviet state and of the "progressive role" of the Red Army. With the same logic which he shows in the editing of *Partisan Review* as in his analysis of the Kronstadt uprising, he discovers that I am "in reality" a minorityite, a Shachtmanite, or a Macdonaldist,

---

* Major portions of Trotsky's article "The Twin-Stars: Hitler-Stalin," were published in the January 27, 1940, issue of *Liberty* magazine. The complete text is in *Writings of Leon Trotsky [1939–40]*, pp. 113–24.

at least when I speak for the bourgeois press and that my contrary declarations, capitulatory toward Stalinism, are made only in the internal bulletins for the purpose of helping Cannon. If we should express Macdonald's discovery in a more articulate manner, it would signify: When Trotsky wishes to adapt himself to the bourgeois public opinion, to make himself agreeable to the readers of *Liberty*, he writes like Shachtman, and almost like Macdonald; but when he speaks to the party, he becomes terribly antiminority. The *Partisan Review* is very interested in psychoanalysis and I permit myself to say that the editor of this review, if he analyzes himself a bit, would recognize that he has uncovered his own subconscious.

Nobody asks from the minority that they analyze in every article and in every speech the contradictory nature of the Soviet state and the contradictory role of the Red Army. What we ask of them is that they understand this nature and this role and that they apply their understanding adequately at every occasion. My article was devoted to Stalin's politics and not to the nature of the Soviet state. In the Mexican bourgeois press, there was published an anonymous statement asserting "from sources near to Trotsky" that I approve Stalin's international politics and that I am seeking a reconciliation with Stalin. I don't know whether such statements appeared also in the United States' press. It is clear that the Mexican press reproduced only in its own manner the terribly serious accusation of Macdonald and company about my capitulation to Stalinism. In order to prevent such a misuse of the internal discussion by the world bourgeois press, I devoted my article in *Liberty* to the unmasking of Stalin's role in international politics and not at all to the sociological analysis of the nature of the Soviet state. I wrote what I found more urgent for that moment. Politics consists not in saying at each occasion everything one knows, but in saying at the given occasion just what is necessary. Possibly I coincided thereby with some assertions of the opposition, but surely the corresponding assertions of the opposition were only a repetition of thoughts that we expressed a thousand times before Macdonald appeared on our horizon.

But we will pass to more serious things. Comrade Abern's letter to me is an absolutely clear enunciation of his will to split. The justification he gives is simultaneously lamentable and scandalous: these are the two mildest words I can find. If "Cannon's clique" should have the majority in the convention, it will, you see, transform Abern and his associates into "second-class" citizens. This is why he, Abern, prefers to have his own state where he will be like Weisbord, Field, and Oehler, the first of the first-class citizens. Who can decide about the places of different "citizens" inside the party? The party itself. How can the party come to a decision? Through a free discussion. Who took the initiative in this discussion? Abern and his associates. Were or are they limited in the use of their pen or their tongue? Not at all. They didn't succeed, it seems from Abern's letter, in convincing the party. Worse than that: they discredited themselves a bit in the eyes of the party and the International. This is very regrettable because they are valuable people. They could reestablish their authority now only by assiduous and serious work in the party. It needs time, patience, and firmness. But it seems that Abern lost hope in ever convincing the party based on the principles of the Fourth International. The split tendency is a kind of desertion. This is why it is so lamentable.

But it is also scandalous! The underlying tone is the contempt of petty-bourgeois elements for the proletarian majority: We are such excellent writers, speakers, organizers, and they, the uncultivated people, are incapable of appreciating us at face value. Better to build our own league of elevated souls!

In the Third International we persisted with all our power to remain a tendency or a faction. They persecuted us, they deprived us of all the means of legal expression, they invented the worst calumnies, in the USSR they arrested and shot our comrades—in spite of all we didn't wish to separate ourselves from the workers. We considered ourselves as a faction to the very last possibility. And all that—in spite of the corrupt totalitarian bureaucracy of the Third International. The Fourth International is the only honest revolutionary organization in the world. We don't have a professional bureaucracy. Our "apparatus" has no means of coercion. Every question is decided and every comrade is appreciated through methods of the most complete party democracy. If the majority of party members are mistaken, the minority can, by and by, educate them. If not before the next convention, then after it. The minority can attract new members to the party and transform itself into a majority. It is necessary only to have a bit of confidence in the workers and a bit of hope that the workers can be imbued with confidence in the leaders of the opposition. But these leaders created in their own milieu an atmosphere of hysteric impatience. They adapt themselves to bourgeois public opinion, but they don't wish to adapt themselves to the rhythm of development of the Fourth International. Their impatience has a class character, it is the reverse side of the contempt of petty-bourgeois intellectuals toward the workers. This is why the split tendency expressed by Abern is so scandalous!

Comrade Abern in his appreciation as in his perspective is moved by hatred. And personal hatred is an abominable feeling in politics. I am sure that Abern's attitude and his split objectives can only repulse every sound member of the opposition. Back to the party, comrades! Abern's way is a blind alley. There is no other way than that of the Fourth International.

Leon Trotsky
COYOACÁN, D.F.

26

'Science and Style'

FEBRUARY 23, 1940

Dear Comrades,

I received Burnham's "Science and Style." The abscess is open and this is an important political advantage. The theoretical backwardness of the American "radical" opinion is expressed by the fact that Burnham repeats only—with some "modernized" illustrations—what Struve wrote in Russia more than forty years ago and to a great degree what Dühring tried to teach German Social Democracy three quarters of a century ago. So much from the point of view of "science." As far as "style" is concerned, I frankly prefer Eastman.

The interest of the document is not at all of a theoretical character: the thousand and first professorial refutation of dialectics has no more worth than all its precedents. But, from the political point of view the importance of the document is indisputable. It shows that the theoretical inspirer of the opposition is not at all nearer to scientific socialism than was Muste, the former associate of Abern. Shachtman mentioned Bogdanov's philosophy. But it is absolutely impossible to imagine Bogdanov's signature under such a document, even after his definite rupture with bolshevism. I believe the party should ask Comrades Abern and Shachtman, as I do at this moment: What do you think of Burnham's "science" and of Burnham's "style"? The question of Finland is important but it is finally only an episode and the change of the international situation, revealing the genuine factors of events, can at once dissipate the divergences on this concrete issue. But can Comrades Abern and Shachtman now, after the appearance of "Science and Style," continue to carry the slightest responsibility, not for the poor document as such, but for Burnham's entire conception on science, Marxism, politics, and "morals." Those minorityites who prepared themselves for a split should consider that they would be connected not for a week and not for the duration of the Soviet-Finnish war, but for years with a "leader" who has in his entire conception nothing in common with the proletarian revolution.

The abscess is open. Abern and Shachtman can no longer repeat that they wish only to discuss Finland and Cannon a bit. They can no longer play blindman's buff with Marxism and with the Fourth International. Should the Socialist Workers Party remain in the tradition of Marx, Engels, Franz Mehring, Lenin, and Rosa Luxemburg—a tradition which Burnham proclaims "reactionary"—or should it accept Burnham's conceptions which are only a belated reproduction of pre-Marxian petty-bourgeois socialism?

We know too well what such revisionism signified *politically* in the past. Now in the epoch of the death agony of the bourgeois society, the political consequences of Burnhamism would be incomparably more immediate and anti-revolutionary. Comrades Abern and Shachtman, you have the floor!

Leon Trotsky
COYOACÁN, D.F.

27

Letter to James P. Cannon‡

FEBRUARY 27, 1940

Dear Friend,

I am answering your letter of February 20. The minority convention is now as I suppose, over and I believe that in the concrete tactical question which you analyze in your letter, your *immediate* moves depend at least to 51 percent on the results of this convention.

You are convinced that the minority as a whole is preparing for a split and that you cannot win over anyone else. I accept this premise. But the more was it necessary to accomplish before the Cleveland convention an energetic gesture of peace in order to change radically your line after their negative answer. I appreciate completely your considerations in favor of the necessity to publish an issue of the *New International* preparing public opinion for the split. But the minority convention took place on the 24th–25th of February and the party convention will not be until the beginning of April. You have enough time at your disposal for the proposal of peace, for the denunciation of the minority's refusal, and for the publication of the issue of the *New International*. We must do everything in order to convince also the other sections [of the Fourth International] that the majority exhausted all the possibilities in favor of unity. This is why we three made the proposition to the International Executive Committee: it is necessary also to put to a test every member of this not unimportant body.

I understand well the impatience of many majority comrades (I suppose that this impatience is not infrequently connected with theoretical indifference), but they should be reminded that the happenings in the Socialist Workers Party have now a great international importance and that you must act not only on the basis of your subjective appreciations, as correct as they may be, but on the basis of objective facts available to everyone.

W. Rork [Leon Trotsky]
COYOACÁN, D.F.

28

Letter to Joseph Hansen[‡]

FEBRUARY 29, 1940

My dear Joe,

If Shachtman affirms that the letter quoted by me about Spain was signed not only by him but also by Cannon and Carter, then he is completely mistaken. I would of course not have hidden the other signatures but they did not exist. As you will see from the photographs, the letter was signed only by Max Shachtman.

In my article I admitted that in different questions the majority comrades could have shared the errors of Shachtman but they never made a system of them, they never transformed them into a factional platform. And that is the whole question.

Abern and Burnham are indignant that I quote their oral declarations without a previous "verification." They mean obviously that instead of publishing these alleged declarations and of giving to both of them the full possibility to confirm or to deny them, I should send an investigating committee from here with five or seven impartial persons and a couple of stenographers. And why the terrible moral noise? Burnham several times identified dialectics with religion. Yes, it is a fact. But on this special occasion he didn't pronounce the sentence I quote (as reported to me).

Oh, horror! Oh, bolshevik cynicism, etc.!

The same with Abern.* In his letter to me he shows clearly that he is preparing for a split. But you see, he never pronounced to Goldman the sentence about split. It is a slander! A dishonest invention! A calumny, etc.!

As far as I remember, my article on morals begins with a remark about the moral sweatings of the disorientated petty bourgeois.† We have now a new occurrence of the same phenomenon in our own party.

The new moralists quote, I heard, my terrible crime concerning Eastman and Lenin's Testament.‡ What despicable hypocrites! Eastman published the document on his own initiative in a moment when our faction decided to interrupt all public activity in order to avoid a premature split. Don't forget it was before the famous Anglo-Russian Trade Union Committee and before the Chinese revolution, even before the appearance of the Zinoviev opposition. We were obliged to maneuver in order to win time. On the contrary,

---

* See Trotsky's letter to Abern, January 29, 1940, on page 253.

† Trotsky, *Their Morals and Ours* [New York: Pathfinder].

‡ In 1925 Max Eastman released for publication in the *New York Times* the text of Lenin's Testament and also included it in his book *Since Lenin Died*. The document, dictated between December 1922 and January 1923, while Lenin was recuperating from a stroke, included a call for Stalin's removal as Communist Party general secretary.

Trotsky later gave the following explanation for his statement at the time disavowing Eastman: "Eastman published this document without consulting me and the others, and by these means he sharpened terribly the inner struggle in the Soviet Union, in the Politburo, which was the beginning of the split. We tried on our side to avoid a split. The majority of the Politburo asked me, demanded of me, to take a position toward this. It was a very diplomatic document that I signed at that time." (*The Case of Leon Trotsky* [New York: Pathfinder, 1968], p. 429.)

the Troika wished to utilize Eastman's publication in order to provoke a kind of oppositional abortion. They presented an ultimatum: Either I must sign the declaration written by the Troika in my name or they will immediately open the fight on the matter. The opposition center decided unanimously that this issue at this moment is absolutely unfavorable, that I must accept the ultimatum and sign my name under a declaration written by the Politburo. The transforming of this political necessity into an abstract moral question is only possible for petty-bourgeois fakers who are ready to proclaim: *Pereat mundus, fiat justicia!* (the world can perish, long live justice!), but who have a far more indulgent bookkeeping for their own daily procedures. And these people imagine that they are revolutionaries! Our old Mensheviks were real heroes in comparison with them.

W. Rork [Leon Trotsky]
COYOACÁN, D.F.

29

Three letters to Farrell Dobbs[‡]

(1)   MARCH 4, 1940

Dear Comrade Dobbs,

It is of course difficult for me to follow from here the feverish political evolution of the opposition. But I agree that they produce more and more the impression of people who are hastening to burn all the bridges behind them. Burnham's article "Science and Style" is not unexpected in itself. But the calm acceptance of the article by Shachtman, Abern, and the others is the most disappointing symptom, not only from the theoretical and political point of view, but also from that of their genuine ideas concerning the unity of the party.

So far as I can judge from here, they wish a split under the name of unity. Shachtman finds, or better to say invents "historical precedents." In the Bolshevik Party the opposition had its own public papers, etc. He forgets only that the party at that time had hundreds of thousands of members, that the discussion had as its task to reach these hundreds of thousands and to convince them. Under such conditions it was not easy to confine the discussion to internal circles. On the other hand the danger of the coexistence of the party and the opposition papers was mitigated by the fact that the final decision depended upon hundreds of thousands of workers and not upon two small groups. The American party has only a comparatively small number of members, the discussion was and is more than abundant. The demarcation lines seem to be firm enough, at least for the next period. Under such conditions for the opposition to have their own public paper or magazine is a means not to convince the party but to appeal against the party to the external world.

The homogeneity and cohesion of a revolutionary propaganda organization such as the SWP must be incomparably greater than that of a mass party. I agree with you that under such conditions the Fourth International should and could not admit a purely fictitious unity under the cover of which two independent organizations address the external world with different theories, different programs, different slogans, and different organizational principles. Under these conditions an open split would be a thousand times preferable to such a hypocritical unity.

The opposition refers also to the fact that we had in certain periods two parallel groups in the same country. But such abnormal situations were temporarily admitted only in two cases: When the political physiognomy of both groups or of one of them was not clear enough and the Fourth International needed time in order to make up its own mind about the matter; or a coexistence of two groups was admitted in the case of a very sharp but limited concrete disagreement (entrance in the PSOP [Workers and Peasants Socialist Party of France], etc.). The situation in the United States is absolutely different. We had a united party with a serious tradition, now we have two organizations one of which, thanks to its social composition and external pressure, entered, during a period of a couple of months, into an irreconcilable conflict with our theory, our program, our politics, our organizational methods.

If they agree to work with you on the basis of democratic centralism, you can hope to convince and to win over the best elements by common practice. (They have the same right to hope to convince you.) But as an independent organization with their own publication they can only develop in Burnham's direction. In this case the Fourth International can not have, in my opinion, the slightest interest in granting them its cover, i.e., to camouflage before the workers their inevitable degeneration. On the contrary, the interests of the Fourth International would be in this case to force the opposition to have its experience absolutely independently from us, not only without the protection of our banner, but on the contrary, with the sharpest warning openly addressed by us to the masses.

This is why the convention has not only the right but the duty to formulate a sharp and clear alternative: Either a genuine unity on the principle of democratic centralism (with serious and large guarantees for the minority *inside* the party) or an open, clear, and demonstrative break before the forum of the working class.*

With best greetings,

W. Rork [Leon Trotsky]

P.S. I just received the Cleveland resolution on party unity. My impression: The rank and file of the minority do not wish a split. The leaders are interested not in a political but a purely journalistic activity. The leaders presented a resolution on party split under the name of a resolution on party unity with the purpose of involving their followers in a split. The resolution says: "Minorities of the Bolshevik Party both

---

* The International Executive Committee should, a long time ago, have presented such an alternative, but unfortunately the IEC does not exist.—L.T.

before and during the First World War" had their own public political journals. What minorities? At what time? What journals? The leaders induce their followers into an error in order to camouflage their split intentions.

All hopes of the minority leaders are based on their literary capacities. They assure one another that their paper would surely excel that of the majority. Such was always the hope of the Russian Mensheviks who as a petty-bourgeois faction had more intellectuals and able journalists. But their hopes were in vain. A fluent pen is not sufficient to create a revolutionary party: a granite theoretical base is necessary, a scientific program, a consistency in political thinking, and firm organizational principles. The opposition as an opposition has nothing of all that; it is the opposite of all that. This is why I agree with you completely: If they wish to present Burnham's theories, Shachtman's politics, and Abern's organizational methods to the external public opinion, they should do it in their own name without any responsibility of the party or of the Fourth International.

W.R.

(2)   APRIL 4, 1940

Dear Comrade Dobbs,

When you receive this letter, the convention will have already progressed and you will probably have a clear idea if the split is unavoidable. In this case the Abern question would lose its interest. But in the case that the minority makes a retreat, I permit myself to insist upon my previous propositions. The necessity of preserving the secrets of the discussions and decisions in the National Committee is a very important interest but not the only one and in the present situation not the most important. About 40 percent of party members believe Abern is the best organizer. If they remain inside the party, you cannot help but give Abern the chance to show his superiority in organizational matters or to compromise himself. In the first session of the new National Committee, the first decision should proclaim that nobody has the right to divulge the internal happenings in the National Committee except the committee as a whole or its official institutions (Political Committee or Secretariat). The Secretariat could in its turn concretize the rules of secrecy. If, in spite of all, a leak occurs, an official investigation should be made and if Abern should be guilty, he should receive a public warning; in case of another offense, he should be eliminated from the Secretariat. Such a procedure, in spite of its temporary disadvantages is, in the long run, incomparably more favorable than to leave Abern, the New York organizer, outside the Secretariat, i.e., outside the real control of the Secretariat.

I understand very well that you are satisfied with the present Secretariat. In case of a split it is possibly the best Secretariat one could wish. But if the unity is preserved, you can't have a Secretariat composed only of majority representatives. You should possibly have a Secretariat even of five members—three majorityites and two minorityites.

If the opposition is wavering, it would be best to let them know in an informal way: we are ready to retain Shachtman as a member not only of the Political Committee but also of our editorial staff; we are even ready to include Abern in the Secretariat; we are willing to consider other combinations of the same kind; the only thing we cannot accept is the transformation of the minority into an independent political factor.

... I received a letter from Lebrun on the IEC. A peculiar

people! They believe that now in the period of the death agony of capitalism, under the conditions of war and coming illegality, bolshevik centralism should be abandoned in favor of unlimited democracy. Everything is topsy-turvy! But their democracy has a purely individual meaning: Let me do as I please. Lebrun and Johnson were elected to the IEC on the basis of certain principles and as representatives of certain organizations. Both abandoned the principles and ignored completely their own organizations. These "democrats" acted completely as bohemian freelancers. Should we have the possibility of convoking an international congress, they would surely be dismissed with the severest blame. They themselves don't doubt it. At the same time, they consider themselves as unremovable senators—in the name of democracy!

As the French say, we must take wartime measures during a war. This means that we must adapt the leading body of the Fourth International to the real relationship of forces in our sections. There is more democracy in this than in the pretensions of the unremovable senators.

If this question comes up for discussion, you can quote these lines as my answer to Lebrun's document.

W. Rork [Leon Trotsky]
COYOACÁN, D.F.

(3)   APRIL 16, 1940

Dear Comrade Dobbs,

. . . We received also your and Joe's communications on the convention. As far as we can judge from here, you did everything you could in order to preserve the unity of the party. If under these conditions the minority nevertheless commits a split, it will only show to every worker how far they are from the principles of bolshevism and how hostile to the proletarian majority of the party. About the details of your decisions, we will judge more concretely when we have more information. . . .

I permit myself to call to your attention another article, namely that of Gerland against Burnham concerning symbolic logic, the logic of Bertrand Russell and the others. The article is very sharp and in the case of the opposition's remaining in the party and Burnham on the editorial board of the *New International* the article should possibly be rewritten from the point of view of "friendliness" of expressions. But the presentation of symbolic logic is very serious and good and seems to me very useful especially for the American readers.

Comrade Weber devoted also an important part of his last article to the same item. My opinion is that he should elaborate this part in the form of an independent article for the *New International*. We should now continue systematically and seriously our theoretical campaign in favor of dialectical materialism. . . .

Jim's pamphlet* is excellent. It is the writing of a genuine workers leader. If the discussion had not produced more than this document, it would be justified.

With friendliest greetings for you all,

W. Rork [Leon Trotsky]
COYOACÁN, D.F.

---

* This refers to "The Struggle for a Proletarian Party" by James P. Cannon.

30

Petty-bourgeois moralists and the proletarian party*

APRIL 23, 1940

The discussion in the Socialist Workers Party of the United States was thorough and democratic. The preparations for the convention were carried out with absolute loyalty. The minority participated in the convention, recognizing thereby its legality and authoritativeness. The majority offered the minority all the necessary guarantees permitting it to conduct a struggle for its own views after the convention. The minority demanded a license to appeal to the masses over the head of the party. The majority naturally rejected this monstrous pretension. Meanwhile, behind the back of the party the minority indulged in shady machinations and appropriated the *New International*, which had been published through the efforts of the entire party and of the Fourth International. I should add that the majority had agreed to

---

* This article was first printed in the *Socialist Appeal* of May 4, 1940. The minority split from the SWP after the party convention in April 1940. Burnham, Shachtman, and Abern, who held posts by party appointment on the party's theoretical organ, the *New International*, and who were trustees for the party in the New International Publishing Company, usurped the name of the magazine and appropriated its mailing rights as their personal property.

assign the minority two posts out of the five on the editorial board of this theoretical organ. But how can an intellectual "aristocracy" remain the minority in a workers party? To place a professor on equal plane with a worker—after all, that's "bureaucratic conservatism"!

In his recent polemical article against me, Burnham explained that socialism is a "moral ideal." To be sure, this is not so very new. At the opening of the last century, morality served as the basis for the "True German Socialism" which Marx and Engels criticized at the very beginning of their activity. At the beginning of our century, the Russian Social Revolutionaries counterposed the "moral ideal" to materialistic socialism. Sad to say, these bearers of morality turned out to be common swindlers in the field of politics. In 1917 they betrayed the workers completely into the hands of the bourgeoisie and foreign imperialism.

Long political experience has taught me that whenever a petty-bourgeois professor or journalist begins talking about high moral standards it is necessary to keep a firm hand on one's pocketbook. It happened this time, too. In the name of a "moral ideal" a petty-bourgeois intellectual has picked the proletarian party's pocket of its theoretical organ. Here you have a tiny living example of the organizational methods of these innovators, moralists, and champions of democracy.

What is party democracy in the eyes of an "educated" petty bourgeois? A regime which permits him to say and write whatever he pleases. What is "bureaucratism" in the eyes of an "educated" petty bourgeois? A regime in which the proletarian majority enforces by democratic methods its decisions and discipline. Workers, bear this firmly in mind!

The petty-bourgeois minority of the SWP split from the proletarian majority on the basis of a struggle against revolutionary Marxism. Burnham proclaimed dialectic materialism to be incompatible with his moth-eaten "science." Shachtman proclaimed revolutionary Marxism to be of no moment from the standpoint of "practical tasks." Abern hastened to hook up his little booth with the anti-Marxist bloc. And now these gentlemen label the magazine they filched from the party an "organ of revolutionary Marxism." What is this, if not ideological charlatanism? Let the readers demand of these editors that they publish the sole programmatic work of the minority, namely, Burnham's article, "Science and Style." If the editors were not preparing to emulate a peddler who markets rotten merchandise under fancy labels, they would themselves have felt obliged to publish this article. Everybody could then see for himself just what kind of "revolutionary Marxism" is involved here. But they *will not dare* do so. They are ashamed to show their true faces. Burnham is skilled at hiding his all-too-revealing articles and resolutions in his briefcase, while Shachtman has made a profession of serving as an attorney for other people's views through lack of any views of his own.

The very first "programmatic" articles of the purloined organ already reveal completely the light-mindedness and hollowness of this new anti-Marxist grouping which appears under the label of the "Third Camp."* What is this animal? There is the camp of capitalism; there is the camp of the proletariat. But is there perhaps a "third camp"—a petty-bourgeois sanctuary? In the nature of things, it is nothing else. But, as always, the petty bourgeois camouflages his "camp" with the paper flowers of rhetoric. Let us lend our ears! Here is one camp: France and England. There's another camp: Hitler and Stalin. And a third camp: Burn-

---

* The first issue of the *New International* following its theft by the minority carried the banner headline "For the Third Camp!"

ham, with Shachtman. The Fourth International turns out
for them to be in Hitler's camp (Stalin made this discovery
long ago). And so, a new great slogan: Muddlers and pacifists of the world, all ye suffering from the pinpricks of fate,
rally to the "third" camp!

But the whole trouble is that two warring camps do not at
all exhaust the bourgeois world. What about all the neutral
and semineutral countries? What about the United States?
Where should Italy and Japan be assigned? The Scandinavian countries? India? China? We have in mind not the
revolutionary Indian or Chinese workers but rather India
and China as oppressed countries. The schoolboy schema
of the three camps leaves out a trifling detail: the colonial
world, the greater portion of mankind!

India is participating in the imperialist war on the side
of Great Britain. Does this mean that our attitude toward
India—not the Indian Bolsheviks but *India*—is the same
as toward Great Britain? If there exist in this world, in addition to Shachtman and Burnham, only two imperialist
camps, then where, permit me to ask, shall we put India?
A Marxist will say that despite India's being an integral
part of the British Empire and India's participating in the
imperialist war; despite the perfidious policy of Gandhi
and other nationalist leaders, our attitude toward India is
altogether different from our attitude toward England. We
defend India against England. Why then cannot our attitude toward the Soviet Union be different from our attitude
toward Germany despite the fact that Stalin is allied with
Hitler? Why can't we defend the more progressive social
forms which are capable of development against reactionary forms which are capable only of decomposition? We not
only can but we must! The theoreticians of the stolen magazine replace class analysis with a mechanistic construction
very captivating to petty-bourgeois intellectuals because of

its pseudosymmetry. Just as the Stalinists camouflage their subservience to National Socialism (the Nazis) with harsh epithets addressed to the imperialist democracies, so Shachtman and company cover up their capitulation to American petty-bourgeois public opinion with the pompous phraseology of the "third camp." As if this "third camp" (What is it? A party? A club? A League of Abandoned Hopes? A "People's Front"?) is free from the obligation of having a correct policy toward the petty bourgeoisie, the trade unions, India, and the USSR!

Only the other day Shachtman referred to himself in the press as a "Trotskyist." If *this* be Trotskyism then I at least am no Trotskyist. With the present ideas of Shachtman, not to mention Burnham, I have nothing in common. I used to collaborate actively with the *New International*, protesting in letters against Shachtman's frivolous attitude toward theory and his unprincipled concessions to Burnham, the strutting petty-bourgeois pedant. But at the time both Burnham and Shachtman were kept in check by the party and the International. Today the pressure of petty-bourgeois democracy has unbridled them. Toward their new magazine my attitude can only be the same as toward all other petty-bourgeois counterfeits of Marxism. As for their "organizational methods" and political "morality," these evoke in me nothing but contempt.

Had conscious agents of the class enemy operated through Shachtman, they could not have advised him to do anything different from what he himself has perpetrated. He united with anti-Marxists to wage a struggle against Marxism. He helped fuse together a petty-bourgeois faction against the workers. He refrained from utilizing internal party democracy and from making an honest effort to convince the proletarian majority. He engineered a split under the conditions of a world war. To crown it all, he threw over this split the

veil of a petty and dirty scandal, which seems especially designed to provide our enemies with ammunition. Such are
these "democrats," such are their "morals"!

But all this will prove of no avail. They are bankrupt. Despite the betrayals of unstable intellectuals and the cheap
gibes of all their democratic cousins, the Fourth International
will march forward on its road, creating and educating a
genuine selection of proletarian revolutionists capable of
understanding what the party is, what loyalty to the banner
means, and what revolutionary discipline signifies.

Advanced workers! Not one cent's worth of confidence
in the "third front" of the petty bourgeoisie!

31

Balance sheet of the Finnish events*

APRIL 25, 1940

They couldn't foresee

"We" foresaw the alliance with Hitler—write Shachtman and Burnham—but the seizure of eastern Poland? the invasion of Finland?—no, "we" couldn't foresee these events. Such completely improbable and utterly unexpected events necessitate, they insist, a complete upheaval in our politics. These politicians labored under the impression apparently that Stalin needed an alliance with Hitler in order to roll Easter eggs with him. They "foresaw" the alliance (when? where?) but couldn't foresee what it was for and why.

They recognize the right of the workers state to maneuver between the imperialist camps and to conclude agreements with one against another. These agreements should, obviously, have as their goal the defense of the workers state, the acquisition of economic, strategical, and other advantages and, if circumstances permit, the extension of the base of the workers state. The degenerated workers state attempts to gain these ends with its own bureaucratic methods, which at

---

* This article was first published in the June 1940 *Fourth International*. The new publication replaced the *New International* as the monthly magazine of the SWP.

every step come into conflict with the interests of the world proletariat. But exactly what is so unexpected and so unpredictable about the Kremlin's attempt to get as much as it could from its alliance with Hitler?

If our ill-starred politicians failed to foresee "this" it is only because they fail to think a single question seriously through to the end. During the protracted negotiations with the Anglo-French delegation in the summer of 1939, the Kremlin openly demanded military control over the Baltic states. Because England and France refused to grant him this control, Stalin broke off negotiations. This alone clearly indicated that an agreement with Hitler would secure Stalin at least control over the Baltic states. Politically mature people the world over approached the matter from precisely this standpoint, asking themselves: Just how will Stalin accomplish this task? Will he resort to military force? And so on. The course of events depended, however, a great deal more on Hitler than on Stalin. Generally speaking, concrete events cannot be predicted. But the main direction of the events as they actually unfolded contained nothing essentially new.

Because of the degeneration of the workers state, the Soviet Union turned out at the threshold of the second imperialist war to be far weaker than it need have been. Stalin's agreement with Hitler had as its objective the securing of the USSR from a German assault and, generally, securing the USSR from being drawn into a major war. While seizing Poland, Hitler had to protect himself on the east. Stalin was compelled, with Hitler's permission, to invade eastern Poland in order to avail himself of some supplementary guarantees against Hitler on the western boundary of the USSR. As a result of these events, however, the USSR acquired a common frontier with Germany, and by virtue of this very fact the danger from a victorious Germany became much more direct, while Stalin's dependence on Hitler was greatly increased.

The episode of the partitioning of Poland had its development and sequel in the Scandinavian arena. Hitler could not have failed to give some intimation to his "friend" Stalin that he planned to seize the Scandinavian countries. Stalin could not have failed to break into a cold sweat. After all, this signified complete German domination of the Baltic Sea, of Finland, and hence constituted a direct threat to Leningrad. Once again Stalin had to seek supplementary guarantees against his ally, this time in Finland. However, he met with serious resistance there. The "military excursion" dragged on. Meanwhile Scandinavia threatened to become the arena of major warfare. Hitler, who had completed his preparations for the blow against Denmark and Norway, demanded that Stalin conclude an early peace. Stalin had to cut his plans short, and renounce sovietizing Finland. These are the salient features of the course of events in the European northwest.

Small nations in the imperialist war

Under the conditions of world war, to approach the question of the fate of small states from the standpoint of "national independence," "neutrality," etc., is to remain in the sphere of imperialist mythology. The struggle involves world domination. The question of the existence of the USSR will be solved in passing. This problem which today remains in the background, will at a certain moment come to the forefront. So far as the small and second-rate states are concerned, they are already today pawns in the hands of the great powers. The sole freedom they still retain, and this only to a limited extent, is the freedom of choosing between masters.

Two governments struggle for a while in Norway: the

government of the Norwegian Nazis, covered by the German troops in the south, and the old Social Democratic government with their king in the north. Should the Norwegian workers have supported the "democratic" camp against the fascist? Following the analogy with Spain, it might at first glance appear as if this question should be answered in the affirmative. In reality this would be the crudest kind of blunder. In Spain there was an isolated civil war; the intervention of foreign imperialist powers, however important in itself, nevertheless remained of secondary character. What is involved in Norway is the direct and immediate clash between two imperialist camps in whose hands the warring Norwegian governments are only auxiliary tools. On the world arena we support neither the camp of the Allies nor the camp of Germany. Consequently we have not the slightest reason or justification for supporting either one of their temporary tools within Norway itself.

The very same approach must be applied to Finland. From the standpoint of the strategy of the world proletariat, Finnish resistance was no more an act of independent national defense than is the resistance of Norway. This was best demonstrated by the Finnish government itself, which preferred to cease all resistance rather than have Finland completely transformed into a military base of England, France, and the United States. Secondary factors like the national independence of Finland or Norway, the defense of democracy, etc., however important in themselves, are now intertwined in the struggle of infinitely more powerful world forces and are completely subordinate to them. We must discount these secondary factors and determine our policy in accordance with the basic factors.

The programmatic theses of the Fourth International on war gave an exhaustive answer to this question six years ago.* The theses state: "The idea of national defense, especially if it coincides with the idea of the defense of democracy, can most readily be utilized to dupe the workers of small and neutral countries (Switzerland, in particular Belgium, the Scandinavian countries . . .)." And further on: "Only petty-bourgeois blockheads (like Robert Grimm) from a God-forsaken Swiss village could seriously believe that the World War into which he will be drawn is a means for defending the independence of Switzerland." Other petty bourgeois equally stupid imagined that world war is a means for defending Finland, that it is possible to determine proletarian *strategy* on the basis of a *tactical* episode such as the invasion of Finland by the Red Army.

Georgia and Finland

Just as during strikes directed against big capitalists, the workers often bankrupt in passing highly respectable petty-bourgeois concerns, so in a military struggle against imperialism, or in seeking military guarantees against imperialism, the workers state—even completely healthy and revolutionary—may find itself compelled to violate the independence of this or that small state. Tears over the ruthlessness of the class struggle on either the domestic or the international arena may properly be shed by democratic philistines but not by proletarian revolutionists.

The Soviet Republic in 1921 forcefully sovietized Georgia, which constituted an open gateway for imperialist assault in the Caucasus. From the standpoint of the principles of national self-determination, a good deal might have been said in objection to such sovietization. From the standpoint of extending the arena of the socialist revolution, military

---

* "War and the Fourth International," in *Writings of Leon Trotsky* [1933–34], pp. 299–329.

intervention in a peasant country was more than a dubious act. From the standpoint of the self-defense of the workers state surrounded by enemies, forceful sovietization was justified: the safeguarding of the socialist revolution comes before formal democratic principles.

World imperialism for a long time utilized the question of violence in Georgia as the rallying cry in mobilizing world public opinion against the Soviets. The Second International took the lead in this campaign. The Entente aimed at the preparation of a possible new military intervention against the Soviets.

In exactly the same way as in the case of Georgia, the world bourgeoisie utilized the invasion of Finland in mobilizing public opinion against the USSR. The Social Democracy in this case too came out as the vanguard of democratic imperialism. The unhappy "third camp" of the stampeding petty bourgeois brings up the rear.

Along with the striking similarity between these two instances of military intervention there is, however, a profound difference—the present USSR is far from being the Soviet Republic of 1921. The 1934 theses of the Fourth International on war declare: "The monstrous development of Soviet bureaucratism and the wretched living conditions of the toilers have extremely reduced the attractive power of the USSR for the world working class." The Soviet-Finnish war revealed graphically and completely that within gunshot of Leningrad, the cradle of the October revolution, the present regime of the USSR is incapable of exercising an attractive force. Yet it does not follow from this that the USSR must be surrendered to the imperialists but only that the USSR must be torn out of the hands of the bureaucracy.

'Where is the civil war?'

"But where is the civil war in Finland which you promised?" demand the leaders of the former opposition, who have now become the leaders of the "third camp." I promised nothing. I only analyzed one of the possible variants of the further development of the Soviet-Finnish conflict. The seizure of isolated bases in Finland was as probable as the complete occupation of Finland. The seizure of bases presupposed maintaining the bourgeois regime throughout the rest of the country. Occupation presupposed a social overturn which would be impossible without involving the workers and poorer farmers in civil war. The initial diplomatic negotiations between Moscow and Helsinki indicated an attempt to solve the question in the way it was solved with the other Baltic states. Finland's resistance compelled the Kremlin to seek its ends through military measures. Stalin could justify the war before the broadest masses only by sovietizing Finland. The appointment of the Kuusinen government indicated that the fate awaiting Finland was not that of the Baltic states but that of Poland, where Stalin— no matter what the amateur columnists of the "third camp" scribble—found himself compelled to provoke civil war and to overthrow property relations.

I specified several times that *if* the war in Finland was not submerged in a general war, and *if* Stalin was not compelled to retreat before a threat from the outside, then he would be forced to carry through the sovietizing of Finland. This task by itself was much more difficult than the sovietizing of eastern Poland. More difficult from a *military* standpoint, for Finland happened to be better prepared. More difficult from a *national* standpoint, for Finland possesses a long tradition of struggle for national independence from Russia, whereas the Ukrainians and the White Russians were fighting against Poland. More difficult from a *social* standpoint, for the Finnish bourgeoisie had in its own way solved the precapitalist agrarian problem through the creation of an agricultural petty bourgeoisie. Nevertheless the military victory of Stalin over

Finland would unquestionably have made fully possible an overthrow of property relations with more or less assistance from the Finnish workers and small farmers.

Why then didn't Stalin carry out this plan? Because a colossal mobilization of bourgeois public opinion began against the USSR. Because England and France seriously posed the question of military intervention. Finally—last but not least in importance—because Hitler could wait no longer. The appearance of English and French troops in Finland would have meant a direct threat to Hitler's Scandinavian plans which were based on conspiracy and surprise. Caught in the vise of a twofold danger—on one side from the Allies and from the other, Hitler—Stalin renounced sovietizing Finland, limiting himself to the seizure of isolated strategical positions.

The partisans of the "third camp" (the camp of the stampeding petty bourgeois) now piece together the following construction: Trotsky deduced the civil war in Finland from the class nature of the USSR; inasmuch as no civil war occurred, that signifies the USSR is not a workers state. In reality there was no necessity whatever for logically "deducing" a possible civil war in Finland from a sociological definition of the USSR—it was sufficient to base oneself on the experience in eastern Poland. The overturn in property relations which was accomplished there could have been achieved only by the state that issued from the October revolution. This overturn was forced upon the Kremlin oligarchy through its struggle for self-preservation under specific conditions. There was not the slightest ground for doubting that *under analogous conditions* it would find itself compelled to repeat the very same operation in Finland. That was all I pointed out. But conditions changed during the course of the struggle. War, like revolution, often develops abrupt turns. With the cessation of military operations on the part of the Red Army, naturally there could be no talk of the unfolding of civil war in Finland.

Every historical prognosis is always conditional, and the more concrete the prognosis, the more conditional it is. A prognosis is not a promissory note which can be cashed on a given date. Prognosis outlines only the definite trends of the development. But along with these trends a different order of forces and tendencies operate, which at a certain moment begin to predominate. All those who seek exact predictions of concrete events should consult the astrologists. Marxist prognosis aids only in orientation. I made reservations several times as to the conditionality of my prognosis as *one* of several possible variants. To clutch now, as the rock of salvation, at the tenth-rate historical fact that the fate of Finland was temporarily determined on the pattern of Lithuania, Latvia, and Estonia rather than the pattern of eastern Poland can occur only to sterile scholastics or—the leaders of the "third camp."

The defense of the Soviet Union

Stalin's assault upon Finland was not of course *solely* an act in defense of the USSR. The politics of the Soviet Union is guided by the Bonapartist bureaucracy. This bureaucracy is first and foremost concerned with its power, its prestige, its revenues. It defends itself much better than it defends the USSR. It defends itself at the expense of the USSR and at the expense of the world proletariat. This was revealed only too clearly throughout the entire development of the Soviet-Finnish conflict. We cannot therefore either directly or indirectly take upon ourselves even a shadow of responsibility for the invasion of Finland, which represents only a single link in the chain of the politics of the Bonapartist bureaucracy.

It is one thing to solidarize with Stalin, defend his policy, assume responsibility for it—as does the triply infamous Comintern—it is another thing to explain to the world working class that no matter what crimes Stalin may be guilty of we cannot permit world imperialism to crush the Soviet Union, reestablish capitalism, and convert the land of the October revolution into a colony. This explanation likewise furnishes the basis for our defense of the USSR.

The attempt of the conjunctural defeatists, i.e., the adventurers in defeatism, to extricate themselves from their difficulty by promising that in the event the Allies intervene they will change their defeatist policy to a defensist one is a contemptible evasion. It is in general not easy to determine one's policies according to a stop watch, especially under wartime conditions. In the critical days of the Soviet-Finnish war, as has now become known—the Allied general staffs reached the conclusion that serious and quick aid to Finland could come only through destroying the Murmansk railway by bombing it from the air. From the point of view of strategy this was quite correct. The question of intervention or nonintervention by the Allied air forces hung by a hair. From the same hair, apparently, the principled position of the "third camp" also dangled. But from the very beginning we considered that it was necessary to determine one's position in accordance with the basic class camps in the war. This is much more reliable.

No surrender to the enemy of positions already won

The policy of defeatism is not punishment of a given government for this or that crime it has committed but a conclusion from the class relationships. The Marxist line of conduct in war is not based on abstract moral and sentimental considerations but on the social appraisal of a regime in its reciprocal relations with other regimes. We supported Abyssinia not because the Negus was politically or "morally" superior to Mussolini but because the defense of a backward country against colonial oppression deals a blow to imperialism, which is the main enemy of the world working class.* We defend the USSR independently of the policy of the Moscow Negus for two fundamental reasons. First, the defeat of the USSR would supply imperialism with new colossal resources and could prolong for many years the death agony of capitalist society. Secondly, the social foundations of the USSR, cleansed of the parasitic bureaucracy are capable of assuring unbounded economic and cultural progress, while the capitalist foundations disclose no possibilities except further decay.

What unmasks the noisy critics most of all is that they continued to consider the USSR a workers state at a time when Stalin was destroying the Bolshevik Party; when he was strangling the proletarian revolution in Spain; when he was betraying the world revolution in the name of "People's Fronts" and "collective security." Under all these conditions they recognized the necessity of defending the USSR as a workers state! But no sooner did this same Stalin invade "democratic" Finland, no sooner did bourgeois public opinion of the imperialist democracies—which covered up and approved all Stalin's crimes against the communists, the workers and the peasants—raise a howl to the skies, than our innovators immediately declared: "Yes, this is intolerable!" And following Roosevelt they declared a moral embargo against the Soviet Union.

Educated witch doctor Burnham's reasoning on the theme that by defending the USSR we *thereby* defend Hitler, is a neat little specimen of petty-bourgeois fatheadedness which seeks to force contradictory reality into the framework of a two-dimensional syllogism. By defending the Soviet Re-

---

* In October 1935 Italian troops invaded Ethiopia (Abyssinia), then ruled by Emperor Haile Selassie (the Negus). By May 1936 the country had been placed under military occupation. Trotsky and other communists supported Ethiopia in the war.

public after the Brest-Litovsk peace did the workers support Hohenzollern? Yes or no? The programmatic theses of the Fourth International on war, which deal in detail with this question, establish categorically that agreements between a soviet state and this or that imperialist state do not place any restrictions upon the revolutionary party of that state. The interests of the world revolution stand above an isolated diplomatic combination, however justifiable the latter may be in and of itself. By defending the USSR we struggle far more seriously against Stalin, as well as Hitler, than do Burnham and company.

It is true, Burnham and Shachtman do not stand alone. Léon Jouhaux, the notorious agent of French capitalism, also waxes indignant over the fact that the "Trotskyists defend the USSR." Who should be indignant if not he! But our attitude toward the USSR is the same as our attitude toward the CGT [General Confederation of Labor]: we defend it against the bourgeoisie despite the fact that the Confederation is headed by scoundrels like Léon Jouhaux who deceive and betray the workers at every step. The Russian Mensheviks likewise are howling: "The Fourth International is in a blind alley!" because the Fourth International still continues to recognize the USSR as a workers state. These gentlemen themselves are members of the Second International, which is led by such eminent traitors as the typical bourgeois mayor Huysmans and Léon Blum, who betrayed an exceptionally favorable revolutionary situation in June 1936 and thereby made possible the present war.* The Mensheviks recognize

---

* In May and June 1936 a massive wave of strikes and factory occupations rocked France. At its height the movement involved two million workers, one-fourth of all wage earners. Trotsky's writings on this upsurge are contained in *Leon Trotsky on France* (New York: Pathfinder, 1979).

the parties of the Second International as *workers* parties but refuse to recognize the Soviet Union as a *workers* state on the ground that at its head stand bureaucratic traitors. This falsehood reeks with brazenness and cynicism. Stalin, Molotov, and the rest, as a social layer, are no better and no worse than the Blums, Jouhaux, Citrines, Thomases, etc. The difference between them is only this, that Stalin and company exploit and cripple the viable economic foundation of socialist development, while the Blums cling to the thoroughly rotted foundation of capitalist society.

The workers state must be taken as it has emerged from the merciless laboratory of history and not as it is imagined by a "socialist" professor, reflectively exploring his nose with his finger. It is the duty of revolutionists to defend every conquest of the working class even though it may be distorted by the pressure of hostile forces. Those who cannot defend old positions will never conquer new ones.

Letter to James P. Cannon[‡]

MAY 28, 1940

Dear Comrades,

... The resignation of Burnham[*] is an excellent confirmation of our analysis and prognosis concerning the ex-minority. We don't believe that it is the last separation.

W.R. [Leon Trotsky]

---

* Burnham's letter proclaiming his open repudiation of socialism and at the same time announcing his resignation from the self-styled "Workers Party," set up by the minority after their split in April 1940, is dated May 21, 1940. The text of this letter, never made public by Burnham's collaborators, was printed in the August 1940 issue of *Fourth International* and is reprinted in the appendix to this book.

Letter to Albert Goldman[‡]

JUNE 5, 1940

Dear Friend,

. . . Burnham doesn't recognize dialectics but dialectics does not permit him to escape from its net. He is caught as a fly in a web. The blow he gave to Shachtman is irreparable. What a lesson on principled and unprincipled blocs! And poor Abern. Four years ago, he found the protector for his family clique in the person of Holy Father Muste and his altar boy Spector; now he repeated the same experiment with the secularized Catholic, Burnham and his attorney, Shachtman. . . . In the good old days we waited, often for years and decades for a verification of a prognosis. Now the tempo of events is so feverish that the verification comes unexpectedly the next day. Poor Shachtman!

With best wishes,

Leon Trotsky
COYOACÁN, D.F.

On the 'Workers' Party‡*

AUGUST 7, 1940

QUESTION: *In your opinion were there enough political differences between the majority and the minority to warrant a split?*

TROTSKY: Here it is also necessary to consider the question dialectically, not mechanically. What does this terrible word *dialectics* mean? It means to consider things in their development, not in their static situation. If we take the political differences as they are, we can say they were not sufficient for a split, but if they developed a tendency to turn away from the proletariat in the direction of petty-bourgeois circles, then the same differences can have an absolutely different value; a different weight; if they are connected with a different social group. This is a very important point.

We have the fact that the minority split away from us, in spite of all the measures taken by the majority not to split. This signifies that their inner social feeling was such that it is impossible for them to go together with us. It is a petty-bourgeois tendency, not a proletarian. If you wish a new

* This article is reprinted from the October 1940 *Fourth International.*

confirmation of this, we have an excellent example in the article of Dwight Macdonald.*

First of all, what characterizes a proletarian revolutionary? No one is obliged to participate in a revolutionary party, but if he does participate, he considers the party seriously. If we dare to call the people for a revolutionary change of society, we carry a tremendous responsibility, which we must consider very seriously. And what is our theory, but merely the tools of our action? These tools are our Marxist theory because up to today we have not found better tools. A worker is not fantastic about tools—if they are the best tools he can get he is careful with them; he does not abandon them or demand fantastic nonexistent tools.

Burnham is an intellectual snob. He picks up one party, abandons it, takes up another. A worker cannot do this. If he enters a revolutionary party, addresses the people, calls them for action, it is the same as a general during a war—he must know where he is leading them. What would you think of a general who said he thought the guns were bad—that it would be better to wait for ten years until they had invented better guns, so everybody had better go home. That is the way Burnham reasons. So he abandoned the party. But the unemployed remain, and the war remains. These things cannot be postponed. Therefore it is only Burnham who has postponed his action.

Dwight Macdonald is not a snob, but a bit stupid. I quote: "The intellectual, if he is to serve any useful function in society, must not deceive either himself or others, must not accept as good coin what he knows is counterfeit, must not forget in a moment of crisis what he has learned over a pe-

---

* Macdonald, a member of the Shachtman-led split, was an editor of the literary magazine *Partisan Review*. The July-August 1940 issue contained his article "National Defense: The Case for Socialism."

riod of years and decades." Good. Absolutely correct. I quote again: "Only if we meet the stormy and terrible years ahead with both *skepticism* and devotion—skepticism towards *all* theories, governments and social systems; devotion to the revolutionary fight of the masses—only then can we justify ourselves as intellectuals."

Here is one of the leaders of the so-called "Workers" Party, who considers himself not a proletarian but an "intellectual." He speaks of skepticism toward all theories.

We have prepared ourselves for this crisis by studying, by building a scientific method, and our method is Marxism. Then the crisis comes and Mr. Macdonald says "be skeptical of all theories," and then talks about devotion to the revolution without replacing it with any new theory. Unless it is this skeptical theory of his own. How can we work without a theory? What is the fight of the masses and what is a revolutionary? The whole article is scandalous and a party which can tolerate such a man as one of its leaders is not serious.

I quote again: "What is the nature of the beast (fascism), then? Trotsky insists it is no more nor less than the familiar phenomenon of Bonapartism, in which a clique maintains itself in power by playing one class off against another, thus giving the state power a temporary autonomous character. But these modern totalitarian regimes are not temporary affairs; they have already changed the underlying economic and social structure, not only manipulating the old forms but also destroying their inner vitality. Is the Nazi bureaucracy a new ruling class, then, and fascism a new form of society, comparable to capitalism? That doesn't seem to be true either."

Here he creates a new theory, a new definition of fascism, but he wishes, nevertheless, that we should be skeptical toward all theories. So also to the workers he would say that the instruments and tools they work with are not important but they must have devotion to their work! I think the workers would find a very sharp expression for such a statement.

It is very characteristic of the disappointed intellectual. He sees the war, the terrible epoch ahead, with losses, with sacrifices, and he is afraid. He begins to propagate skepticism and still he believes it is possible to unify skepticism with revolutionary devotion. We can only develop a revolutionary devotion if we are sure it is rational and possible, and we cannot have such assurances without a working theory. He who propagates theoretical skepticism is a traitor.

We analyzed in fascism different elements:

1. The element which fascism has in common with the old Bonapartism is that it used the antagonisms of classes in order to give to the state power the greatest independence. But we have always underlined that the old Bonapartism was in a time of an ascending bourgeois society, while fascism is a state power of the declining bourgeois society.

2. That fascism is an attempt of the bourgeois class to overcome, to overstep, the contradiction between the new technique and private property without eliminating the private property. It is the "planned economy" of fascism. It is an attempt to save private property and at the same time to check private property.

3. To overstep the contradiction between the new, modern technique of productive forces within the limited borders of the national state. This new technique cannot be limited by the borders of the old national state and fascism attempts to overcome this contradiction. The result is the war. We have already analyzed all these elements.

Dwight Macdonald will abandon the party just as Burnham did, but possibly because he is a little lazier, it will come later.

Burnham was considered "good stuff" at one time? Yes, the proletarian party in our epoch must make use of every intellectual who can contribute to the party. I spent many months on Diego Rivera, to save him for our movement, but did not succeed. But every International has had an experience of this kind. The First International had troubles with the poet, Freiligrath, who was also very capricious. The Second and Third Internationals had trouble with Maxim Gorky. The Fourth International with Rivera. In every case they separated from us.

Burnham was, of course, closer to the movement, but Cannon had his doubts about him. He can write, and has some formal skill in thinking, not deep, but adroit. He can accept your idea, develop it, write a fine article about it—and then forget it. The author can forget—but the worker cannot. However, so long as we can use such people, well and good. Mussolini at one time was also "good stuff"!

COYOACÁN, D.F.

35

Letter to Albert Goldman‡

AUGUST 9, 1940

Dear Friend:

I don't know whether you have seen Dwight Macdonald's article in the August issue of his *Partisan Review*. This man was a disciple of Burnham, the intellectual snob. After Burnham deserted, Dwight Macdonald was left in Shachtman's party as the lone representative of "Science."

On the question of fascism, Macdonald serves up a poor compilation of plagiarisms from our arsenal, which he represents as his own discoveries and to which he opposes some banalities that he characterizes as our ideas. The whole— without perspective, without proportion, and without elementary intellectual honesty.

However, this is not the worst. Burnham's orphan proclaims: "We must examine again with a cold and skeptical eye, the most basic premises of Marxism." Page 266. And what must the poor "Workers Party" do during this period of "examination"? What must the proletariat do? They should wait, of course, for the result of Dwight Macdonald's study. This result will probably be Macdonald's desertion himself into the camp of Burnham.

The last four lines of the article can be nothing but preparation for personal desertion. "Only if we meet the stormy

and terrible years ahead with both skepticism and devotion—
skepticism towards all theories, governments, and social
systems; devotion to the revolutionary fight of the masses—
only then can we justify ourselves as intellectuals."

Revolutionary activity based upon theoretical skepticism
is the most awkward of inner contradictions. "Devotion to
the revolutionary fight of the masses" is impossible without
theoretical understanding of the laws of this revolutionary
fight. Revolutionary devotion is possible only if one gains
the assurance that his devotion is reasonable, adequate; that
it corresponds to its aim. Such assurance can be created
only by theoretical insight into the class struggle. "Skepticism towards all theories" is nothing but preparation for
personal desertion.

Shachtman remains silent; as "general secretary" he is
too busy to defend the "most basic premises of Marxism"
from petty-bourgeois philistines and snobs. . . .

Fraternally yours,

L. Trotsky

36

Letter to Chris Andrews‡

AUGUST 17, 1940

Dear Chris:

. . . I very much enjoyed your appreciation of the antipacifist position accepted by the party. There are two great advantages to this position: first, it is revolutionary in its essence and based upon the whole character of our epoch, when all questions will be decided not only by arms of critics, but by critiques of arms; second, it is completely free of sectarianism. We do not oppose to events and to the feelings of the masses an abstract affirmation of our sanctity.

The poor *Labor Action** of August 12 writes: "In his fight against conscription we are with Lewis 100 percent." *We* are not with Lewis for even a single percent, because Lewis tries to defend the capitalist fatherland with completely outdated means. The great majority of the workers understand or feel that these means (professional voluntary armament) are outdated from a military point of view and extremely dangerous from a class point of view. That is why the workers are for conscription. It is a very confused and contradictory form of adhering to the "arming of the proletariat." We do not flatly reject this great historical change, as do the sec-

---

* *Labor Action* was the weekly paper of the Workers Party.

tarians of all kinds. We say "Conscription? Yes. But made by ourselves." It is an excellent point of departure.

With best greetings, I am,

Fraternally,

Your Old Man [Leon Trotsky]

Science and style

A REPLY TO COMRADE TROTSKY

By James Burnham

FEBRUARY 1, 1940

Dear Comrade Trotsky:

I find the open letter which you have addressed nominally to me more than a little disarming. It is not easy, I confess, for me to undertake an answer.

In reading it I was reminded of a conversation I had some while ago with one of our good comrades from Central Europe. We were discussing, in that idle and profligate way we intellectuals have, the possible conflicts between the aesthetic sense, the feeling for beauty, and the demands of political action. He told me a story.

A number of years ago, the country in which he lived was going through a period of social crisis. The masses were surging forward, heading, it seemed, toward revolt. One morning, near the height of the movement, a crowd of many thousand workers gathered on one side of the wonderful great square of the capital city of that country. Our comrade was assigned as captain to direct one wing of the workers' detachments.

The sky was dark blue, with the white morning sun throwing across the square the shadows of the buildings that lined its sides. From the side of the square opposite the workers, the troops of the police filed out and took formation: in straight rows, mounted on their tense horses, equipment gleaming. At the shout of command, in a single swift gesture their sabres were drawn, and flashed in the rays of that white sun. The second command came: forward against the workers.

The instant had come for reply: for our comrade, to launch his wing of the workers into a driving counterattack. But for a long moment he found his will paralyzed and his voice stopped by the sensuous beauty of the unfolded scene. And all that day, while the bitter struggle lasted—more than fifty were killed that day, hundreds wounded, our comrade among them—he could not forget that sun, those shadows, that blue sky, those whirling horses and flashing sabres.

So, too, on this verbal battleground, pale reflex—and indispensable spark—of the battles in the streets, I, when all my will should be concentrated in launching my ranked arguments into counterattack against your letter (so wrong, so false, so very false), find I must stop awhile in wonder: at the technical perfection of the verbal structure you have created, the dynamic sweep of your rhetoric, the burning expression of your unconquerable devotion to the socialist ideal, the sudden, witty, flashing metaphors that sparkle through your pages.

How unpleasant and thankless a duty to submit that splendid structure to the dissolving acids from those two so pedestrian, so unromantic flasks: logic and science!

Comrade Trotsky, while reading and thinking about this letter, I recalled also the first time that I had ever given really serious attention to your work: in a lengthy review of the first volume of your *History* [*of the Russian Revolution*], published in the July 1932 issue of the *Symposium*. I reread that review, which I had not done for many years. There, too, I found that I had been compelled to discuss first of all your *style*, your wonderful style, which in fact I analyzed at considerable length. And I saw more clearly than ever before what is, in my eyes, an important truth: that you have a too *literary* conception of proof, of evidence; that you deceive yourself into treating persuasive rhetoric as logical demonstration, a brilliant *metaphor* as argument. Here, I believe, is the heart of the mystery of the dialectic, as it appears in your books and articles: the dialectic, for you, is a *device of style*—the contrasting epithets, the flowing rhythms, the verbal paradoxes which characterize your way of writing.

Comrade Trotsky, I will not match metaphors with you. In such a verbal tournament, I concede you the ribbon in advance. Evidence, argument, proof: these only are my weapons.

The skeleton undraped

I will now summarize your argument:

With reference to your own position, you assert the following:

(a) The philosophy of dialectical materialism is true.

(b) Marxian sociology, in particular the Marxian theory of the state, is true.

(c) Russia is a workers state.

(d) A tactic of defense of the Russian state in the present war is correct.

With reference to the position of the opposition—or, more exactly, of Burnham who you claim expresses the "essence" of the opposition—you assert the following:

(1) Burnham is a bourgeois democrat.

(2) Burnham rejects dialectics.

(3) Burnham rejects Marxian sociology, in particular the Marxian theory of the state.

(4) Burnham denies that Russia is a workers state.

(5) Burnham's practical politics are "abstentionist."

(6) Burnham rejects bolshevik organization theories and methods.

But you not merely assert these individual propositions. You are even more concerned to assert certain *connections* which you allege hold among these propositions.

With reference to your own position, you thus assert the following additional propositions:

(A) From dialectical materialism, *it follows that* Marxian sociology, in particular the Marxian theory of the state, is true.

(B) From the Marxian theory of the state, *it follows that* Russia is a workers state.

(C) From Russia's being a workers state, *it follows that* a tactic of defense of the Russian state in the present war is correct.

With reference to Burnham's position, you assert the following connections:

(I) From Burnham's being a bourgeois democrat, *it follows that* he rejects dialectics.

(II) From his rejection of dialectics, *it follows that* he rejects Marxian sociology, in particular the Marxian theory of the state.

(III) From his rejection of the Marxian theory of the state, *it follows that* he denies that Russia is a workers state.

(IV) From his denial that Russia is a workers state (and from 1 and 2), *it follows that* his practical politics are "abstentionist."

(V) From his being a bourgeois democrat and his rejection of dialectics, *it follows that* he rejects bolshevik organization theories and methods.

So far as I have been able, I have been scrupulously fair in presenting here your central *argument*. These eighteen propositions constitute that "unified conception" whose absence you so deplore in the point of view of the opposition. But as soon as these propositions are made *explicit*, as soon as they are brought to the surface from beneath the shrouds of metaphor and rhetoric, it is clear that *each* of them stands on its own feet, that each would have to be proved independently of the others. Moreover, the structure of your argument, of your "unified conception" and "explanation," stands or falls on the truth of *all* of these propositions. And who, even of your most ardent supporters, would be so brash as to claim that you have *proved all* of them to be true?

Examination shows, more specifically, that these eighteen propositions are either trivial or irrelevant or obviously false or at the least unproved. It would be wearisome, and unnecessary, to demonstrate this with reference to each of these propositions; every comrade has, indeed, material at his disposal to carry out the analysis for himself. I shall confine my attention to only a few of those which raise special problems.

Dialectics as a red herring

"Since in the course of the factional struggle," you write, "the question (of dialectics) has been posed point-blank. . . ." How innocent, objective, and impersonal, Comrade Trotsky! Dialectics, suddenly, like Banquo's ghost, thrust its wild face into our political midst, to dismay all skeptics. But, alas, as in the case of all ghosts, it was a very human hand that manipulated the apparatus producing our supernatural phenomenon; and that hand was yours, Comrade Trotsky. Like all good mediums, you attribute the visitation to the working of another and a higher realm—to the "logic of events," the "historical course of the struggle"—but like all good observers, we will admire the artistry, and smile at the explanation.

I can understand, and even sympathize with, your recourse to dialectics in the current dispute. There is little else for you to write about, with every appeal you make to

actual events refuted the day after you make it, with each
week's developments in the war smashing another pillar
of your political position. An argument about dialectics is
100 percent safe, a century ago or a century hence. Among
those lofty generalities, no humble and inconvenient *fact*
intrudes; no earthy test or observation or experiment mar
their Olympian calm; those serene words remain forever
free from the gross touch of everyday events.

I have participated in a number of previous faction fights,
some very bitter, some in which you also were concerned,
Comrade Trotsky. Where was dialectics then? How did it
happen that no word came from you in those times about
the dangers of my rejection of dialectics? Can it be (the suggestion is so banal as to be unseemly in these philosophical
days) that the difference has some connection with the fact
that in those previous disputes I happened to be on the same
side as you? Is the speculation altogether absurd that if, by
a chance that cannot be completely excluded, I happened
today to be with you and Cannon, dialectics might not have
appeared so, shall we say, prominently on the scene?

Comrade Trotsky, I regard you as one of the most competent historians and political scientists in the world. I did
so yesterday, when I agreed with you on most points, today
when I disagree on a number of very important questions,
and will doubtless tomorrow. My beliefs, tolerant scientist
that I am, are not at the service of my immediate factional
interests. But your qualifications in these fields do not automatically assure your competence also in the fields of philosophy, logic, natural science, and scientific method.

I find about 75 percent of what Engels wrote in these latter
fields to be confused or outmoded by subsequent scientific
investigation—in either case of little value. It seems to me
(and as a Marxist I do not find it astonishing) that in them
Engels was a true son of his generation, the generation of

Herbert Spencer and Thomas Huxley, of the popularizers of Darwin who thought that by a metaphorical extension of the hypothesis of biological evolution they had discovered the ultimate key to the mysteries of the universe. Nevertheless, Engels made a real effort to acquaint himself with the philosophy, logic, and science of his day, and wrote with this acquaintance in mind.

You, however, serve up to us only a stale rehash of Engels. The latest scientist admitted to your pages is—Darwin; apart from Aristotle, the only "logic worthy of attention" is that of—Hegel, the century-dead arch-muddler of human thought. Comrade Trotsky, as we Americans ask: where have you been all these years? During the 125 years since Hegel wrote, science has progressed more than during the entire preceding history of mankind. During that same period, after 2,300 years of stability, logic has undergone a revolutionary transformation: a transformation in which Hegel and his ideas have had an influence of exactly zero.

You ask me: "Do you hold that the progress of the sciences, including Darwinism, Marxism, modern physics, chemistry, etc., have not influenced in any way the forms of our thought?" But it is to yourself that you should address this question, not to me. *Of course* I hold that they have (and one way that they have influenced it is to show that Hegelian dialectics has nothing whatever to do with science). *How* the sciences have influenced the forms of thought no one will ever discover by spending even a lifetime on the tortuous syntax of the reactionary absolutist, Hegel, but only by studying modern science and mathematics, and the careful analysts of modern science and mathematics.

In a most sarcastic vein, you keep asking me to "take the trouble to inform us just who following Aristotle analyzed and systematized the subsequent progress of logic," "perhaps you will call my attention to those works which should

supplant the system of dialectic materialism for the proletariat . . ." as if this demand were so obviously impossible of
fulfillment that I must collapse like a pricked balloon before
it. The sarcasm is misplaced, for the demand is the easiest
in the world to fulfill. Do you wish me to prepare a reading
list, Comrade Trotsky? It would be long, ranging from the
work of the brilliant mathematicians and logicians of the
middle of the last century to one climax in the monumental
Principia Mathematica of Russell and Whitehead (the historic turning point in modern logic), and then spreading out
in many directions—one of the most fruitful represented by
the scientists, mathematicians, and logicians now cooperat-
ing in the new *Encyclopedia of Unified Science.* For logic in
its narrower sense, C.I. Lewis's *Survey of Symbolic Logic*
is an excellent, though not easy, introduction. I am afraid,
however, that in all of these works you will find scarcely a
single reference to Hegelian (or Marxian) dialectics; nor will
you in those of a single reputable contemporary scientist—
except the Soviet scientists, whose necks depend upon such
references, or one or two Kremlin hangers-on, like J.B.S.
Haldane, in other nations. The study of these works would
be not uninteresting; but I am afraid that when we finished
we would be not much nearer the solution of the question
of the role of Russia in the war.

You have an altogether incorrect idea of logic, Comrade
Trotsky. You draw an analogy between a machine or instrument and logic: "Just as a machine shop in a plant supplies
instruments for all departments, so logic is indispensable
for all spheres of human knowledge." This analogy is false.
For our politics, the analogy to a machine or instrument or
tool is not logic or "method," but the *party*; the party, the
actual party, is the instrument we use to achieve our political goals. Logic is indispensable to human knowledge only
in this respect: that logic states the conditions of intelligible

discourse, so that we "violate" logic only at the risk of talking nonsense. But no one has to know the science of logic in order to make sense or even to be a great empirical scientist—in fact very few people know logic, which is a highly specialized and, when divorced from empirical knowledge, rather useless subject. *Perhaps* a clear knowledge of logic ("method") will aid someone to make sense, to be a better scientist (especially in highly theoretical science does this seem possible); but experience does not indicate that this happens as often or as importantly as logicians would like to think it does. Otherwise we may be sure that there would be much less unemployment among logicians.

Nor is there any such thing as an "unconscious logician." I read your passage on "unconscious dialecticians"—your peasant woman and fox—with amazement, hoping to discover that the entire section was meant only humorously. But I was forced to the conclusion that you intended it seriously also. By your reasoning, a toad—or for that matter a stone—must be a scientist, because, forsooth, they both act in accordance with the law of gravity! What makes a scientist (differentiating him from a savage or a stone) is not that he behaves in accordance with scientific law—which all things do equally; and if they don't, the scientific laws are altered to explain better how they do act—but the fact that the scientist *knows* the laws, and knows them not "unconsciously" (whatever that could mean) but quite consciously, deliberately.

You tell us that workers, proletarians, are "naturally inclined to dialectical thinking." Where are these workers, Comrade Trotsky? It seems to me that you are presenting a very damaging advertisement for dialectics. The only workers I, or anyone else, know anything about are those human beings found in the mines of Kennecott Copper, the mills of U.S. Steel, the ships of the merchant marine. . . . These workers, in spite of what has been happening in the world, continue to trust John L. Lewis and Citrine and Jouhaux and Stalin, continue to vote Democratic or Republican, continue to believe in capitalism. I think they will change their thinking, perhaps one day very quickly. But I find their thought, for the most part, false or where not false, confused. If this is what you mean by "dialectical thinking," I can agree with you.

In all the elaborated confusion of your new remarks on dialectics, you make only one attempt at an *argument* in favor of dialectics; and this argument, upon examination, turns out to be both irrelevant and *reactionary*. "All the great and outstanding revolutionists," you write, "—first and foremost, Marx, Engels, Lenin, Luxemburg, Franz Mehring—stood on the ground of dialectic materialism"; whereas many deserters from the revolution began with an attack on dialectics. Is this weapon not identical in form with the weapon *in extremis* of all reaction: do you dare to disbelieve when our fathers believed, and their fathers and forefathers before them? Has not virtually every single one of us had to break through this very argument in taking our place on the side of socialism? The argument is not an iota more valid when a socialist employs it.

Even if it were true—as it is not—that *every* revolutionist believed in dialectics and *everyone* who was against the revolution disbelieved, this fact (interesting as it would be from a psychological and historical point of view) would not have the slightest relevance to the question of the truth, falsity, or scientific meaninglessness of dialectics. These are two entirely different *types* of question.

You yourself are well able to recognize this difference when you are not subordinating truth to factional rhetoric; indeed, you have often most tellingly insisted upon it. For example: in analyzing the Moscow trials, you (and all of us) showed that the confessions of the defendants could be proved false by the available evidence, by their internal contradictions, and by an understanding of the historical process which culminated in the trials. The Stalinists replied—and very effectively from the point of view of many persons—by pointing to the undoubted fact that they all did confess. We said: this is a different question altogether, independent of the question of the truth or falsity of the confessions themselves; we also have our hypotheses about why they confessed, but even if these latter are incorrect, it has nothing to do with the truth of what is said in the confessions.

Why Marx, Engels, and Lenin believed in dialectics is a problem for psychological and historical examination, and stands on its own feet.

But your account of "who believed what?" is, shall I say, a little incomplete. You turn a couple of pages of somersaults explaining away the awkward fact that Liebknecht did not accept dialectics while Plekhanov did. But how about the Mensheviks pretty much as a whole, Comrade Trotsky? I have always read that they devoted as much or more attention to writing about and defending dialectics as even the ultradialectical Bolsheviks. And, much more pertinently: what of the Stalinist theoreticians, Comrade Trotsky? The bibliography of Stalinist writings on dialectics would fill a shelf or two, I assure you. And, very conspicuously, the sectarians. Did you know, Comrade Trotsky, that of those who have been in our ranks during the past decade, the one by far most concerned of all over dialectics was Hugo Oehler? (It was Oehler, come to think of it, who was the only predecessor of yours in attacking me for anti-dialectics during a political dispute. That was over the problem of SP [Socialist Party] entry; somehow, at that time, you, Cannon, and even Comrade Wright, failed to recognize that your bloc with me was unprincipled and that principled politics demanded that you should line up with Oehler until the "fundamental question" of dialectics was cleared up. Instead, we hung together on the "conjunctural," episodic, merely empirical tactic of entry. Fortunately, we have learned principles since that day.) Isn't it remarkable that when our bookstore, under its new impulse, begins advertising treatises on dialectics, the list is mostly of Mensheviks, Brandlerites, Stalinists even . . . ? And how about Shachtman and Abern, whose dialectics haven't prevented them from going astray with me? Now I naturally understand that all these turncoats—"are not really dialecticians," are just giving lip-service to dialectics, etc.

Can it be, Comrade Trotsky, that the only really *real* (conscious and unconscious) dialecticians are: those who agree with you *politically*?

You reproach me as derelict in not taking up arms against the opium of religion-dialectics. Well, Comrade Trotsky, I will match my writings on dialectics during the past decade with yours against religion (or for dialectics); we are, I suspect, fellow sinners with respect to our antinarcotic duties.

Nevertheless, *you* have placed dialectics on the agenda. Very well. I will debate the question with you. But I will do so only when the two conditions already given in my recent article ("The Politics of Desperation") are fulfilled: First, that you make clear *what* we are debating about by formulating significantly the laws and principles of dialectics. I am not, let me repeat, merely going to juggle words with you. Second, that we discuss dialectics and not utilize dialectics as a red herring to throw the party and the International off the track of the political issues before us.

I do not recognize dialectics, but, as you say, dialectics recognizes me. Evidently, if Cannon has a majority at the convention, this recognition will be a blow on the head in the form of a resolution adding acceptance of dialectics as part of the programmatic basis of the party—if I interpret your remarks correctly, you have answered my challenge on this point even before receiving it. I do not know whether to find this plan more ludicrous or shocking. Let me ask, in an off-the-record, nonfactional aside: Whatever the merits of dialectics, do you imagine, have you so lost your intellectual bearings as to imagine, that such a question can be settled by the present sort of factional dispute, followed by a vote at a convention—a vote, moreover, which would be determined by hard factional lines drawn on quite other issues? But perhaps I can answer my own question, for there *is* a sense in which such questions get settled in such a manner—yes, the history of the past two decades has taught us how to decide even that 2 plus 2 equal 5.

I return, finally, to the query I raised in my previous article. I will grant you your "logic of evolution," from quantity to quality to united opposites, from the distant stars all the way to your dialectical peasant cook and foxes. And now, Comrade Trotsky, please, please, explain to me and all of us: how, just how, does there *follow from* any and all of this the answer to the political dispute we are arguing, a dispute over the *strategical orientation of our movement during the first phase of the Second World War?* Your inability to answer this question—and you will not be able to answer it—proves that your introduction of dialectics is an evasion, a perfumed trap for the unwary.

What are fundamentals?

It is a popular illusion of ancient lineage that the "fundamental questions" are these dealing with the grand and often-capitalized nouns like God, Freedom, Immortality, Universe, Reality, Creation, and the like. The churches have always been anxious to sustain this illusion, since these pretended questions, being outside the domain of science, can then be claimed as the peculiar province of the church, and thus the church alone gives answer to man's fundamental problem. I judge, Comrade Trotsky, from your attack on the opposition for "neglecting fundamentals," that you remain a victim of this illusion.

Since you and Cannon, following the example of Hardman, Oehler, Muste, and Jack Altman, have by now pretty clearly established the fact that I am a teacher, I shall take the liberty of drawing for a moment from my teaching experience. Many students who enter my introductory courses in philosophy have heard vaguely that philosophy deals somehow with "fundamentals"; and they register for the course with the hope of hearing "answers" to just such questions as I have referred to. To their surprise, and often to their dismay, they discover that their attention is turned to quite another set of topics: they learn to become critical of their beliefs, and how to test them; they learn the difference between significant statement and nonsense; they learn how to clarify problems and how to answer them—when they can be answered; they learn how science has developed and what the scientific enterprise means, what a hypothesis is, how it is confirmed or refuted; they learn how the vast "fundamental questions" are not genuine questions at all, but requests for emotional satisfaction—and how the abuse of the intense feelings surrounding these capitalized words has for many ages been used by church and authority, by priest and philosopher and tyrant, to serve obscurantist and reactionary ends. A number of the students resent what they have learned, feel cheated in the expectations they had formed of the course (expectations, in actuality, of verbal balm for their wounded and disoriented feelings), and they do not reregister for the second term. But others, and I believe the best of them, gradually realize that they are reaching daylight from a land of mists, and they find a new confidence like a man whose brain clears after a drunken stupor.

There are no fundamental questions "in general," Comrade Trotsky. Within each systematized field of knowledge there are certain principles which can be regarded, from the point of view of that field, as fundamental: either in the logical sense of being the basic axioms, postulates, and theorems upon which the logical structure of the field rests; or in the instrumental sense of being the directing aim or purpose which the field serves. But in each field to which we may refer, there are *different* "fundamentals."

The only fundamentals relevant to our present dispute are the fundamentals of *politics*—presumably we are not banded together as a society of mathematicians or a school of art. The fundamentals of politics are constituted by: the central *aim*, together with the most important means which are regarded as necessary in achieving that aim. Isn't that obvious? In order to remain members of one political organization, we of the Fourth International must agree on our central aim: namely, socialism. And we must agree on the most important means which we regard as necessary for achieving that aim: the dictatorship of the proletariat, the revolutionary overthrow of capitalist society, the building of the party, etc. What means are "important" and how closely must we agree on them? This we cannot answer in advance; only experience can show us, and the limits of required agreement may vary from time to time. Experience has already shown that persons cannot long remain in the same political party if they differ over such a means toward socialism as involved in the dispute over the revolutionary or parliamentary road; it has similarly shown that they can remain in the same organization when they differ over such a means as a labor party.

Our basic program (and the same analysis holds for any political party) is properly speaking simply the statement of our central aim and the most important means regarded as necessary to achieve it. It is this, for example, that, in fact, determines the conditions of membership and directs our activities. In addition, of course, in order to meet the requirements of day-to-day or even year-to-year practical activity, the basic program is supplemented by guiding statements on means regarded as less crucial or more temporary (labor party, New Deal, . . . etc.). These, though binding as guides for the party, need not demand agreement from all members, nor constitute conditions of membership.

But what about Marxian sociology (the theory of the state) and dialectics? For it is upon the alleged rejection of the former and Burnham's rejection of the latter that you condemn the opposition's "disregard of fundamentals."

In the first place, it is a direct falsehood to say that I, or any other member of the opposition, rejects the Marxian theory of the state. We disagree with your *interpretation* and *application* of the Marxian theory of the state; but all of us proceed in our analysis from the basis, among other factors, of the Marxian theory of the state. Since when have we granted one individual the right of infallible interpretation? All of the opposition disagree with your application of the theory to the role of Russia in the present war; some of us (for example, Carter and myself) believe further that the application of the theory to the whole problem of the proletarian dictatorship requires clarification. But none of us denies the theory (though naturally, for my own part, I accept it as a hypothesis, not as revealed dogma). What else but my insistence on the theory do you suppose would have led me to call my column "Their Government"—a name I selected some time *before* joining the Fourth Internationalist movement?

However, the theory of the state is not a "fundamental" of politics in precisely the same sense that I have explained. If it is fundamental, it is so from this point of view: that it has been pretty clearly demonstrated that from no other hypothesis can we consistently reach such conclusions as are embodied in many of the planks of our basic program (rejection of parliamentary road, attitude toward imperialist war, dictatorship of the proletariat, etc.), whereas any other theory of the state leads to different (and wrong) conclusions about the necessary means for achieving socialism. Thus it would seem that acceptance of our basic program logically entails acceptance of the Marxian theory of the state, though this may not be clear at every stage to every person. Nevertheless, so far as *politics* goes, it is the program and the empirical consequences that follow from it which are fundamental in relation to the theory of the state, rather than the theory fundamental in relation to the program.

But there is no sense *at all* in which dialectics (even if dialectics were not, as it is, scientifically meaningless) is fundamental in politics, none at all. An opinion on dialectics is no more fundamental for *politics* than an opinion on non-Euclidean geometry or relativity physics. By claiming that it is, you from your side, and Eastman from his, are alike submitting to the same vulgar and damaging illusion to which I referred at the beginning of this section.

You are wrong, Comrade Trotsky. The opposition is very much concerned with fundamentals, but with *political fundamentals*. Our political fundamentals are expressed by and large in the program of the International and the party. We are proposing to revise one section of that program, just as we have revised other sections in the past; but we propose to revise it precisely from the point of view of the basic and fundamental planks of the program: the central aim of world socialism and the crucial means which we jointly regard as necessary for the achievement of that aim.

Comrade Trotsky, you have absorbed too much of Hegel, of his monolithic, his totalitarian, vision of a block universe in which every part is related to every other part, in which everything is relevant to everything else, where the destruction of a single grain of dust means the annihilation of the Whole. I am as opposed to totalitarianism in philosophy as in the state or in the party.

It is false that we reject Marxian sociology; it is false that I reject fundamentals in rejecting dialectics. It is doubly false when you try to bolster up your shaky case on "fundamentals" with the pretended story that with reference to the events of the present war, the opposition has had a purely episodic position that changed and veered with every change in passing events—that "the tasks in Finland" were split from "our position on Poland," and so on. It is not we but you, Comrade Trotsky, and much more grossly Cannon, who, since the war began, have confused the party, those who read our press, and you yourselves, with a succession of bewildering shifts in position which have shown nothing but the helplessness of your doctrine in the face of events. Anyone who has read the *Appeal* knows this to be most blatantly the case. We, on our side, from the time when, shortly after the war began, we saw clearly what kind of a war it was and Russia's role in it, have consistently analyzed events in the light of a single strategical orientation—which we call the strategy of the third camp, it in turn based upon our fundamental objectives. We have made no "principled" distinctions between Poland and the Baltic countries and Finland; but you and the Cannons and Goldmans have done so, issuing from week to week, self-contradicting analyses and directives. You cannot help doing so, because your central strategical orientation—defense of the Stalinist state and its army—is now in direct conflict with the fundamental objectives of our movement, and you are attempting the impossible—to juggle them both in the same hand.

Your appeal to "fundamentals" is of exactly the same character as your essays on dialectics: a red herring to divert attention from the political issues at stake.

The namelessness of science

You make very merry, Comrade Trotsky, over the anonymity, the namelessness, of the science for which I stand. You find it most droll when our document advocates "bold, flexible, critical, and experimental politics—in a word, scientific politics." "With this formula," you remark, "one can enter any democratic salon." I want no misunderstanding, none whatever and no chance of any, on this point.

You find these adjectives "pretentious and deliberately abstruse." What is pretentious and abstruse about them, Comrade Trotsky? They are words that every child is acquainted with.

Do they describe science or not, Comrade Trotsky? And if Marxism is part of science, do they describe Marxism or not? Is it the word-magic you find lacking? Where is the dispute clarified by calling for "Marxist" politics? The dispute is over *what* kind of politics, in the present instance, Marxist politics happens to be. And for me, certainly, "Marxist politics," means "scientific politics"; if it did not, then I would reject Marxist politics.

But more may lurk here than we have yet brought to light.

Does science as you understand it, and the truths it demonstrates, have a name? What name? "Proletarian" science and "proletarian" truth, *class* science and *class* truth?

If that is right—and I cannot fathom the point of your sneers if it is not—then indeed there is a gulf between us.

Yes, most certainly, the science and the truths I stand for are anonymous, nameless. They are the monopoly of no man or group or class, but a common human possession; for them all men are equal. The truths that science tells are as true for Stalin as for Trotsky, for Morgan as for Cannon, for Roosevelt as for Browder. Naturally, the psychological and social interests (including, conspicuously, their *class* interests) of men may constitute obstacles, even insurmountable obstacles, to their discovering or admitting these truths; but the truths themselves are based solely on the evidence, and the evidence is available to all men.

You are on treacherous ground, Comrade Trotsky. The doctrine of "class truth" is the road of Plato's philosopher-kings, of prophets and popes and Stalins. For all of them, also, a man must be among the anointed in order to know truth. It leads in a direction diametrically opposite to that of socialism, of a truly *human* society.

You issue many warnings to the young comrades of our movement. I add an ominous warning to the list: Beware, beware, comrades, of anyone or any doctrine that tells you that any man, or group of men, holds a monopoly on truth, or on the ways of getting truth.

'I don't smoke . . .'

"Throughout all the vacillations and convulsions of the opposition, contradictory though they may be, two general features run like a guiding thread from the pinnacles of theory down to the most trifling political episodes . . . the second general feature intimately bound to the first, namely, a tendency to refrain from active participation, a tendency to self-elimination, to abstentionism, naturally, under cover of ultraradical phrases. . . ." Again the mighty wind of the rhetoric, the sweeping style, backed here with the delicious wit of the repeated phrase, "Thank you, I don't smoke."

The unsuspicious might gather from the mountainous style in this passage that here at last a real point was being established, and that acres of evidence, of proof, will be spread before us to justify the rhetoric. But the analytic microscope is able to disclose: exactly two, two and no more, items offered for exhibit; two taken singly, and utterly unrelated to the hundreds of other items that constitute the political course of the members of the opposition, taken singly or as a group. The opposition is "abstentionist" in practical politics because: (a) Burnham was opposed to Trotsky's appearing before the Dies Committee; and (b) the opposition rejects both sides equally in the Finnish-Russian conflict. Even if both specific charges were justified, when they are compared with the cosmic general conclusion, I can only remark with Prince Hal, as he read over the list of the colossal quantity of wine that Falstaff had ordered as compared with the tiny piece of bread: "Oh, monstrous! But one poor half-pennyworth of bread to this intolerable deal of sack!"

But let us consider also the two items.

There is not the slightest reason for considering the Dies question as relevant to the general politics of either of the two contending factions. Again you proceed from a *totalitarian* conception, which relates everything to everything, with iron bonds. The NC opposition members divided on this issue; in the ranks, the attitudes expressed crossed the faction lines in both directions. In the eyes of any sensible person, it was certainly a question about which a difference of opinion was natural, and where—assuming that there was a clearly correct opinion—a mistake is to be understood easily as merely a mistake.

But it is surprising to me, Comrade Trotsky, that you are so ill-advised as to bring up this miserable episode in the present context—as an argument against the opposition!

You have a curious way of reasoning. It is in keeping with revolutionary principle to utilize bourgeois parliamentary institutions as a forum. This is not in dispute, and never has been in our ranks. But then you go on to *deduce* from this that it was correct to accept the Dies invitation; and that, *irrespective of results*, the decision was correct, and opposition to it was a proof of violation of revolutionary politics. Your reasoning here is very similar to that which you employ in connection with dialectics and the theory of the state.

But our principle does not hold that it is *always* correct to try to utilize *every* bourgeois parliamentary institution. That would be a completely absurd interpretation. We recognize that principle does not exclude, for example, our going to court against even a working-class opponent; but we are very cautious indeed in applying this principled permission. We will sit in Congresses, but not always or in every Congress: sometimes we *boycott* a Congress, as you, certainly, should very well remember. The principle does little more than to leave the question open; the specific decision always has to be based on an estimate of how the specific situation is related to our political aims, and which tactic under the given circumstances will best serve those aims.

When the invitation to the Dies Committee came before the PC, the problem was to estimate what the consequences would be with respect to our aims; there was no problem over principle. Comrade Bern and I made one estimate; the rest of the committee, and yourself, another.

Who was right? One could not be very sure then—it was in part a guess. *But one can be sure, in my opinion, now,* because now we have the actual consequences to judge by.

I was prepared, indeed anxious (as I stated before the New York membership), to be proved *wrong*. But, unfortunately, Bern and I were proved even more correct than we had imagined.

The truth is that Dies won hands down. That is obvious to anyone who looks at events and not at abstract dogmas.

What were the actual consequences:

In the first place, we were compelled to tell a base lie to our members and sympathizers. This lie took the form of an editorial in the *Appeal* in answer to Zack, pretending that we had changed our views on the Dies Committee because of this, that and the other consideration, when in truth it was because Trotsky had been asked to testify.

The further consequences were that, through the publicity connected with the invitation and the later withdrawal, we in effect gave a partial whitewash to the committee and its purposes, to the renegades who had appeared before it; we, you might say, *legitimized* the committee *in the eyes of the radical workers* (not of the democrats, who were most of them well enough pleased with the committee for some time back). And we also gave what could only seem as a sample of cynical opportunism in our own agitation.

If you had actually appeared before the committee, this *might* have been counterbalanced by your testimony— though, having watched the committee's procedure carefully, and the publicity it received, I continue to doubt it. But you did not. Do you think your statement in the *Appeal*, with its few thousand readers, compensated for all the damage?

(Your way of reasoning here is identical with that which you employ in connection with the invitation to Hook, Eastman, et al. given at the end of our article, "Intellectuals in Retreat." Shachtman and I had sufficient wisdom to understand that none of our opponents would be bold enough to accept the invitation—we discussed the question carefully beforehand. When you read the invitation, you, misjudging the men we were dealing with, flew into a panic, and wrote in horror that we were turning the magazine over to the democrats. Experience proved that we were right and you mistaken. And now you have the temerity to accuse *us* of a lack of political sagacity!)

As for your second exhibit in substantiation of your charge of abstentionism—our policy with respect to the present war. We, you say, "withdraw from the struggle," "do not take part in this filthy business." Here your rhetoric and your content equally betray you, Comrade Trotsky. Your reasoning on the matter of the Dies Committee is of a type so peculiar that I have seldom heretofore met with it; but your reasoning on this second item comes from a well known, a very well known variety. It is the eternal charge of reaction when it attacks the supporters of *the third camp*. How many times do we find it in the writings of 1914–18! And today it reappears from all sides. In this country, the *New Leader* is perhaps the most skillful exponent, and I particularly recommend the column of Charles Yale Harrison for instances of its shrewd manipulation. How Harrison rips into the "pacifists" and "utopian socialists" and all the other "idealists"—you could have borrowed your very phrases from him. You've got to take sides now, he shouts; no more standing in your ivory tower! True enough, he takes Mannerheim's side and you Stalin's. But both of you now unite in the attempt to hide from the sight of the workers the only side that can deserve socialist loyalty: the side of the third camp. No, Comrade Trotsky, we do not withdraw from the struggle, or advocate any withdrawal. But we are concerned with whom we struggle, and for what. And we will not fight alongside the GPU for the salvation of the counterrevolution in the Kremlin.

So much, then, for the two items of pretended "evidence" by which you bolster your grandiose charge of abstentionism.

But to bring such a charge against the present opposition, and myself in particular, is—apart from your two items—to put things at their mildest, absurd. Without any hesitation, I can say with no chance of motivated denial from anyone, that of all leading members of the party, the charge of abstentionism has the remotest application to me. I am, indeed, almost notorious in the party for trying to find ways of participating in almost anything that shows itself on the political horizon: from Ludlow amendments to elections; from Ham and Eggs to labor parties; from conferences to anti-Nazi demonstrations. If any charge were to be seriously brought against me, it would—and with a certain measure of justification—be the exact opposite of abstentionism. Unlike Cannon and Cochran, I am not one of those who are able to boast about how I never make political mistakes. But my mistakes are not *abstentionist* mistakes. Even the most sung of my mistakes of the past year—over policy in auto—was the insistence that we had to head toward one of the conventions (Martin's) as against the initial Cochran-Clarke policy which was that of *boycotting both conventions.*

In this respect, furthermore, I am not at all an exception, but typical of the leading members of the opposition. During the past few years, it is from them that virtually all proposals for active participation in actions of all kinds have come, as against the passive, negative approach of Cannon-Goldman-Lewit. This difference is for the most part written into the record of the party. The record of the leaders of the YPSL [Young People's Socialist League] is most illuminating in this connection. This charge of abstentionism, like your other charges, is the product only of the nightmare you are imaginatively creating out of your own false doctrine, and has no relation to reality.

The verdict on the evidence: Proposition (5), like Propositions (3), (C), (II), (III), (IV) . . . —*unproved*; further: false, utterly false.

What are the issues?

The dominant issues dividing the ranks of our party and the International are not dialectics or sociology or logic. To pose the question in this manner is an evasion or a fraud. It is with the greatest impatience and reluctance that I have written on them to the extent that I have.

The dominant, the *fundamental* issues, in the present dispute are two, one involving the entire International, the other particularly concerning the Socialist Workers Party.

The first is the central political issue. This has been clarified and simplified by the course of events and the discussion. What it concerns is *the problem of the strategical orientation of the Fourth International in the present phase of the Second World War.* It is an issue which every single party member can understand clearly, without any obfuscation from Hegel and dialectical foxes.

The practical politics of every active and serious political organization is normally governed by what might be called a *strategical focus*, an axis around which the major part of agitation and action revolves. The popular front, for example, constituted such a focus, or axis, for the Stalinist movement during a number of years: the agitation, actions, proposals, analyses of the CI [Communist International] and its sections revolved around this strategic center. For our movement, during several years, the orientation toward the Second International was such a focus.

Today there are two tendencies in the Fourth International. They are differentiated by the fact that they propose two sharply different strategical orientations, different axes to govern our practical politics.

Trotsky-Cannon propose *the strategy of defense of the Stalinist bureaucracy as the lesser evil.* It doesn't make any difference what Trotsky-Cannon *say* about their policies; this is what it comes down to in practice. This focus governs their major specific proposals, their agitation, their interpretation of events, their predictions (not always, not consistently, but on the whole—sufficiently to determine the practical direction), their *weighting* of agitation (in the *Appeal,* for example), and so on. Let any party member retrace in his mind the events of the past months, let him read the party press and internal documents, remember the speeches and committee proposals; and he will see for himself how an understanding of this underlying strategical orientation provides a clear pattern which makes the events intelligible.

The opposition, nationally and internationally (for the dispute has of course already spread beyond the borders of our own party, as it should), proposes *the strategy of the third camp.* Any party member who makes a similar review of the actions of the opposition during this period, their proposals and speeches and articles, their interpretations of what is happening in the world, their emphases and stresses, will similarly see for himself how an understanding of this opposed strategical orientation provides an adequate pattern and guide.

This conflict of strategical orientations is the central political issue, and nothing else. When once this key is grasped, a decision should not be hard for the membership of the party and the International. Ninety-five percent of the polemical output of Trotsky-Cannon can be estimated for what it really is: irrelevance, evasion, smokescreen. The distinguishing feature of the present factional struggle is not the difficulty of the question at dispute—it is an unusually simple and direct question, but the difficulty of understanding what the question is. This difficulty results from the fact that Trotsky-Cannon, standing on a hopeless position, indefensible on its own merits, are compelled to devote their entire factional energies to the attempt to prevent the membership from seeing what the question is.

The second central issue is the question of the regime in the Socialist Workers Party. This question has been thoroughly treated in the document, "The War and Bureaucratic Conservatism." No reply has been made to this document; and it is safe to predict that no serious reply will be forthcoming.

These are the issues. The course of our movement will depend on the answers given to *them*.

Morality and polemics

Comrade Trotsky, in the course of your intervention in the present dispute, you have struck such heavy blows against the Fourth International that, for my own part, I am not convinced that the International will be able to survive them. I say advisedly that your blows have been directed "against the Fourth International"; from the narrower factional interests of the opposition they have altogether failed of the effect you have intended; the ranks of the opposition have increased and their determination been strengthened as a result of them, and it is only Cannon's followers who have been disconcerted.

You have done these injuries directly, in your own name; and indirectly, by lending your illustrious name as a cloak for the rotten clique of Cannon.

You have elected to defend a false theory and a wrong policy; and to stand as attorney for a cynical group of small-time bureaucrats. No one can choose such a course and hope to avoid its consequences; as evidenced by your recent articles and letters, these consequences step by step are swamping you.

The truth can only destroy a false doctrine; and therefore you are compelled to evade the truth, and to hide it.

To evade the truth? Witness: Your systematic failure to take up the actual problems posed not only by the opposition but by the realities of the war. Your unscrupulous dragging in of dialectics as a polemical maneuver. Your endless discussions of everything under the sun—except the actual issues which the party is facing.

To hide the truth? Yes: Your failure to mention, even, that a belief in dialectics has been professed by Stalinists, Mensheviks, sectarians, and others among the enemies of the proletarian revolution. Your never saying a word about property relations in the three Baltic countries which are now Stalin's provinces. Your failure to say a word about the shifts and contradictions in the policy of Cannon toward the war, as shown in committee votes and *Appeal* articles from the days of Poland onward. Your silence, your so very diplomatic silence, on the *specific* charges which the opposition has brought against the Cannon clique.

At the very beginning of the struggle, you made not the slightest effort to discover *what* the position of the opposition was; at every stage you have made no effort to *verify* a single report relayed to you by Cannon and his followers. In your documents you have not once tried to present fairly the position of the opposition, but have invariably given a carefully distorted account of its position—in direct contrast to us, who have always used the most scrupulous care in trying to show exactly what your position is (precisely because only in that way can the membership be genuinely educated). Similarly, on a broader scale, you have distorted what is happening in the war. You attribute to me a position on Russia, on Marxian sociology, in philosophy, which does not have the slightest resemblance to that which I actually hold, and which is well known to you. In your open letter you have gravely distorted the history of the relations between Mensheviks and Bolsheviks to accord with your immediate polemical aim.

The distortions breed offspring in their own image. In your article, "A Petty-Bourgeois Opposition . . . ," you discovered a nonexistent civil war going on in Finland. Then, in later articles, you have tried to get out of the bad hole you had dug for yourself by denying you had said what you said, by giving it another significance than that contained in the clear words of your first statement. You invented an origin in the Communist Party for the "Abern group," and make no effort to abandon the invention now that it has been undeniably disproved. You wrote of the opposition's resolution on Finland, "As to just how these three 'concrete' circumstances (in Finland and Russia) will be 'taken into account,' the resolution doesn't give the slightest inkling . . . ," when the very next lines of the resolution outline the answer to this very problem.

Your defense of a false doctrine drives you away from the truth; your defense of a bureaucratic clique compels you toward the methods of such a clique. When in the history of our movement was a more infamous, and more gratuitous, slander introduced than that footnote to the letter signed "Rork" (on the "press"), where the opposition is so clearly linked with "Stalinist influence"? Where is there a record of a more disloyal sneer than the one you direct against Abern (who has devoted his entire life to the movement) on the basis of a remark *falsely* attributed to him by the gossips of the Cannon clique?

You sin more grievously than you even understand, Comrade Trotsky. In a cheap manner you twice grimace at Shachtman for trying to "conduct the revolution" from "the Bronx." Not merely are you here appealing to a usual reactionary provincialism, directed against the metropolis. Do you know what *further* meaning "the Bronx" has in this country, Comrade Trotsky? Do you know that to nearly every American it means not only a New Yorker, but a *Jew*? And are you so naive as to think that our party—yes, even our party—is altogether immune to influence from such an association? The weapons you are now using have a fearful habit of backfiring.

You attribute to the opposition a practice of gossip and scandal-mongering. This is simply another of your "deductions" from your airy theory: the opposition is petty-bourgeois; petty-bourgeois individuals go in for gossip; therefore the opposition gossips. Now I will not pretend that in a long faction fight either side can avoid completely a certain amount of personal gossip: to gossip seems to be a fairly general human trait. However, to state that the opposition uses gossip as a *method* is simply *false*, like so much else of what you say with no evidence whatever. It is not the opposition, but the Cannon clique which employs gossip as a tool, an instrument in the struggle, and, furthermore, its chief instrument. For some while, even before the present faction struggle began, it has been systematically corrupting the minds of its followers by the circulation of the vilest personal gossip. This is today its main stock-in-trade.

I find it revealing in the extreme that the structure of your open letter is draped around three tidbits of gossip—all naturally unverified—in which remarks are assigned to myself, to Abern, and to Shachtman. This is symptomatic. The truth is that your open letter, in spite of its pretentious theorizing and its grandiose rhetoric, is in reality only a kind of apotheosis, a supersophisticated rendering, of the gutter-gossip of the Cannon clique. Stripped of its irrelevancies, this is what your open letter comes down to: Shachtman is a clownish and superficial Bronx intellectual; Abern a sly and treacherous *intriguant*; Burnham a professor. You deal with the "dialectical" variations on these themes. The Cannon hangers-on provide the juicy filling that makes them so tasty a sidedish for evening coffee.

From what source springs this unending reiteration of "academic," "school bench," "professor," "pedant," "democratic salon" . . . ? I have met this often before, Comrade Trotsky, in political struggle; and without any exception it has been a mark of reaction.

Please don't try to tell me that even the gossip of the Cannon clique represents, in a somewhat distorted form, a "healthy" and "progressive" response of the "proletarian rank and file." We know too well the originators of this gossip, and how close they are to being "healthy proletarians." The proletariat does well, I grant you, to distrust petty bourgeois, very much including intellectuals and professors. This is in particular true where it is a question of personnel, of organizational leadership. But this does not in the least alter the reactionary character of making, as you do, the sly introduction of appeals to this feeling the central focus of your attack on our *position*, our *arguments*, our policy. In the actual context of the actual struggle, these appeals to antimetropolitan, anti-intellectual prejudices have exclusively reactionary effects: they pander to backward provincialism, to antitheoretical, antipolitical even, bias. And these effects will be felt far beyond the close of the present fight. Yes, they will plague you in months and even years to come when the political disintegration already well on its way among the Cannon forces reaches maturity. Perhaps even you will be discovered to be an intellectual and a big-city man, Comrade Trotsky.

A large section of the Cannon clique—especially its articulate spokesmen—are already deeply sunk in cynicism. They have no perspective beyond their votes. This mood expresses itself in the acceptance of the principle: "Anything goes!" They act in accordance with this principle. Lies, slanders, gossip, denunciation, contradictions, brutality, fake indignation, rhetoric turned on and off with an actor's spigot. . . . Anything goes! I watched these manifestations with dismay at, for example, the New York city convention. And they do more than corrupt the members of the Cannon clique itself. Many comrades came to me during the course of the New York city convention and remarked that they "were certainly learning a lot about politics through the faction fight"; alas, the lesson that Cannon and Cochran and Lewit and Gordon were teaching them was the lesson of "anything goes." You have done nothing to counteract that lesson.

You attempt to turn aside all criticism of your "methods" by two devices: You say that all who mention methods do so because they are losing on the field of political principles. You say that anyone who objects is doing so from the point of view of God or the Kantian categorical imperative or "the eternal norms of petty-bourgeois morality." This is sometimes, even often, the case. But I have no intention of remaining silent about the methods you are now using out of any fear of being called a petty bourgeois. My moral norms are not drawn from either religion or Kant, and we have refuted your present political policy with arguments and evidence, with a finality that I do not expect you even to try to challenge on its merits.

Yes, I judge a political struggle *morally* as well as politically. Socialism is a moral ideal, which reflective men choose deliberately, by a moral act. Cold and sober scientific analysis convinces me that this ideal dictates an appropriate morality which must govern the struggle for it. Just as we say that the white man cannot be free while the black man is enslaved, so a social order based upon truth and freedom and loyal cooperation cannot be won by those who in their relations with each other base their methods of action on lies and disloyalty and slander. It is dangerous to have a false political policy. But it need not be fatal: for the policy can be changed, if a critical, democratic, and loyal *morale* prevails, when experience makes clearer the need for change. But it is disastrous if the very springs of action are poisoned.

You conclude your letter on a strange note, Comrade Trotsky. "If," you say to me, "we can arrive at an agreement with you on the basis of these principles, then without difficulty we shall find a correct policy in relation to Poland, Finland, and even India. At the same time, I pledge myself to help you conduct a struggle against any manifestation whatsoever of bureaucratism and conservatism. . . ." In the face of the events of these past months, you will understand why such a pledge can carry little weight for me. As to agreement on principles: There is only one way in which such agreement is possible for me—when I am convinced that my principles are wrong, and others are right. And I am afraid that the metaphors, even of a Shakespeare, would not be enough to convince me.

Letter of resignation of James Burnham from the Workers Party

To the National Committee of the Workers Party:

I am compelled to place before the committee the question of my status in relation to the newly formed Workers Party.

The faction fight in the Socialist Workers Party, its conclusion, and the recent formation of the Workers Party have been in my own case, the unavoidable occasion for the review of my own theoretical and political beliefs. This review has shown me that by no stretching of terminology can I any longer regard myself, or permit others to regard me, as a Marxist.

Of the most important beliefs, which have been associated with the Marxist movement, whether in its reformist, Leninist, Stalinist, or Trotskyist variants, there is virtually none which I accept in its traditional form. I regard these beliefs as either false or obsolete or meaningless; or in a few cases, as at best true only in a form so restricted and modified as no longer properly to be called Marxist.

This communication is not meant to be an elaborate analysis or a lengthy personal credo. Nevertheless, I wish to illustrate my opinion with a few specific examples:

I reject, as you know, the "philosophy of Marxism," dialectical materialism. I have never, it is true, accepted this philosophy. In the past I excused this discrepancy and compromised

341

this belief with the idea that the philosophy was "unimportant" and "did not matter" so far as practice and politics were concerned. Experience, and further study and reflection, have convinced me that I have been wrong and Trotsky—with so many others—right on this score; that dialectical materialism though scientifically meaningless, is psychologically and historically an integral part of Marxism, and does have its many and adverse effects upon practice and politics.

The general Marxian theory of "universal history," to the extent that it has any empirical content, seems to me disproved by modern historical and anthropological investigation.

Marxian economics seems to me for the most part either false or obsolete or meaningless in application to contemporary economic phenomena. Those aspects of Marxian economics which retain validity do not seem to me to justify the theoretical structure of the economics.

Not only do I believe it meaningless to say that "socialism is inevitable" and false that socialism is "the only alternative to capitalism"; I consider that on the basis of the evidence now available to us a new form of exploitive society (what I call "managerial society") is not only possible as an alternative to capitalism but is a more probable outcome of the present period than socialism.

As you know, I do not believe that Russia can be considered a "workers state" in any intelligible sense of the term. This opinion, however, is related to far more basic conclusions: for example, that Stalinism must be understood as one manifestation of the same general historical forces of which fascism is another manifestation. There is still doubt in my mind as to whether this conclusion applies also to Leninism and Trotskyism.

I disagree flatly and entirely, as Cannon has understood for a long while, with the Leninist conception of a party—not merely with Stalin's or Cannon's modifications of that

conception, but with Lenin's and Trotsky's. I disagree with
the theory of the party, but even more, and more important,
with the established pattern of behavior which displays the
character of the party as a living reality. The Leninist type
of party seems to me incompatible with genuine scientific
method and genuine democracy.

In the light of such beliefs, and others similar to them, it
goes without saying that I must reject a considerable part of
the programmatic documents of the Fourth Internationalist
movement (accepted by the Workers Party). The "transition
program" document seems to me—as it pretty much did
when first presented—more or less arrant nonsense, and a
key example of the inability of Marxism, even in the hands
of its most brilliant intellectual representative, to handle
contemporary history.

These beliefs, especially in their negative aspect—that is,
insofar as they involve disagreement with Marxism—are not
at all "sudden" or episodic, nor are they products merely of
the recent faction struggle. Several I have always held. Many
others I have held for some years. Others have, during the
past year or two, changed from doubt and uncertainty into
conviction. The faction fight has only served to compel me
to make them explicit and to consider them more or less in
their entirety. I understand, naturally, that many of them
are not "new" or "original," and that in holding some of
them I find myself in very bad company. However, I have
never been able to judge the truth of beliefs by the moral
character of those who hold them.

The newly formed Workers Party is a Marxist party, and
more particularly a bolshevik, a Leninist party. This is not
a mere matter of definition. It is guaranteed alike by its pro-

grammatic documents (especially the key document on "The Aims, the Tasks, and the Structure of the Workers Party"), by the statements and convictions of the overwhelming majority of its leadership and of a substantial majority of its membership, and by the habits of action of this majority. It is strikingly symbolized by the statement on the masthead of *Labor Action* that the party is a section of the Fourth International, by the definition of its theoretical magazine as "an organ of revolutionary Marxism," by the reiterated appeal in the key document above mentioned to "the revolutionary traditions of Marx, Engels, Lenin, and Trotsky" and to the "principles of Marxism," and by the convention episode of the cable to Trotsky. Nothing whatever in the faction fight indicated a decisive tendency away from this orientation; on the contrary, every sharp suggestion in such a direction was at once blocked. In reality, the split from the Socialist Workers Party was not based upon anything fundamental, and the Workers Party exists now as a faction of the Trotskyist movement. This was the actual cause of the extreme difficulty which the faction found in drawing up its position on "the nature of the party," and in differentiating that position from Cannon's. This was hard to do, was in fact not done, because the two positions, except in details and emphases, did not really differ.

I do not, of course, wish to mitigate my own share of responsibility of what happened in the immediate and the more distant past. I wish here to record the facts as I see them, among which is the fact that I have not been a full-time political worker and have not accepted a full share of organizational responsibility.

From the facts about my own present beliefs and the character of the Workers Party, the following conclusion

inescapably follows: I cannot be a loyal member of the
Workers Party; I cannot accept its program or discipline; I
cannot speak or act for it. Naturally I do not disagree with
everything for which the Workers Party stands. I believe
that socialism would be a good thing if it can be achieved
(though "socialism as a moral ideal" is in bad repute among
Marxists, we learn). I agree with the Workers Party attitude toward the war, at least insofar as this was involved
in the just concluded faction dispute. But I share agreement
on those points with many other organizations and tens
of thousands of individuals wholly apart from the Workers Party. To the extent that I function politically, I cannot
confine what I say and do to rhapsodies on the desirability
of socialism and denunciations of both camps in the war.
This was brought home to me with particular keenness by
the first public mass meeting of the Workers Party. For I
tried to figure out what I could say, and I could not find
any way of saying what I felt I ought to say and still appear
on the platform as a loyal spokesman of the group. I finally
compromised once more, spoke "safely" on the third camp,
and felt like a liar when I had finished.

Two alternatives only, therefore, present themselves
to me:

Continuing as a member of the party, I can immediately
launch a faction struggle along the lines suggested by this
document. This struggle would, of course, be, from a political and theoretical standpoint, far broader and more
fundamental than the struggle just concluded with Cannon
and would have as its general aim, from my standpoint, to
break the group altogether away from Marxism.

Or I can simply separate from the Workers Party.

From the usual conception of "principled" and "responsible" politics, the first course is incumbent upon me.
However, I do not believe that it makes sense under the

actual circumstances. On the one hand, a sharp faction struggle now in the Workers Party (in which my point of view would be supported by a very small minority) would mean the breakup of the group, at the very least its reduction to impotence and it begins with foundations none too firm. What could be gained would not be worthwhile, would simply not mean anything politically. On the other hand, I personally am not willing to undertake leadership in such a struggle. I am not, have not been, and cannot be a "practical politician" and "organization man," above all not a leader.

Thus the second course alone remains.

It will be thought and said by many that my present beliefs and the decision which follows from them are a "rationalization" of, on the one side, the pressure of a soft and bourgeois personal environment, and, on the other, the influence of the terrible defeats of labor, and mankind during the past twenty years, and of the war crisis.

I should be the last to pretend that any man should be so brash as to imagine that he knows clearly the motives and springs of his own actions. This whole letter may be an overelaborate way of saying the single sentence: "I feel like quitting politics." It is certainly the case that I am influenced by the defeats and betrayals of the past twenty and more years. These form part of the evidence for my belief that Marxism must be rejected: at every single one of the many tests provided by history, Marxist movements have either failed socialism or betrayed it. And they influence also my feelings and attitudes, I know that.

As for my "personal life," how is one ever to know which is chicken and which egg, whether unwillingness fully to enter Marxist politics confuses beliefs, or whether clear beliefs keep one from entering Marxist politics fully? I am a little tired, I confess, of the habit of settling accounts with opponents and critics, of deciding scientific disputes by smug references to "rationalizations" and the "pressure of alien classes and influences." Because this habit is a well-established part of the tradition of Marxism is not the least of my objections to Marxism.

My beliefs are facts; and the defeats and betrayals, and the mode of my life and my tastes are also facts. There they are, whatever the truth about sources and origins and motives.

On no ideological, theoretic, or political ground, then, can I recognize, or do I feel, any bond or allegiance to the Workers Party (or to any other Marxist party). That is simply the case, and I can no longer pretend about it, either to myself or to others.

Unfortunately, one factor still remains. This factor is a sense of moral obligation and responsibility to my past self—seven years dominated, however inadequately but on the whole, by Marxism or any comparable structure, cannot be wiped out by a few minutes at the typewriter—and more especially to other *persons*, to those with whom I have joined in loyal collaboration on both sides, and to others who have been influenced in their ideas and acts by me. Trotsky and Cannon will exploit my decision as a confirmation of their *views*—Burnham's quitting will be, by their remarkable but humanly understandable logic, evidence for the truth of their opinions on the character of the war, the nature of the Russian state, and the role of Russia in the war. To many members of the Workers Party, my separation will appear as a desertion. From a moral and personal point of view, I cannot but agree that there will be a good deal of truth in this latter judgment.

But this factor, weighed against the others, is no longer sufficient to decide my actions. Indeed, it now seems clear to me that if it had not been for these moral and personal considerations, I should properly have left the party some while ago. On the grounds of beliefs and interests (which are also a fact) I have for several years had no real place in a Marxist party.

This communication constitutes my definitive resignation from the group. However, because of the obligations which I recognize, I am, within strict limitations, prepared to discuss with the committee, if the committee so wishes, the manner of my separation. There are four alternatives:

1. The committee can expel me. There would be no difficulty in finding grounds for expulsion: I have already written an article, which, if published in the nonparty press (and there is the opportunity for such publication), would be adequate grounds.

2. I can simply withdraw, without any special notice being taken on either side, from the group and its activities.

3. I can be, nominally, granted a "leave of absence" for six months. If this alternative were chosen, there should be no misunderstanding. The future is never certain, but the probability of such a leave's coming to an end would be very slight indeed.

4. I am, finally, prepared, if the committee feels that it would make any serious difference in this first period of the group's independent existence, to carry out a form of partial collaboration during the next two months. This would consist primarily of writing signed and unsigned articles for the party press, consistent with the party's position; and during that time refraining from public acts contrary to the party and its program. At the conclusion of these two months, any of the three other alternatives could be put into effect.

I would not like this fourth solution, to be quite honest, but, as I have stated, I am prepared to accept it.

Writing this letter has been a painful and difficult task for me. It is in no way an impulsive act, but has been preceded by the most careful and lengthy deliberation. I am above all anxious that I avoid giving any impression that I seek to excuse or extenuate myself, my own weaknesses or deficiencies or failures. I do not propose to blame others or history for my faults. When I say that I reject Marxism, I do not at all mean that I am scornful of or consider myself "superior to" Marxists. Not at all. I am humble, believe me, before the loyalty, sacrifice, and heroism of so many Marxists— qualities found so widely within the ranks of the Workers Party. But I cannot act otherwise than I do.

Believing as I do, I cannot wish success to the Workers Party; but I can and do wish its members well. To the extent that each of us, in his own way and arena, preserves the values and truth and freedom, I hope that we shall continue to regard ourselves as comrades, whatever names we use and whatever labels may be tied around our necks.

Fraternally yours,

James Burnham
NEW YORK

Abern, Martin (1898–1949) – a founder of U.S. Communist Party and member of its Central Committee; expelled 1928 with Cannon and Shachtman for support of Bolshevik-Leninist opposition; founding member of Communist League of America; a leader of minority faction in 1940 SWP split.

Altman, Jack (b. 1905) – a leader of Socialist Party and head of its New York Local; helped carry out expulsion of left-wing caucus in 1937.

Andrews, Chris (Christy Moustakis) (1911–1989) – SWP member assigned as armed guard at Trotsky home in Mexico; left SWP after World War II.

Anglo-Russian Trade Union Unity Committee – founded May 1925 by leadership of British and Soviet trade unions; criticized by Trotsky as providing cover to policies of British union bureaucracy; dissolved September 1927 when British members walked out.

Berdyaev, Nikolai A. (1874–1948) – reactionary Russian mystic; claimed in his early writings to be influenced by Marxism.

Bern, Irving (Paul Bernick) (b. 1915) – SWP member and leader of Young People's Socialist League; supported minority in 1940 split.

Bernstein, Eduard (1850–1932) – prominent member of Social Democratic Party in Germany; after 1896 a leading proponent of class collaborationism.

Blum, Léon (1872–1950) – leader of Socialist Party of France; premier in first People's Front government 1936–37.

Bogdanov, A.A. (1873–1928) – leader of an ultraleft and philosophically idealist current in Bolshevik Party after 1905 revolutions; expelled 1909.

Bolshevik Party – originated 1903 as majority faction of Russian Social Democratic Labor Party; led October 1917 revolution; became Communist Party of Russia (Bolsheviks) in 1918.

Bonapartism – a regime that originates in a period of social crisis and concentrates executive power in the hands of a "strong man"; the Bonapartist leader presents himself as standing above contending class forces, with the aim of maintaining the power of the dominant social class or layer; term originates from the regime of Louis-Napoleon Bonaparte in France 1852–70.

Bordiga, Amadeo (1889–1970) – founder of Italian CP and leader of ultraleft current in Comintern; collaborated briefly with International Left Opposition after his expulsion from CP in 1930; led small ultraleft current until his death.

Brockway, Fenner (1890–1988) – leader of Independent Labour Party of Britain; secretary of centrist London Bureau; opponent of Fourth International.

Browder, Earl (1891–1973) – general secretary of Communist Party of U.S. 1930–45; expelled 1946 as scapegoat for CP's openly pro-imperialist policy dictated by Stalin in World War II.

Bruno R. (Bruno Rizzi) (1901–1977) – former member of Italian CP; briefly collaborated with Fourth International; author of book analyzing Soviet Union as bureaucratic collectivist.

Bulgakov, Sergei (1871–1944) – Russian economist and philosopher influenced by Marxism during 1890s.

Burnham, James (1905–1987) – philosophy professor at New York University; participated as leader of American Workers Party in 1934 fusion with Communist League;

member of SWP Political Committee; a leader of minority faction in April 1940 split; resigned from newly formed Workers Party May 1940; author of *The Managerial Revolution* 1941; subsequently became open anti-communist and worked for Central Intelligence Agency; later editor of *National Review*.

Cannon, James P. (1890–1974) – founding leader of SWP; originally IWW organizer and leader of SP left wing; founder of Communist Party and a central leader during 1920s; expelled 1928 for supporting Bolshevik-Leninist opposition; first editor of *Militant*; founding leader of Communist League of America 1929; national secretary of SWP 1938–53; subsequently national chairman.

Carter, Joseph (1910–196?) – member of SWP National Committee; with Burnham, held that USSR was neither capitalist nor workers state in 1937 discussion; supported minority in 1940 split.

Chamberlain, Neville (1869–1940) – Conservative Party prime minister of Britain 1937–40; signer of 1938 Munich pact with Hitler.

Cheka – abbreviated name of Soviet police force set up after October revolution to combat counterrevolutionary terror and sabotage; later renamed GPU.

Ciliga, Anton (1898–1992) – leader of Yugoslav CP imprisoned in USSR until 1935 for support to Left Opposition, which he collaborated with subsequently in exile; broke with Marxist movement in late 1930s.

Citrine, Walter (1887–1983) – general secretary of Trades Union Congress of Britain 1926–46.

Clarke, George (1913–1964) – joined Communist League of America 1929; member of SWP National Committee; supporter of majority in 1939–40 fight; left SWP in 1953.

Cochran, Bert (1915–1984) – joined Communist League of America 1934; member of SWP National Committee and leader of party's participation in struggles of auto workers' union; supporter of majority in 1939–40 fight; left SWP in 1953.

Comintern (Communist or Third International) – organized
1919 as world revolutionary party following capitulation
to imperialism by Social Democratic (Second)
International; under Stalin became counterrevolutionary
instrument of Soviet foreign policy and furthered
interests of the privileged caste; dissolved in 1943.

Corey, Lewis (1894–1953) – writer and professor; as Louis
Fraina, founding leader of Communist movement in
U.S.; left CP in early 1920s; repudiated Marxism in
1940.

Dan, Fyodor Ilyich (1871–1947) – a central leader of Russian
Mensheviks; leading opponent of October revolution;
later became editor of émigré Menshevik journal.

Darwin, Charles (1809–1882) – founder of evolutionary
biology; author of *Origin of Species*.

Dewey Commission – Commission of Inquiry into the
Charges Made against Leon Trotsky in the Moscow
Trials, chaired by U.S. liberal educator John Dewey
(1859–1952); held hearings in 1937; its findings were
contained in 1938 report titled *Not Guilty*.

Dies Committee – House Un-American Activities Committee
(HUAC) chaired by Rep. Martin Dies; held hearings to
expose "extremist" organizations.

Dobbs, Farrell (1907–1983) – joined Communist League of
America 1934; a leader of 1934 Minneapolis Teamsters
strikes and Teamsters union organizer during 1930s;
became SWP labor secretary in 1939; SWP national
secretary 1953–72.

Dubrovinsky, I.F. (1877–1913) – a leader of Bolshevik Party in
Moscow; supporter of conciliation with Mensheviks.

Dunne, Vincent R. (1890–1970) – founding member of
Communist Party; expelled 1928 for support of
Bolshevik-Leninists; founding member of Communist
League of America; a central leader of 1934
Minneapolis Teamsters strikes; supporter of majority in
1939–40 fight; longtime leader of SWP.

Eastman, Max (1883–1969) – editor of *Masses* before World

War I and supporter of Russian revolution; early
sympathizer of Trotsky in 1920s and translator of
several of his works; renounced socialism by end of
1930s; later became open anticommunist and an editor
of *Reader's Digest.*

Economists – supporters of a reformist trend in Russian Social
Democracy at turn of century; counterposed fight
around immediate economic issues to the social and
political struggle for working-class emancipation.

Engels, Frederick (1820–1895) – lifelong collaborator of Karl
Marx and cofounder with him of modern communist
workers movement.

Field, B.J. (1900–1977) – member of Communist League of
America expelled 1932 for indiscipline; readmitted 1933
on Trotsky's urging; expelled 1934 for indiscipline in
New York hotel workers' strike; subsequently leader of
League for a Revolutionary Workers Party.

Fourth International – formed 1938 by forces seeking to
rebuild international communist movement; most
prominent leader was Trotsky.

Freiligrath, Ferdinand (1810–1876) – noted German poet;
member of Communist League and collaborator of
Marx and Engels; withdrew from political activity in
1850s.

Frey, Josef (1882–1957) – a leader of communist opposition
group in Austria; was briefly affiliated to International
Left Opposition in early 1930s.

Gandhi, Mohandas (1869–1948) – leader of Indian
independence movement from British rule; advocated
pacifist civil disobedience as political strategy.

Gerland (Jean Van Heijenoort) (1912–1986) – a secretary to
Trotsky 1932–39; moved to New York November 1939
to take on responsibilities for International Secretariat
of Fourth International; left Marxist movement in 1946.

Goldman, Albert (1897–1960) – a leader of SWP and Trotsky's
U.S. lawyer; supporter of majority in 1939–40 fight; left
SWP 1946.

Gordon, Sam (1910–1982) – joined Communist League of America 1930; member of SWP National Committee and supporter of majority in 1939–40 fight.

Gorky, Maxim (1868–1936) – prominent Russian writer; sympathizer of Bolsheviks before 1917; critical of Soviet regime in its early years; later publicly supported Stalin.

Gould, Nathan (b. 1913) – member of SWP National Committee; national secretary Young People's Socialist League; supported minority in 1940 split.

GPU – originally known as Cheka, which was set up after October revolution to combat counterrevolutionary terror and sabotage; transformed into Stalin's secret political police and terror squad; later renamed KGB.

Green, William (1873–1952) – president of American Federation of Labor 1924–52.

Hansen, Joseph (1910–1979) – joined Communist League of America 1934; secretary to Leon Trotsky 1937–40; longtime leader of SWP until his death; served as editor of the *Militant, International Socialist Review,* and *Intercontinental Press.*

Hardman, J.B.S. (J.B. Salutsky) (1882–1968) – educational director for Amalgamated Clothing Workers union 1920–40; leader of American Workers Party led by A.J. Muste; opponent of 1934 fusion with Communist League and quit the new organization.

Hegel, Georg Wilhelm (1770–1831) – philosopher whose writings systematized, from an idealist viewpoint, the dialectical character of development in nature and society.

Hitler, Adolf (1889–1945) – leader of National Socialist Workers Party (Nazis); became head of German state in 1933; organized fascist forces to smash workers movement and later carry out extermination campaign against Jews, Gypsies, and others.

Hook, Sidney (1902–1989) – professor of philosophy at New York University; sympathizer of communist movement in 1930s; a leader of American Workers Party founded by A.J. Muste; became vocal anticommunist in 1940s.

Huysmans, Camille (1871–1968) – leader of Belgian Workers Party; secretary of Second International 1905–22; served in Belgian government after World War II.

ILP (Independent Labour Party) – founded 1893; broke with British Labour Party and Second International in 1932 and briefly advocated new revolutionary International; reaffiliated to Labour Party in 1939.

Iskra (The Spark) – first all-Russian Marxist newspaper; founded by Lenin and others in 1900.

Johnson, J.R. (C.L.R. James) (1901–1989) – noted author from Trinidad; supporter of Fourth International who moved to U.S. from Britain in 1938 and joined SWP; supported minority in 1940 split; rejoined SWP 1947 but left in 1951.

Jouhaux, Léon (1879–1954) – head of General Confederation of Labor of France 1909–40, 1945–47.

Kamenev, Lev B. (1883–1936) – longtime Bolshevik Party leader; opposed course toward seizure of power on eve of October 1917 revolution; joined with Stalin in anti-Trotsky bloc 1923–25; joined Trotsky and Zinoviev in United Opposition 1926–27; recanted 1928; executed during Moscow frame-up trials.

Kant, Immanuel (1724–1804) – liberal philosopher who developed theory of ethics based on universal moral law, the "categorical imperative."

Kautsky, Karl (1854–1938) – leading member of Social Democratic Party in Germany; collaborator of Engels; author of works on history and Marxist theory; leading apologist for prowar leaders of Second International during World War I; opposed October 1917 Russian revolution.

Kerensky, Alexander (1881–1970) – prime minister of capitalist Provisional Government in Russia from July 1917 until Bolshevik-led seizure of power by soviets in October.

Kuusinen, Otto (1881–1964) – member of Finnish soviet government 1918; founding member of Finnish CP; key figure in Comintern under Stalin; named head of Soviet-created Finnish "government" 1939; president of Soviet Finno-Karelian Republic 1940–56.

Labriola, Antonio (1843–1904) – Italian Marxist; author of *Essays on the Materialist Conception of History* and *Socialism and Philosophy.*

Landau, Kurt (1903–1937) – a central leader of Left Opposition in Germany; led split from German section in 1931.

Lebrun (Mario Pedrosa) (1905–1982) – leader of Brazilian section of Fourth International and member of International Executive Committee; supported minority in 1940 SWP split.

Left Opposition – organized 1923 by Trotsky and other communists fighting to maintain Lenin's revolutionary course in face of political counterrevolution led by privileged bureaucratic caste in Soviet Union; organized on international basis in 1930 following Trotsky's exile from Soviet Union; became Fourth International in 1938.

Lenin, Vladimir Ilyich (1870–1924) – founder of Bolshevik Party; chair of Council of People's Commissars (Soviet government) 1917–24; central leader of Communist International.

Lewis, John L. (1880–1969) – president of United Mine Workers union 1919–60; president of CIO 1935–40.

Lewit, Morris (Morris Stein) (1903–1998) – member of SWP National Committee and supporter of majority in 1939–40 fight.

Liebknecht, Karl (1871–1919) – only Social Democratic member of German parliament to vote against funding for World War I in 1914; imprisoned 1916–18 for antiwar activities; a founding leader of Communist Party of Germany; murdered by army officers instigated by Social Democratic government.

Luxemburg, Rosa (1871–1919) – leader of revolutionary wing of German Social Democratic Party; jailed 1915 for opposing World War I; founder of Spartacus League and Communist Party of Germany; murdered by army officers instigated by Social Democratic government.

Lyons, Eugene (1898–1985) – left-wing author and editor in 1920s and 1930s; United Press correspondent in Moscow and author of *Assignment in Utopia* (1937); subsequently became anticommunist.

Macdonald, Dwight (1906–1982) – author, journalist, contributor to *Partisan Review*; joined SWP 1939; supported minority in 1940 split; subsequently renounced Marxism; editor of *Politics* during 1940s; later wrote for *New Yorker*.

Mannerheim, K.G. (1867–1951) – headed counterrevolutionary forces in 1918 Finnish civil war and subsequent White terror; commanded Finnish army against Soviet forces in 1939; president of Finland 1944–46.

Martov, L. (Julius) (1873–1923) – a central leader of Russian Mensheviks; opposed October revolution; emigrated in 1920.

Marx, Karl (1818–1883) – founder with Frederick Engels of modern communist workers movement.

Mehring, Franz (1846–1919) – an editor of German Social Democratic theoretical magazine; defended Marxism against opportunist currents; leader of Spartacus League and founding member of Communist Party of Germany.

Menshevik Party – originated as right-wing faction in 1903 split in Russian Social Democratic Labor Party; opposed October 1917 revolution.

Molinier, Raymond (1904–1994) – a leader of Fourth Internationalists in France; expelled 1935 for violating party decisions.

Molotov, Vyacheslav M. (1890–1986) – Soviet foreign minister 1939–49, 1953–56.

Mussolini, Benito (1883–1945) – Italian Socialist Party member expelled 1914 for supporting World War I; founded fascist movement 1919; Italian dictator 1922–43.

Muste, A.J. (1885–1967) – leader of American Workers

Party, which fused with Communist League in 1934 to form Workers Party of U.S.; member of faction opposing entry into SP; broke with Marxism and left revolutionary movement in 1936.

Negrín, Juan (1889–1956) – prime minister of Republican government of Spain 1937–39, during Spanish civil war.

Novack, George (William F. Warde) (1905–1992) – longtime leader of SWP; joined Communist League of America 1933; national secretary of American Committee for the Defense of Leon Trotsky, which helped organize Dewey Commission; supported majority in 1939–40 faction fight; author of *An Introduction to the Logic of Marxism* and other books defending materialist world outlook.

October revolution (1917) – Bolshevik-led insurrection that brought workers and peasants to power in Russia; it followed February 1917 revolution that abolished tsarism and instituted bourgeois coalition government.

Oehler, Hugo (1903–1983) – leader of Communist League of America; led sectarian split in 1935; formed Revolutionary Workers League, which dissolved in 1950s.

People's Front (Popular Front) – name given in 1935 to coalition in France of workers' parties and bourgeois Radical Party; the Stalin-led Comintern subsequently generalized it as a universal strategy subordinating political independence and program of workers parties to coalitions with liberal capitalist parties.

Pivert, Marceau (1895–1958) – served as aide to Popular Front government in France in 1936–37; left Socialist Party and set up centrist Workers and Peasants Socialist Party (PSOP) in 1938; later rejoined SP.

Plekhanov, Georgiy (1856–1918) – founder of Russian Social Democratic movement 1883; author of numerous works defending Marxism; Menshevik after 1903; opposed October 1917 revolution.

POUM (Workers Party of Marxist Unification) – centrist

socialist organization during Spanish civil war; signed popular front pact and joined bourgeois government in 1936; outlawed and suppressed 1937 at instigation of Stalinists.

Radek, Karl (1885–1939) – leading member of Communist Party of Russia after October 1917 revolution; member of Left Opposition 1923–29; capitulated to Stalin 1929; arrested during Moscow trials and died in prison.

Rivera, Diego (1886–1957) – noted muralist; member of Mexican section of Fourth International 1937–39.

Robespierre, Maximilien (1758–1794) – leader of Jacobins in French Revolution; head of revolutionary government 1793–94.

Roosevelt, Franklin D. (1882–1945) – Democratic Party president of U.S. 1933–45; supported as a progressive by Stalinists, social democrats, and most trade union officials.

Russell, Bertrand (1872–1970) – mathematician and liberal philosopher.

Rykov, Aleksey I. (1881–1938) – longtime leader of Bolshevik Party; leader of Soviet state after October revolution; aligned with Bukharin in Right Opposition to Stalin 1928–29; executed during Moscow trials.

SAP (Socialist Workers Party) – centrist split-off from Social Democratic Party of Germany; joined briefly in call for Fourth International in 1934, then moved toward reformism.

Second International (Social Democracy) – founded 1889 as international association of workers parties; collapsed at outbreak of World War I when majority of leaders supported their respective governments; reorganized 1923 as Labor and Socialist International; revolutionary left wing founded Third, Communist International in 1919.

Serge, Victor (1890–1947) – active in anarchist movement in western Europe; moved to Russia after October 1917 revolution and joined Communist Party; member of Left

Opposition in Russia from 1923; arrested twice before being allowed to leave USSR in 1936; broke with Fourth International in 1937.

Shachtman, Max (1904–1972) – a leader of Communist Party in 1920s; expelled 1928 with Cannon and Abern for support of Bolshevik-Leninist opposition; a founding leader of Communist League of America; editor of *Socialist Appeal* and *New International* 1938–39; led minority faction in 1940 SWP split; organized Workers Party, which later became Independent Socialist League; fused with Socialist Party in 1958; subsequently became right-wing social democrat.

Sneevliet, Henk (1883–1942) – founder of Marxist movement in Indonesia and leader of Dutch Communist Party and Left Opposition; broke with Fourth International in 1938; executed by Nazis in World War II.

Social Democracy. See Second International.

Socialist Appeal – weekly, briefly twice-weekly, newspaper of SWP; changed name to *Militant* in 1941.

Socialist Workers Party (SWP) – originated in 1928 expulsion from Communist Party of supporters of Bolshevik-Leninist opposition led by Trotsky; existed as Communist League of America 1929–34; Workers Party of U.S. 1934–36; left wing in Socialist Party 1936–37; formed on January 1, 1938.

Social Revolutionaries (Socialist Revolutionary Party) – Russian petty-bourgeois party founded 1901–2 in opposition to tsarism; had strong base of support among peasantry; right wing of party opposed October 1917 revolution; left wing initially supported it but later went into armed opposition.

Souvarine, Boris (1893–1984) – a founding leader of CP of France; expelled 1924 for support of Trotsky; broke with International Left Opposition 1929; renounced Marxism in 1930s.

Spector, Maurice (1898–1968) – national chairman of Communist Party of Canada 1924–28; founder of Left

Opposition in Canada; later moved to New York and supported Muste faction in Workers Party opposed to entry in SP; left SWP 1939.

Stalin, Joseph (1879–1953) – Soviet Communist Party general secretary; presided over bureaucratic degeneration of Soviet workers state and Comintern and their rejection of revolutionary internationalist course; organized frame-up trials in 1930s and murder of majority of Bolshevik leaders of Lenin's time.

Stanley, Sherman (1915–1981) – member of SWP in New York; supported minority in 1940 split.

Struve, Peter B. (1870–1944) – founding member of Russian Social Democratic Party; subsequently became leader of liberalism; active opponent of October 1917 revolution.

SWP. See Socialist Workers Party

Thermidor – month in French revolutionary calendar when radical Jacobins were overthrown, opening up a period of reaction that could not, however, reinstitute the feudal regime toppled by the French Revolution; Trotsky applied the term to the seizure of power by the Stalinist bureaucratic caste within the framework of nationalized property relations established following the October 1917 revolution.

Thomas, Norman (1884–1968) – leader of Socialist Party from late 1920s until his death; six-time SP presidential candidate; pacifist.

Treint, Albert (1889–1972) – leader of CP of France expelled in 1928; member of French section of International Left Opposition until 1932.

Urbahns, Hugo (1890–1946) – leader of CP of Germany expelled in 1926; organized group that was affiliated to International Left Opposition until 1930.

Vereecken, Georges (1896–1978) – leader of sectarian tendency of Left Opposition in Belgium in 1930s.

Weber, Jack (b. 1896) – member of SWP National Committee; supporter of majority in 1939–40 fight; left SWP 1944.

Weisbord, Albert (1900–1977) – Communist Party member

expelled 1930; led Communist League of Struggle
1931–37.

Wright, John G. (Joseph Vanzler) (1902–1956) – leading
member of SWP from 1933 until his death; supporter of
majority in 1939–40 fight; translator of many books by
Trotsky.

YPSL (Young People's Socialist League) – Socialist Party
youth organization; majority was expelled by SP
leadership in 1937 as supporters of left wing; became
fraternal organization of SWP in 1938; affiliated with
Shachtman-led Workers Party following 1940 split.

Zack, Joseph (1897–1963) – leader of Communist Party trade
union work, expelled 1934; a member of Workers Party
of U.S. 1934–35; later served as government witness
during anticommunist witch-hunt.

Zinoviev, Gregory (1883–1936) – longtime Russian Bolshevik
leader; opposed course toward seizure of power on eve
of October 1917 revolution; chairman of Communist
International 1919–26; joined with Stalin in anti-
Trotsky bloc 1923–25; joined Trotsky and Kamenev in
United Opposition 1926–27; recanted 1928; executed
during Moscow frame-up trials.

Index

Abern, Martin, 26, 31, 41, 131–
32, 133–34, 141, 143–44, 160,
164, 167, 177, 196, 214, 236,
239, 246–47, 253–54, 255–56,
260–62, 263, 267, 268, 270,
274, 297, 318, 336, 337–38,
351; clique, 26–27, 177, 196,
197, 239, 246–48; and organi-
zational questions, 130–35, 160,
273–74; and origins in Commu-
nist Party, 132, 336
Abyssinia, 292
Afghanistan, 80, 203
Alma Ata, 22
Alsace-Lorraine, 218, 219
Altman, Jack, 320, 351
Andrew, Chris, 305, 351
Anglo-Russian Trade Union Unity
Committee, 268, 351
Anti-Dühring (Engels), 210
Aristotelian logic, 116–17, 165
Aristotle, 313
August Bloc (1912), 241–42

Balkans, 80
Baltic states, 80, 81, 101, 231, 284–
85, 324, 335
Baluchistan, 203
Barnes, Jack, 19

Berdyaev, Nikolai, 152, 351
Berlin, 81
Bern, Irving, 328–29, 351
Bernstein, Eduard, 152, 158, 351
Bloody Sunday (1905), 171
Blum, Léon, 294–95, 352
Bogdanov, A.A., 207, 238–39, 263,
352
Bolshevik-Leninist faction in Socialist
Party (United States), 194
Bolshevik-Leninists (USSR), 72
Bolshevik Party, 13, 23, 75, 159,
207, 237–40, 241–42, 243, 248,
270–71, 272–73, 293, 352
Bolshevism, 22, 178, 183, 238–40,
241–43, 263, 276
Bordigists, 127, 352
Brandlerites, 318
Brest-Litovsk, 81–82, 294
Brockway, Fenner, 127, 352
Browder, Earl, 326, 352
Bruno. *See* Rizzi, Bruno
Buffon, G., 162
Bukharin, Nikolai, 104
Bulgakov, Sergei, 152, 352
"Bureaucratic collectivism," 25, 39,
46, 57–59, 62, 88, 122
"Bureaucratic conservatism," 181,
217, 238, 243–44, 246, 278

Burnham, James, 25–30, 31–34, 37–39, 109, 131–33, 139–42, 145, 180, 182, 184, 204, 205, 206, 214, 221, 247, 263, 264, 267, 272, 276, 278, 279, 281, 293, 294, 299, 301–2, 303, 309–10, 327, 352–53; "On the Character of the War," 25; and dialectical materialism, 29, 35, 36–37, 113–15, 121–24, 144, 148–49, 174, 204–8, 297, 309–26, 341–42; and intellectuals, 34–35, 125–27; "Intellectuals in Retreat," 34–35, 109, 151, 204, 329–30; *The Managerial Revolution*, 38; "The Politics of Desperation," 318; resignation from Workers Party, 37, 296, 341–49; and Russian question, 23–28, 37–39, 41, 121–27, 130–31, 283–84, 293–95, 333, 342, 347; "Science and Style," 30–31, 263–64, 270, 279; "The War and Bureaucratic Conservatism," 143–44, 192–93, 334; "What Is at Issue in the Dispute on the Russian Question," 143. *See also* Eastman, Max
Byelorussia, 71, 171, 226–30

Cannon, James P., 18, 28, 32, 95, 105, 131–34, 136, 156, 181–82, 196–98, 201–2, 243–50, 253, 255–56, 258–60, 264, 267, 276, 302, 312, 318–20, 326, 331–39, 342, 345, 353
Capital, 37
Carter, Joseph, 267, 322, 353
Case of Leon Trotsky, The, 268
Caucasus, 287
CGT (General Confederation of Labor, France), 294

Chamberlain, Neville, 75, 222, 353
Changing Face of U.S. Politics, The (Barnes), 19
Chicago, 104
China, 15, 280
Chinese Revolution (1925–27), 79, 268
Ciliga, Anton, 49, 353
Citrine, Walter, 295, 316, 353
Clarke, George, 331, 353
Cleveland convention (1940), 256–57, 265, 272
Cochran, Bert, 331, 339, 353
Comintern. *See* Third International
Common Sense, 164
Communist International. *See* Third International
Communist Manifesto, The, 37
Communist Party (Finland), 231–33
Communist Party (United States), 132, 336
Communist Party (USSR), 13, 22
Corey, Lewis, 34, 354
Coulondre, Robert, 88–89
Cuban revolution, 40

Dan, F.I., 159–60, 228–29, 236, 354
Darwin, Charles, 119–24, 165–66, 208, 313, 354
Democratic centralism, 28, 32–33, 90, 175–77, 193, 242–43, 272, 275
Denmark, 285
Dewey Commission, 198, 268, 354
Dialectical materialism, 29, 34–38, 40, 41–42, 108–24, 148–79, 185, 276, 279, 298–301, 309–19, 335, 341–42; ABCs of, 116–21,

224–26; abstract and concrete, 205–11; and Aristotelian syllogism, 165; and Dies Committee, 167–69; and economics and politics, 204–12; and formal logic, 116–21, 165–66; and relation to Marxism, 34–37, 109, 203–7, 316–18; and religion, 148–49; and symbolic logic, 276, 314; and theory of evolution, 123–24, 165–67, 312–13. See also Burnham, and dialectical materialism; Hegel; Marxism; and USSR, character of

Dies Committee, 140, 167–69, 175, 327–30, 354

Dobbs, Farrell, 18, 181–82, 270–76, 354

Dubrovinsky, I.F., 238, 354

Dühring, Eugen, 210, 263

Dunne, Vincent R., 204, 354

Eastman, Max, 34–37, 109–10, 125, 142, 148, 152–53, 163–64, 198–99, 200, 263, 268–69, 323, 329, 354–55

Economism, 158, 355

Encyclopedia of Unified Science, 314

Engels, Frederick, 31, 142–43, 152, 210, 218–20, 264, 278, 312–13, 316–17, 344, 355

England, 11, 29, 65, 66, 79, 81, 86, 88, 92–93, 202, 235, 279–80, 284

Entente, 288

Estonia, 227, 231, 291

Evolution. See Dialectical materialism

Field, B.J., 251, 260, 355

Finland, 29–30, 101, 124–30, 146–47, 169–75, 179, 193, 203, 219, 226, 230–36, 264, 283–95, 324–27, 336, 340

First International, 302

Ford, Henry, 109, 163

Fourth International, 26, 27–34, 41, 57, 60, 65, 71–72, 74, 84–86, 95, 99–103, 115–16, 130–31, 139, 151, 177, 178, 179, 188–89, 204, 230, 237, 246, 251–52, 254, 256, 257, 260–62, 264, 265, 271–72, 277–80, 294, 302, 321, 332–33, 334, 343, 344, 355; founding, 22, 31, 99–103, 251; IEC, 266, 272, 274–75; and intellectuals, 302; and petty-bourgeois sectors, 179, 205, 245–46; and Russian question, 24, 48–51, 57, 65, 71–73, 84–85, 115–16; and splits in national sections, 271–72

Fourth International, 38, 283, 296, 298

France, 11, 16, 66, 79, 81, 86, 88, 202, 219, 235, 250, 279, 284

Franco, Francisco, 84

Freiligrath, Ferdinand, 302, 355

French Revolution, 119

Freud, Sigmund, 77

Frey, Josef, 251, 355

Galicia, 230

Gandhi, Mohandas, 280, 355

General strike in England (1926), 79

Georgia, 101, 287–88

Gerland, J., 185, 276, 355

Germany, 11, 22, 65, 84, 104, 218–19, 280, 284–86

Goldman, Albert, 142, 253, 258, 268, 331, 355

Gordon, Sam, 339, 356

Gorky, Maxim, 302, 356

Gould, Nathan, 96, 356
GPU, 101, 125, 155, 243, 330, 356
Green, William, 244, 356
Grimm, Robert, 287

Hacker, L., 34
Haldane, J.B.S., 314
Hansen, Joseph, 19, 21, 133, 146–47, 356
Hardman, J.B.S., 320, 356
Harper's Magazine, 164, 199
Harrison, C., 330
Hegel, G.W., 119, 122, 166, 313, 324, 332, 356
Helsingfors, 172
Hitler, Adolf, 24, 38, 48, 58, 68–72, 75, 76, 82–84, 88–89, 100, 124, 125, 172, 228, 279–80, 283–85, 290, 293–94, 356
Hohenzollern, 219
Hook, Sidney, 34–37, 41, 125, 142, 152, 163, 329, 356
Hugo, Victor, 83
Humphrey, Hubert, 41
Hungary, 10
Huxley, Thomas, 313
Huysmans, Camille, 294, 357

ILP (Independent Labour Party, Great Britain), 194, 357
Independent Socialist League (U.S.), 38, 41
India, 179, 203, 280
Internal Bulletin, 28, 99, 192, 246
Iskra, 158, 357
Italy, 16, 280

James, C.L.R. See Johnson, J.R.
Japan, 125, 280
Jewish Bund, 146, 171

Johnson, J.R., 275, 357
Jouhaux, Léon, 294, 316, 357

Kamenev, Lev B., 22, 142, 240, 357
Kant, Immanuel, 152, 153, 339, 357
Kautsky, Karl, 152, 357
Kerensky, Alexander, 236, 357
Kolkhoz, 65
Kremlin. See USSR, bureaucracy
Kronstadt uprising, 258
Kuusinen, Otto, 146, 172, 236, 289, 357–58

Labor Action, 305, 344
Labriola, Antonio, 210, 358
Landau, Kurt, 251, 358
Latvia, 203, 227, 231, 291
Lebrun, A., 274–75, 358
Left Opposition, 22, 95, 132, 192, 243, 358
Lenin, V.I., 21–22, 31, 36, 37, 40, 76, 152, 154, 159, 207, 212–17, 222, 237–43, 248, 252, 264, 316–17, 343–44, 358; testament of, 268–69
Leningrad, 86, 285
Lewis, C.I., 314
Lewis, John L., 244, 305–6, 316, 358
Lewit, Morris, 331–32, 339, 358
Liberty, 258–60
Liebknecht, Karl, 153–54, 317, 358
Linnaeus, 120, 122
Lithuania, 227, 231, 291
Ludlow Amendment, 331
Luxemburg, Rosa, 31, 152–54, 264, 316, 358–59
Lyons, Eugene, 125, 163–64, 199–200, 359

Macdonald, Dwight, 258–60, 299–301, 359
Majority, 25, 31–32, 40, 74–75, 90–91, 93, 106, 132, 135, 189–90, 193, 236–40, 243–45, 248, 257, 260–61, 273, 277–79, 298–99
Managerial Revolution, The (Burnham), 38
Mannerheim, K.T., 29, 173, 175, 330, 359
Martin, Homer, 331
Martov, L., 159, 359
Marx, Karl, 31, 37, 112, 119–22, 152, 155, 166–67, 208, 218–20, 278, 316–17, 344, 359
Marxism, 21–23, 29–41, 86–88, 100, 105, 109, 122, 144–45, 150–57, 161–67, 177–78, 183, 204–7, 210–11, 263–64, 278–79, 281, 313, 341–42
Meany, George, 41
Mehring, Franz, 31, 152–56, 264, 316, 359
Mensheviks, 21, 24, 146, 159, 170–71, 228–29, 236, 241–42, 243, 248, 269, 294, 317–18, 336, 359
Menshevism, 238
Mexico, 13, 203, 245, 247
Minority. *See* Petty-bourgeois opposition
Modern Monthly, 116, 164
Molinier, Raymond, 95, 131, 182, 250–52, 359
Molotov, V.M., 295, 359
Morgan, J.P., 326
Moscow, 81, 86
Moscow Trials, 316–17
Murmansk railway, 292
Mussolini, Benito, 40, 58, 292, 302, 359
Muste, A.J., 133, 177, 263, 297, 320, 359–60

Napoleon, 69
Narodniki, 158
National Review, 39
National Socialism, 57
Negrín, Juan, 223–24, 360
New Deal, 46, 57, 209, 322
New International, 33, 34, 109, 112, 125, 139, 163–64, 198–200, 204–5, 265, 276, 277, 281
New Leader, 330
Newton, Isaac, 208
New York Times, 230, 235, 268
Nixon, Richard, 41
Norway, 285–86
Novack, George. *See* Warde, William F.

O'Brien, V.T., 74
October revolution. *See* Russian revolution
Oehler, Hugo, 260, 317, 320, 360
Opposition. *See* Petty-bourgeois opposition

Paris Soir, 88
Partisan Review, 258, 299
People's Front, 45, 237, 281, 293, 332, 360
People's Government (Finland), 232–34
Persia, 80–81
Petty-bourgeois opposition, 23–42, 74–76, 90–91, 106–7, 108–35, 139–45, 183, 186–87, 188–203, 223, 242–46, 249–50, 258–62, 265, 270–76, 277–82, 285; characteristics of, 28–29, 133; and democratic centralism, 32–33, 90, 175–77, 272; and intellectuals, 34–38, 142, 261, 280–81, 298–302, 303–4; and organizational questions, 130–35; and Russian

question, 23–28, 39–40, 124–27, 258–62; and Soviet-Finnish War, 126–29; and Spanish Revolution, 223; and split, 41–42, 186–87, 260–62, 263–64, 270–76, 278–79, 296. *See also* Eastman, Max; Finland

Pivert, Marceau, 127, 360

Plekhanov, Georgiy, 153, 154, 156, 210, 317, 360

Poland, 17, 26, 68–70, 80, 82, 88, 101, 146–47, 169–75, 179, 193, 219, 220, 226–30, 283–85, 289–91, 324, 335, 340

Polish Ukraine. *See* Ukraine

Politburo, 268

Popular Front. *See* People's Front

POUM (Workers Party of Marxist Unification, Spain), 194, 360–61

PPS (Polish Socialist Party), 146, 170–71

Principia Mathematica, 314

Prinkipo, 247

Proletarian tendency. *See* Majority

Prussia, 218–19

PSOP (Workers and Peasants Socialist Party, France), 271

Radek, Karl, 240–41, 361

Red Army, 26, 27, 68–69, 71–72, 85, 101, 125, 128–29, 146–47, 170–74, 220, 226–36, 258–59, 286–87, 290

Referendum, 90–91, 97–98

Rivera, Diego, 302, 361

Rizzi, Bruno, 25, 34, 46, 49–50, 57, 58–59, 352; *La Bureaucratisation du Monde*, 46, 57

Robespierre, Maximilien, 83, 361

Romania, 81, 146, 170

Roman state, 80

Roosevelt, Franklin, 57, 209, 293, 326, 361

Russell, Bertrand, 59, 276, 314, 361

Russian question. *See* USSR, defense of

Russian revolution (1905), 64; (1917), 21–24, 37, 64, 77–78; October, 21, 57, 61–62, 63–65, 75–76, 100–102, 123, 142, 210–11, 222, 227, 288, 291–92, 360

Rykov, Aleksei, 238, 361

SAP (Socialist Workers Party, Germany), 194, 361

Savoy Monarchy (Italy), 40

Scandinavia, 173, 285, 287, 290

Second International, 21, 189, 194, 288, 294–95, 302, 333, 361–62

Serfdom, 69

Serge, Victor, 34, 361–62

Shachtman, Max, 26–28, 31, 34–35, 37, 38–39, 40–41, 74, 92–93, 95, 99–105, 109, 130–32, 141–42, 143, 151–54, 160–67, 177, 183, 184, 186, 255–56, 263–64, 267, 270, 274, 277–82, 294, 297, 303–4, 318, 329, 337, 362; as Burnham's attorney, 30, 166, 279; "The Crisis in the American Party—An Open Letter to Comrade Leon Trotsky," 183, 184, 190–96, 255–56; and democratic centralism, 175–77, 242–44; and dialectical materialism, 27, 29, 30, 36–37, 109, 110–15, 154, 164–67, 202–7, 208; and intellectuals, 34–35, 109, 126–27, 167, 200–201, 329; "Intellectuals in Retreat," 34–35, 109, 151,

204, 329; and Russian question,
24, 93, 99–105, 170–74, 206–
37, 283–84; and Socialist Party
(USA), 194–95; "The State and
the Character of the War," 207;
and theory of "Blocs," 211–16,
236–49; "Towards a Revolutionary Socialist Party," 194–95. *See
also* Eastman, Max
Shanker, Albert, 41
Sneevliet, Henk, 95, 127, 131, 251,
362
Social Democracy. *See* Second
International
Social Democracy (German), 263
Social Democracy (Russian), 248
Social Democrats, 24
Socialist Appeal, 139, 141, 164, 199–
201, 277, 324, 329, 333, 362
Socialist Party (France), 140
Socialist Party (United States), 93,
137, 194, 203
Socialist Workers Party, 13–18, 22,
30, 32, 33–34, 38, 126–27, 139,
161, 177–78, 188, 200–202, 203,
204, 244, 246, 260, 263–64, 271,
318, 332, 341, 344, 362; National
Committee, 24–25, 92–95, 108,
135, 141, 185, 187, 244, 247, 257,
273–74; New York Branch, 99,
137, 189, 197, 203; Political Com-
mittee, 24–25, 33, 94, 257, 274,
328. *See also* Majority; Petty-
bourgeois opposition
Souvarine, Boris, 34, 116, 362
Soviet Army. *See* Red Army
Soviet-Finnish war. *See* Finland
Sozialisticheski Vestnik, 236
Spain, 84, 126, 174, 267, 286
Spanish Civil War, 192
Spanish Revolution, 54, 79, 126,
223

Spector, Maurice, 133, 177, 297,
362–63
Spencer, Herbert, 313
Stalin, Joseph, 13, 15, 22, 45–46,
62–63, 71–72, 82–84, 88, 102,
103, 124, 126, 170, 171–72, 175,
220–21, 258–59, 279–80, 283–
95, 316, 326, 330, 335, 363
Stalin-Hitler Pact, 24–27, 38, 45,
48–50, 68–69, 76, 88–89, 100,
102, 103, 104, 124, 197, 220,
280, 284
Stalinism, 9–16, 24, 46, 58–59,
62, 105, 124, 126, 195, 220,
259, 342
Stanley, Sherman, 74–76, 92–95,
129–30, 143, 363
*Struggle for a Proletarian Party,
The* (Cannon), 17–18, 276
Struggle for World Power, The
(Burnham), 38
Struve, Peter B., 152, 263, 363
Suicide of the West (Burnham),
38
Survey of Symbolic Logic, 314
Symposium, The, 308

Terrijoki, 172, 173
"Third camp," 279–81, 288–92,
324, 330, 333, 345
Third International, 12, 22, 48, 67,
69, 73, 82, 100, 101, 182, 189,
194, 230, 261, 302, 332, 354
Thomas, Norman, 194–95, 295,
363
Treint, Albert, 251, 363
Trotsky, Leon, 12–18, 21–23, 25,
27–28, 32–33, 34–38, 41, 45–
46, 77, 88, 102, 103, 104, 106–
7, 193, 243, 259, 290, 307–40,
342, 343, 344; "Again and Once
More Again on the Nature of

the USSR," 27, 104; "Balance Sheet of the Finnish Events," 33; "From a Scratch to the Danger of Gangrene," 23, 30; "An Open Letter to Comrade Burnham," 29, 337–38; "A Petty-Bourgeois Opposition in the Socialist Workers Party," 28, 138, 336; "The USSR in War," 25–26, 27, 28, 88; *The War and the Fourth International*, 286–87, 293–94
"True German Socialism," 278
Turkey, 22

Ukraine, 10, 71, 82, 84, 100, 171, 226–27, 233, 289; Polish, 227–28
Union of Soviet Socialist Republics (USSR), 9–16, 24, 25, 27–28, 31, 38, 39–40, 42, 45, 46, 90, 100, 103–4, 140, 220–36, 268, 280–81; bureaucracy, 48–73, 80, 81, 82–83, 84–85, 87–88, 101, 102–3, 122–24, 128, 146–47, 155, 172, 173, 176, 181, 193, 211–12, 215–16, 226–30, 243–44, 288, 290, 291; class character of, 23–27, 39–40, 47–73, 77–89, 92, 113–16, 121–23, 132, 157, 160, 164, 207–17, 224–36, 256, 257, 258–62, 290, 309; defense of ("Russian question"), 23–25, 39–40, 41, 47–73, 92–95, 102–5, 124–27, 134, 143–44, 213–14, 220–26, 280–81, 291–95, 323–24, 325; foreign policy of, 26–27, 125–30, 157, 162, 175, 207, 226–36, 258–62, 283–95.

See also Finland; Poland; Red Army
United States, 11, 12, 13, 18–19, 29, 79, 93, 109–10, 204, 271, 280
Unprincipled combination, 26–27
Urbahns, Hugo, 57, 64, 363
USSR. *See* Union of Soviet Socialist Republics

Vereecken, Georges, 95, 127, 131, 182, 251, 363
Versailles treaty, 59
Vperyodists, 241–42

Warde, William F., 19, 21, 198, 203, 360
Warsaw, 81
Weber, Jack, 276, 363
Weisbord, Albert, 251, 260, 363–64
Whitehead, A., 314
"Whites," 199, 233
Workers Party (U.S.), 33, 38, 41, 296, 298–302, 303, 341–49
World War I, 21, 153, 273
World War II, 14–15, 17, 22, 23, 24, 31, 39, 63–64, 285, 332
Wright, John G., 146, 181, 185, 364

YPSL (Young People's Socialist League, U.S.), 331, 364
Yugoslavia, 10–11

Zack, Joseph, 329, 364
Zbrucz, 229
Zinoviev, Gregory, 142, 240–41, 268, 364

FROM PATHFINDER

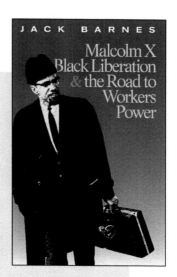

Malcolm X, Black Liberation, and the Road to Workers Power

JACK BARNES

The foundations for the explosive rise of the Black liberation struggle in the US beginning in the mid-1950s were laid by the massive migration of Blacks from the rural South to cities and factories across the continent, drawn by capital's insatiable need for labor power—and cannon fodder for its wars.

Malcolm X emerged from this rising struggle as its outstanding single leader. He insisted that colossal movement was part of a worldwide revolutionary battle for human rights. A clash "between those who want freedom, justice, and equality and those who want to continue the systems of exploitation."

Drawing lessons from a century and a half of struggle, this book helps us understand why it is the revolutionary conquest of power by the working class that will make possible the final battle for Black freedom—and open the way to a world based not on exploitation, violence, and racism, but human solidarity. A socialist world. $20. Also in Spanish and French.

Building a PROLETARIAN PARTY

The Changing Face of U.S. Politics
Working-Class Politics and the Trade Unions
JACK BARNES

Building the kind of party working people need to prepare for coming class battles through which they will revolutionize themselves, their unions, and all society. A handbook for those seeking the road toward effective action to overturn the exploitative system of capitalism and join in reconstructing the world on new, socialist foundations. $24. Also in Spanish, French, and Swedish.

Their Trotsky and Ours
JACK BARNES

To lead the working class in a successful revolution, a mass proletarian party is needed whose cadres, well beforehand, have absorbed a world communist program, are proletarian in life and work, derive deep satisfaction from doing politics, and have forged a leadership with an acute sense of what to do next. This book is about building such a party. $16. Also in Spanish and French.

The History of American Trotskyism, 1928–1938
Report of a Participant
JAMES P. CANNON

"Trotskyism is not a new movement, a new doctrine," Cannon says, "but the restoration, the revival of genuine Marxism as it was expounded and practiced in the Russian revolution and in the early days of the Communist International." In twelve talks given in 1942, Cannon recounts a decisive period in efforts to build a proletarian party in the United States. $22. Also in Spanish and French.

What Is To Be Done?
V.I. LENIN

The stakes in creating a disciplined organization of working-class revolutionaries capable of acting as a "tribune of the people, able to react to every manifestation of tyranny and oppression, no matter where it appears, to clarify for all and everyone the world-historic significance of the struggle for the emancipation of the proletariat." Written in 1902. In *Essential Works of Lenin*. $12.95

The Struggle for a Proletarian Party
JAMES P. CANNON

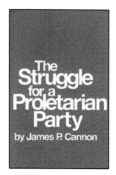

On the eve of World War II, a founder of the communist movement in the US and leader of the Communist International in Lenin's time defends the program and proletarian course of Bolshevism. A companion volume to Leon Trotsky's *In Defense of Marxism*. $22. Also in Spanish.

The Founding of the Socialist Workers Party
JAMES P. CANNON AND OTHERS

At founding gatherings of the Socialist Workers Party in 1938–39, revolutionists in the US codified two decades of experience in building a communist party. They charted a working-class course in resisting the coming imperialist war, fighting fascism and Jew-hatred, the struggle for Black rights, forging an alliance with exploited farmers, and the battle to transform the unions into revolutionary instruments of struggle by working people. $26

Revolutionary Continuity
Marxist Leadership in the United States
FARRELL DOBBS

How successive generations of fighters took part in struggles of the US labor movement, seeking to build a leadership that could advance the class interests of workers and small farmers and link up with fellow toilers around the world.

The Early Years: 1848–1917, $20; *Birth of the Communist Movement, 1918–1922*, $19.

www.pathfinderpress.com

OTHER WRITINGS BY LEON TROTSKY

THE CASE OF LEON TROTSKY
REPORT OF HEARINGS ON THE CHARGES
MADE AGAINST HIM IN THE MOSCOW TRIALS

Was the regime of Joseph Stalin and his
heirs a continuation of the Bolshevik-
led workers and peasants government
established by the October 1917
Revolution? No! says Bolshevik leader
Leon Trotsky in testimony before a 1937
international commission of inquiry
into Stalin's Moscow frame-up trials.
Reviewing forty years of working-class
struggle in which Trotsky was a participant and leader,
he discusses the fight to restore V.I. Lenin's revolutionary
internationalist course and why the Stalin regime
organized the Moscow Trials. He explains working
people's stake in the unfolding Spanish Revolution, the
fight against fascism in Germany, efforts to build a world
revolutionary party, and much more. $30

THE CHALLENGE OF THE LEFT OPPOSITION

This three-volume series documents the fight of the
communist opposition from 1923 to 1929 against the
reactionary political and economic policies of the rising
bureaucratic caste in the Soviet Union. Vol. 1: 1923–25,
$30; vol. 2: 1926–27, $34; vol. 3: 1928–29, $30

THE TRANSITIONAL PROGRAM FOR
SOCIALIST REVOLUTION

Contains discussions between leaders of the US Socialist
Workers Party and exiled revolutionary Leon Trotsky in
1938. The product of these discussions, a program of
immediate, democratic, and transitional demands, was
adopted by the SWP later that year. This program for
socialist revolution remains an irreplaceable component of
a fighting guide for communist workers today. $20

WRITINGS OF LEON TROTSKY

Fourteen volumes covering the period of Trotsky's exile
from the Soviet Union in 1929 until his assassination at
Stalin's orders in 1940. $375

WWW.PATHFINDERPRESS.COM

Russian Revolution's world example

Lenin's Final Fight
Speeches and Writings, 1922–23
V.I. LENIN

In 1922 and 1923, V.I. Lenin, central leader of the world's first socialist revolution, waged what was to be his last political battle. At stake was whether that revolution, and the international movement it led, would remain on the proletarian course that had brought workers and peasants to power in October 1917. Indispensable to understanding the world class struggle in the 20th and 21st centuries. $20. Also in Spanish.

The First Five Years of the Communist International
LEON TROTSKY

During its first five years, the Communist International, guided by V.I. Lenin, Leon Trotsky, and other central Bolshevik leaders, sought to build a world movement of Communist Parties capable of leading the toilers to overthrow capitalist exploitation and colonial oppression. This two-volume collection contains Trotsky's speeches and writings from the first four Comintern congresses. Volume 1, $28; volume 2, $29

The History of the Russian Revolution
LEON TROTSKY

A classic account of the social and political dynamics of the first socialist revolution as told by one of its central leaders. "The history of a revolution is first of all a history of the forcible entrance of the masses into the realm of rulership over their own destiny," says Trotsky. Unabridged, 3 vols. in one. $38. Also in Russian.

The Revolution Betrayed
What Is the Soviet Union and Where Is It Going?
LEON TROTSKY

In 1917 the workers and peasants of Russia carried out one of the greatest revolutions in history. Yet within ten years a political counterrevolution by a privileged social layer whose chief spokesperson was Joseph Stalin was being consolidated. This study of the Soviet workers state and the degeneration of the revolution illuminates the roots of the social and political crisis shaking the former USSR today. $20. Also in Spanish.

EXPAND *Your Revolutionary Library*

The Working Class and the Transformation of Learning
The Fraud of Education Reform under Capitalism
JACK BARNES

"Until society is reorganized so that education is a human activity from the time we are very young until the time we die, there will be no education worthy of working, creating humanity." $3. Also in Spanish, French, Swedish, Icelandic, Farsi, and Greek.

Is Socialist Revolution in the U.S. Possible?
A Necessary Debate
MARY-ALICE WATERS

Not only is socialist revolution in the US possible, says Waters. Revolutionary struggles by working people are inevitable—initiated not by the toilers, but by the crisis-driven assaults of the propertied classes. As a fighting vanguard of the working class emerges in the US, the outlines of these coming battles—whose outcome is not inevitable—can already be seen. The future depends on us. $7. Also in Spanish, French, and Swedish.

Problems of Women's Liberation
EVELYN REED

Six articles explore the social and economic roots of women's oppression from prehistoric society to modern capitalism and point the road forward to emancipation. $15

www.pathfinderpress.com

Women in Cuba:
The Making of a Revolution
Within the Revolution

*From Santiago de Cuba and the Rebel Army, to
the Birth of the Federation of Cuban Women*

VILMA ESPÍN, ASELA DE LOS SANTOS,
YOLANDA FERRER

The social revolution that in 1959 brought
down the bloody Batista dictatorship began
in the streets of cities like Santiago de Cuba
and the Rebel Army's liberated mountain
zones of eastern Cuba. The unprecedented
integration of women in the ranks and leadership of this struggle was a true measure of
the revolutionary course it has followed to
this day. Here, in firsthand accounts by women who helped make it, is the story
of that revolution—and "the revolution within." Introduction by Mary-Alice
Waters. $20. Also in Spanish.

Malcolm X Talks to Young People

"You're living at a time of revolution," Malcolm told
young people in the United Kingdom in December 1964.
"And I for one will join in with anyone, I don't care what
color you are, as long as you want to change the miserable condition that exists on this earth." Four talks and
an interview given to young people in Ghana, the UK,
and the United States in the last months of Malcolm's
life. $15. Also in Spanish and French.

The Jewish Question
A Marxist Interpretation

ABRAM LEON

Traces the historical rationalizations of anti-Semitism
to the fact that, in the centuries preceding the domination of industrial capitalism, Jews emerged as a "people-
class" of merchants, moneylenders, and traders. Leon
explains why the propertied rulers incite renewed Jew-
hatred in the epoch of capitalism's decline. $22

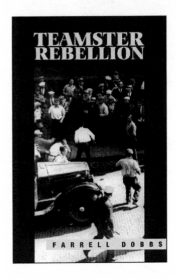

Teamster Rebellion

FARRELL DOBBS

The first of a four-volume participant's account of how strikes and organizing drives across the Midwest in the 1930s, initiated by leaders of Teamsters Local 574 in Minneapolis, paved the way for industrial unions and a fighting working-class social movement. These battles showed what workers and farmers can achieve when they have the leadership they deserve. Dobbs was a central part of that class-struggle leadership. $19. Also in Spanish, French, and Swedish.

The Cuban Five
Who They Are, Why They Were Framed, Why They Should Be Free

MARTÍN KOPPEL, MARY-ALICE WATERS, AND OTHERS

Held in US prisons since 1998, five Cuban revolutionists were framed up for being part of a "Cuban spy network" in Florida. Gerardo Hernández, Ramón Labañino, Antonio Guerrero, Fernando González, and René González were keeping tabs for the Cuban government on rightist groups with a long record of armed attacks on Cuba from US soil. Articles from the *Militant* on the truth about the frame-up and the international fight against it. $5. Also in Spanish.

Understanding History
Marxist Essays

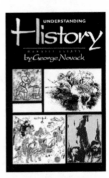

GEORGE NOVACK

How did capitalism arise? Why and when did this exploitative system exhaust its potential to advance civilization? Why revolutionary change is fundamental to human progress. $20

BY KARL MARX AND FREDERICK ENGELS

The Communist Manifesto *Karl Marx, Frederick Engels*
Founding document of the modern working-class movement, published
in 1848. Explains why communism is not a set of preconceived principles
but the line of march of the working class toward power, "springing from
an existing class struggle, a historical movement going on under our very
eyes." $5. Also in Spanish, French, and Arabic.

Capital *Karl Marx*
Marx explains the workings of the capitalist system and how it produces
the insoluble contradictions that breed class struggle. He demonstrates
the inevitability of the revolutionary transformation of society into one
ruled for the first time by the producing majority: the working class.
Volume 1, $18; volume 2, $18; volume 3, $18.

Anti-Dühring *Frederick Engels*
Modern socialism is not a doctrine, but a movement of the working class that
arises as one of the social consequences of the establishment of large-scale
capitalist industry. This defense of materialism and the fundamental ideas of
scientific communism explains why. A "handbook for every class-conscious
worker"—V.I. Lenin. In Marx and Engels *Collected Works,* vol. 25. $35

The Poverty of Philosophy *Karl Marx*
Written by the young Marx in collaboration with working-class fighters
in the League of the Just, this polemic against Pierre-Joseph Proudhon's
middle-class socialism gave Marx the opportunity to "develop the basic
features of his new historical and economic outlook," Frederick Engels
notes in his 1884 preface. $9.95

ORDER AT WWW.PATHFINDERPRESS.COM

New International

A MAGAZINE OF MARXIST POLITICS AND THEORY

NEW INTERNATIONAL NO. 12

CAPITALISM'S LONG HOT WINTER HAS BEGUN

Jack Barnes

and "Their Transformation and Ours,"
Resolution of the Socialist Workers Party

Today's sharpening interimperialist conflicts are fueled both by the opening stages of what will be decades of economic, financial, and social convulsions and class battles, and by the most far-reaching shift in Washington's military policy and organization since the US buildup toward World War II. Class-struggle-minded working people must face this historic turning point for imperialism, and draw satisfaction from being "in their face" as we chart a revolutionary course to confront it. $16. Also in Spanish, French, Swedish, and Arabic.

NEW INTERNATIONAL NO. 14

REVOLUTION, INTERNATIONALISM, AND SOCIALISM: THE LAST YEAR OF MALCOLM X

Jack Barnes

"In addition to the lead article, "The Last Year of Malcolm X," this issue contains "The Clintons' Antilabor Legacy: Roots of the 2008 World Financial Crisis." Jack Barnes explains how the Clinton administration, and both Republican and Democratic administrations before it, stepped up assaults on working people and, at the same time, helped bring on the massive mortgage, household, corporate, and government debts that are by-products of today's world crisis of capitalist production. The results for workers and farmers worldwide are devastating.

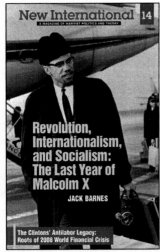

Also in No. 14: "The Stewardship of Nature Also Falls to the Working Class"; and "Setting the Record Straight on Fascism and World War II." $14. Also in Spanish, French, and Swedish.

WWW.PATHFINDERPRESS.COM

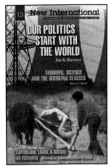

NEW INTERNATIONAL NO. 13
OUR POLITICS
START WITH THE WORLD
Jack Barnes

The huge economic and cultural inequalities between imperialist and semicolonial countries, and among classes within almost every country, are produced, reproduced, and accentuated by the workings of capitalism. For vanguard workers to build parties able to lead a successful revolutionary struggle for power in our own countries, says Jack Barnes in the lead article, our activity must be guided by a strategy to close this gap.

Also in No. 13: "Farming, Science, and the Working Classes" *by Steve Clark.* $14. Also in Spanish, French, and Swedish.

NEW INTERNATIONAL NO. 11
U.S. IMPERIALISM HAS LOST THE COLD WAR
Jack Barnes

Contrary to imperialist expectations at the opening of the 1990s in the wake of the collapse of regimes across Eastern Europe and the USSR claiming to be communist, the workers and farmers there have not been crushed. The toilers remain an intractable obstacle to imperialism's advance, one the exploiters will have to confront in class battles and war. $16. Also in Spanish, French, Swedish, and Icelandic.

NEW INTERNATIONAL NO. 8
CHE GUEVARA, CUBA, AND THE ROAD TO SOCIALISM
Articles by Ernesto Che Guevara, Carlos Rafael Rodríguez, Carlos Tablada, Mary-Alice Waters, Steve Clark, Jack Barnes

Exchanges from the opening years of the Cuban Revolution and today on the political perspectives defended by Guevara as he helped lead working people to advance the transformation of economic and social relations in Cuba. $10. Also in Spanish.

NEW INTERNATIONAL NO. 5
THE COMING REVOLUTION
IN SOUTH AFRICA
Jack Barnes

Writing a decade before the white supremacist regime fell, Barnes explores the social roots of apartheid in South African capitalism and tasks of urban and rural toilers in dismantling it, as they forge a communist leadership of the working class. $14. Also in Spanish and French.

PATHFINDER AROUND THE WORLD

Visit our website for a complete list of titles and to place orders

www.pathfinderpress.com

PATHFINDER DISTRIBUTORS

UNITED STATES
(and Caribbean, Latin America, and East Asia)
> *Pathfinder Books, 306 W. 37th St., 10th Floor,*
> *New York, NY 10018*

CANADA
> *Pathfinder Books, 7107 St. Denis, Suite 204,*
> *Montreal, QC H2S 2S5*

UNITED KINGDOM
(and Europe, Africa, Middle East, and South Asia)
> *Pathfinder Books, First Floor, 120 Bethnal Green Road*
> *(entrance in Brick Lane), London E2 6DG*

AUSTRALIA
(and Southeast Asia and the Pacific)
> *Pathfinder, Level 1, 3/281-287 Beamish St., Campsie, NSW 2194*
> *Postal address: P.O. Box 164, Campsie, NSW 2194*

NEW ZEALAND
> *Pathfinder, 4/125 Grafton Road, Grafton, Auckland*
> *Postal address: P.O. Box 3025, Auckland 1140*

Join the Pathfinder Readers Club
to get 15% discounts on all Pathfinder titles
and bigger discounts on special offers.
Sign up at www.pathfinderpress.com
or through the distributors above.